Called to Suffer

Called to Suffer

*The Necessity of Suffering
in Christian Formation in First Peter*

FRANS-JOHAN PIENAAR
Foreword by Corné J. Bekker

WIPF & STOCK · Eugene, Oregon

CALLED TO SUFFER
The Necessity of Suffering in Christian Formation in First Peter

Copyright © 2022 Frans-Johan Pienaar. All rights reserved. Except for brief quotations in critical publications or reviews, no part of this book may be reproduced in any manner without prior written permission from the publisher. Write: Permissions, Wipf and Stock Publishers, 199 W. 8th Ave., Suite 3, Eugene, OR 97401.

Wipf & Stock
An Imprint of Wipf and Stock Publishers
199 W. 8th Ave., Suite 3
Eugene, OR 97401

www.wipfandstock.com

PAPERBACK ISBN: 978-1-6667-3751-6
HARDCOVER ISBN: 978-1-6667-9703-9
EBOOK ISBN: 978-1-6667-9704-6

SEPTEMBER 15, 2022 3:35 PM

Contents

Preface | vii

Foreword by Corné J. Bekker | ix

Abbreviations | xiii

Introduction | 1

CHAPTER 1
Introduction to the Topic of Suffering in First Peter | 15

CHAPTER 2
Literature Review | 29

CHAPTER 3
Exegetical Analysis | 67

CHAPTER 4
Conclusion | 126

Bibliography | 141

Preface

THIS BOOK IS ABOUT SUFFERING. More pointedly it is about the role of suffering in Christian formation. To point the subject of the book even further, it is about the role of suffering in Christian formation in First Peter. As a result, one might read it and say, "What about joy or love or celebration?" This book is about a very specific topic in a very specific letter and as such it does not seek to provide a holistic model for Christian formation. It stands as a corrective supplement to all the other works on Christian formation, shining the light on something that they have, for the most part, omitted. So please read it as such.

As a guide to my readers. This book is intended to reach a wider audience than the original Master of Divinity thesis it is based upon. However, my high school mathematics teacher always chided me, saying "Show your work. I need to see how you got to the answer." Therefore, due to the nature of exegetical argumentation in New Testament studies I have reproduced the original Greek text in almost all of the citations so as to give the academic reader easy access to the primary text. However, for the lay reader, please just skip over the Greek to the English quotation which follows directly below it.

I pray that the Lord would bless you as you engage with this book. May it inspire hope and endurance as you follow in his footsteps.

Frans-Johan Pienaar
Summer 2022

Foreword

THE CHRISTIAN FAITH FINDS its truest test and most profound dimension in suffering. Towards the end of his life, Martin Luther wrote a lengthy critique of the church of his day and her desperate need for revival and reformation. In the conclusion of this treatise, Luther identifies seven marks of the true church. He lists suffering as the culminating identifier of true Christianity. Luther[1] writes:

> Seventh, the holy Christian people are externally recognized by the holy possession of the sacred cross. They must endure every misfortune and persecution, all kinds of trials and evil from the devil, the world, and the flesh . . . in order to become like their head, Christ. And the only reason they must suffer is that they steadfastly adhere to Christ and God's word, enduring this for the sake of Christ.

Luther roots his theology of suffering firmly within the apostolic and faithful teachings of the church, building on the foundation of Christ, who warned his disciples that suffering was an essential part of following him (Luke 9:21–27), and the apostle Paul, who explained to early Christians that they were called to suffer for Christ's sake (Phil 1:27–30). This biblical truth, that "God's people are a suffering people,"[2] is central to Luther's understanding of the dynamics of a faith reformed and a church renewed. Nowhere is this clearer than in Luther's exegesis of the First Letter of Peter in the New Testament. Luther considered 1 Peter among the "noblest books in the New Testament"[3] and said it contained the "pure gospel."[4]

---

1. Pelikan and Lehmann, *Luther's Works*, 41:164–65 (hereafter LW).
2. Woo, "Suffering as a Mark of the Church," 307.
3. Foreword to "Sermons on the First Epistle of St. Peter," LW 30:4.
4. "Epistel S. Petri gepredigt und ausgelegt, 1523," in *D. Martin Luthers Werke:*

FOREWORD

In Luther's detailed and rich exegesis of 1 Peter, he links suffering most deeply with the power and the centrality of God's word in his church, "God's Word cannot be without God's people, and conversely, God's people cannot be without God's Word."[5] It is when Christians cling to the word of God that they often experience suffering that is "unjust" (1 Pet 2:19), when they are "zealous for what is good" (1 Pet 3:13), and "for the name of Christ" (1 Pet 4:14).[6] It is because Christians cling to the word of God that they experience suffering so that they might themselves learn to rejoice in the sufferings of Christ and "be glad when his glory is revealed" (1 Pet 4:13). Luther sees in this suffering the promise of the transformative power of the gospel, the link between Christ-centered suffering and sanctification:

> [God] lays the holy cross on our backs to strengthen us and make faith powerful in us. The holy Gospel is a powerful Word. Therefore it cannot do its work without trials, and only he who tastes it is aware that it has such power . . . God inflicts no glowing fire or heat-cross and suffering, which make you burn-on you for another purpose than 'to prove you,' where you also cling to His Word . . . When you suffer, you have communion with the Lord Christ.[7]

For Luther, we as Christians experience transformative suffering because "we hold to the Word of God, preach it, hear it, learn it, and practice it."[8] Suffering not only comes because we seek to imitate Christ as we obey his word; part of this suffering that transforms is when we wrestle with the content of God's word and its implications in our world. Luther sees this constant struggle with God's holy word as essential in the process of faithful exegesis. When speaking about the importance of this struggle (Latin *tentatio*, German *anfechtung*)[9] in the process of interpretation, Luther writes:[10]

> This is the touchstone which teaches you not only to know and understand, but also to experience how right, how true, how sweet, how lovely, how mighty, how comforting God's wisdom is, wisdom beyond all wisdom.

Kritische Gesantausgabe (Weimar: H. Böhlau, 1914), 12:260. (Hereafter WA).

5. LW 41:149–50.
6. Woo, "Suffering as a Mark of the Church," 314.
7. LW 30:12–27.
8. "Sermon at Coburg on Cross and Suffering, 1530," LW 51:200–201.
9. Woo, "Suffering as a Mark of the Church," 321.
10. "Preface to the Wittenberg Edition of Luther's German Writings, 1539" in LW 34:286–287.

Foreword

For Luther, it is the twin processes of experiencing the inner tension *(tentatio/anfechtung)* of grappling with Christ's example and the experience of suffering as we seek to imitate him that brings transformation to us.

Peter centers his message on the innocent suffering Christ (1 Pet 4:1) in his first letter. This message is an acute and challenging appeal to the early followers of Jesus who lived as "elect exiles" (1 Pet 1:1) in first-century Asia Minor and who "endured severe suffering for their faith."[11] Peter structured his message around a robust reflection on crucial Old Testament texts;[12] Isaiah 53 as the foundation for his Christology of the suffering Savior and the Greek text (LXX) of Psalm 33 (Ps 34 in the Hebrew and English texts) for his exhortation on how to endure suffering in ways that glorify God. In this letter, Peter sees the Godly suffering of David in Psalm 33 (LXX) as a divine prefiguring of the innocent suffering of Christ.[13] Peter finds in the wrestling of faith *(tentatio)* of David in Psalm 33 (LXX) the prophetic prefiguring of the kenotic suffering of Christ. When Christians seek to imitate the example of Christ in his sinless suffering, they are blessed and rewarded as "the Spirit of glory and of Christ rests" (1 Pet 4:14) on them. Rebecca Skaggs[14] comments on the role of the Holy Spirit in 1 Peter regarding the suffering of God's elect when she writes, "the Spirit functions as agent, bringing the blessing as the reward of suffering." God's Spirit sustains and transforms us amid our suffering.

In his own time, Martin Luther, deeply disturbed by the temporal corruption and theological drift the church, turned to 1 Peter to make sense of the purpose of his suffering as he sought to bring reform and renewal to the people of God. Frans-Johan Pienaar turns to the same ancient text and, through careful exegetical analysis and robust theological conversation with the extant research literature, uncovers the clear message of Peter for our time. His engaging and challenging book reminds us of Peter's eternal message, "But rejoice insofar as you share Christ's sufferings, that you may also rejoice and be glad when his glory is revealed" (1 Pet 4:13 ESV). Pienaar's reading of 1 Peter is bristling with the desire to see the church renewed and reformed. Like Luther, he longs for a pure and true church. Like Peter, he maintains that the God of all grace will "restore, confirm, strengthen,

---

11. Jung, "Between Texts and Sermon," 57.
12. Jobes, "'O Taste and See,'" 241.
13. Christensen, "Solidarity in Suffering and Glory," 351.
14. Skaggs, "Spirit in 1 Peter," 538.

and establish" (1 Pet 5:10) us only through a mimetic solidarity with Christ and his suffering (1 Pet 5:10).

May we have ears to hear, and hearts open to receiving this ancient and biblical message. May God's church be renewed in solidarity with the suffering of Christ through the power of the Holy Spirit.

"To Him be the dominion forever and ever. Amen." (1 Pet 5:11 ESV)

Corné J. Bekker
Dean and Professor,
Regent University School of Divinity

Abbreviations

ANF	*Ante-Nicene Fathers*
ANRW	*Aufstieg und Niedergang der römischen Welt: Geschichte und Kultur Roms im Spiegel der neueren Forschung*. Part 2, *Principat*. Edited by Hildegard Temporini and Wolfgang Haase. Berlin: de Gruyter, 1972–.
BECNT	Baker Exegetical Commentary on the New Testament
BNTC	Black's New Testament Commentaries
CBC	Cambridge Bible Commentary
CTQ	*Concordia Theological Quarterly*
Int	*Interpretation*
JOTT	*Journal of Translation and Textlinguistics*
JSNT	*Journal for the Study of the New Testament*
JSNTSup	Journal for the Study of the New Testament Supplement Series
NAC	New American Commentary
NICNT	New International Commentary on the New Testament
RevExp	*Review and Expositor*
SBL	Society of Biblical Literature
TDNT	*Theological Dictionary of the New Testament*. Edited by Gerhard Kittel and Gerhard Friedrich. Translated by Geoffrey W. Bromiley 10 vols. Grand Rapids: Eerdmans, 1964–76.
WBC	Word Biblical Commentary

Introduction

IS SUFFERING PART OF God's plan for the Christian life? This question is one that every Christian will ponder at some point. Many answer this question with a resounding "No!" Some argue that God's promise of abundant life (John 10:10) implies that suffering cannot come from him. We struggle to reconcile a good God known for his loving-kindness and steadfast mercy (e.g., Ps 100:5) with Job's life (God never did explain to Job why he had to suffer; Job 38:1—40:2), or with Paul's words to the Philippians: "For it has been granted to you that for the sake of Christ you should not only believe in him but also suffer for his sake" (Phil 1:29). Other books on spiritual formation might have themes like spiritual disciplines or communal engagement in common, but suffering is often not included as a crucial element of Christian growth.[1] We resign ourselves to the fact that this life can be brutal, but we try to avoid suffering at all costs and get stuck in questions of theodicy—How can a good God allow evil things to happen?[2] Certain contemporary Christian leaders also struggle to embrace the idea that suffering might be sent by God for the purpose of formation. Kenneth Copeland labels the idea that God can use suffering for our benefit as "absolutely against the Word of God."[3] Joel Osteen seems to believe that suffering is the result of having the wrong mindset, and that if one merely thinks in the correct way everything will fall into place as one desires them to.[4] In other words, a person's thoughts and words become determinative for the outcome of their life; reality is, therefore, self-generated instead of chosen

---

1. Chandler, *Christian Spiritual Formation*; Earley and Dempsey, *Spiritual Formation Is*; Pettit, *Foundations of Spiritual Formation*; Miller, *Spiritual Formation of Leaders*.

2. This book does not try to address the question of theodicy in a systematic way. For a short analysis see, Blomberg, *Can We Still Believe in God?*, 1–16.

3. Copeland, "Why Do Bad Things Happen?," para. 2.

4. Osteen, *Next Level Thinking*, 1–13.

by God. In another monograph, Osteen desires every day to be "a Friday."[5] Happiness, for Osteen, is to cease from work and receive the fulfilment of all your desires. This theology of positive thinking is similar to what one finds in Word of Faith circles.

These communities conclude that suffering is antithetical to God's kingdom in Christ and must be banished at all costs.[6] However, they need a way to explain the suffering that is evident in everyday life. Instinctively, they know that it is not wise to blame God, so they opt for blaming it on the believer's lack of faith.[7] At the core of their belief system lie four themes: "*faith, health, wealth,* and *victory.*"[8] If someone has enough faith, whatever they declare becomes reality.[9] This kind of faith is most clearly demonstrated by personal prosperity and health.[10] The glaring problem is that God's will for the believer's life is synonymous with their every desire, and that everything outside the realm of their desires is simply present because of weak faith.

This type of thinking, or various adaptations thereof, is pervasive amongst Christian preachers in the West.[11] The reader may be tempted to dismiss these preachers out of hand, viewing them as being on the fringes of the Christian movement, but that would be a grave mistake. Jones and Woodbridge show in an extensive volume that out of the 262

---

5. Osteen, *Every Day a Friday*.

6. Rouse, *Why Suffering Cannot Be God's Will*, 1–199; Magno, *Suffering Is Not God's Will*, 1–226; Kenneth Copeland, "Should I Expect?" "Kenneth Copeland has taught that there was a time in history when the whole body of Christ was under a unique attack of the enemy. During that time, many believers received the anointing of God to endure martyrdom (dying for Jesus). He believes the anointing was there to experience this without pain. (Stephen, for example, simply fell asleep in Acts 7:60.) Unfortunately, when God stopped that spirit of death, much of the body of Christ still kept a 'martyrdom mentality.' Believers were so used to suffering, they continued to think this was necessary even though that level of persecution had stopped" (Copeland, "Should I Expect?," lines 1–5). In *Next Level Thinking*, Osteen believes that if one just thinks in the correct way all things will fall into place as one desires them to.

7. Savelle, *If Satan Can't*; Copeland, "Understanding Chastisement."

8. Bowler, *Blessed*, 7 (emphasis original).

9. Bowler, *Blessed*, 7.

10. Bowler, *Blessed*, 7.

11. Bowler, *Blessed*, 253, provides a list of preachers who would fall within the category of "prosperity" preachers. Benny Hinn, Joel Osteen, Creflo Dollar, Kenneth Hagin, and Kenneth Copeland, to name a few, all have audiences in the millions. Thus, to dismiss it as merely a fringe movement would be a grave mistake.

INTRODUCTION

largest congregations in America, fifty actively promote this theology.[12] Joel Osteen's television program is available in 100 countries and more than a million people download his sermons every week.[13] Countless people are left without the capacity to make sense of suffering in a helpful manner and are wholly unable to embrace it as a formative tool; in fact, the inevitable suffering that comes their way hampers them in their Christian walk as they turn inward and try to find answers for why their faith is failing.

Our capacity to process suffering is also stunted by the unprecedented prosperity and health that many people, at least those in the developed world, have come to accept as normal over the past sixty years. In Rome, between 200 BC, and AD 200, 30 percent of infants would die before they turned one year old.[14] Moreover, half of the remaining 70 percent who made it past one year would die before turning fifteen years old.[15] That is an astronomical number, and a brutal reality to live in. In the 1950s, the global infant mortality rate almost halved to 16 percent, and the youth mortality rate similarly dropped to 27 percent.[16] This is still an astronomical number by today's standards. Today's mortality rates are 2.9 percent for infants and 4.6 percent for youths.[17] Thus, where it would have been highly likely for parents to lose at least one child to death during their lives, it has now become a devastating exception. To add to this, in the USA the average individual's income doubled from 1940 to 2012, and the average household income almost tripled in the same period.[18] Affluence and modern medical practices, not to mention the widespread availability of utilities like electricity (in 1932, only 10 percent of rural America had access to electricity), [19] have enabled many to limit suffering that would have been historically unavoidable. We are not as exposed to disease, we are able to survive financially, and our individual freedoms have caused us to buy into the notion that we can (and should!) create our own realities and choose

---

12. Jones and Woodbridge, *Health, Wealth, and Happiness*, 17.
13. Joel Osteen Ministries, "Our Ministry."
14. Roser, "Mortality Rates of Children," chart #1.
15. Roser, "Mortality Rates of Children," para. 7.
16. Roser, "Mortality Rates of Children," chart #1.
17. Roser, "Mortality Rates of Children." para. 7.
18. Russell Sage Foundation, "Real Mean and Median Income," See first chart. Individual income grew from $19, 549 to $40, 563, whilst household income grew from $27, 255 to $71, 274. All figures have been adjusted to show real income.
19. Wallace, "Power from the People," para. 2.

our own paths. When coupled with an understanding of the Christian God as one who exists to make us even more prosperous and healthy, we become wholly unable to conceive of suffering as a necessary part of Christian formation.

As much as we try, we cannot get away from the centrality of suffering in the biblical text as is shown by this book's analysis of 1 Peter. Changes in the world around us, such as widespread instability brought on by COVID-19 over the last two years, also seem to indicate that the relative stability we have come to trust may be less stable than we would like. The illusion of control that people in the West have lulled themselves into through the accumulation of wealth and a plethora of insurance schemes is crumbling. Suddenly, the stock market can plummet overnight because of a new variant. Medical technology cannot guarantee that someone will survive an infection with the virus, regardless of health, age, or demographic. As always, God shakes that which is shakable so that his reality, that which is unshakeable, remains.[20] Suffering suddenly seems unavoidable. So, what do we do now? We must reflect psychologically, socially, and, most importantly, biblically on the purpose of suffering. We then must allow what we discover to shape our perceptions and determine our disposition.

Luckily for us, psychologists have been reflecting on the purpose of suffering for decades. Haidt and Lukianoff, in *The Coddling of the American Mind: How Good Intentions and Bad Ideas Are Setting Up a Generation for Failure*, note a great "untruth" that is ravaging society:[21] "The Untruth of Fragility: What Doesn't Kill You Makes You Weaker."[22] They demonstrate how we have largely embraced the notion that humans are inherently fragile, and that suffering hampers us from flourishing. They do so by observing how the terms related to safety (i.e., danger, trauma, abuse, and so forth) have taken on new meanings. In the twentieth century, "safety" generally referred to safety from physical abuse or danger. However, in the twenty-first century this term has undergone what Nick Haslam, a noted psychologist, calls "concept creep": an expanding of the term's intended meaning.[23] This creep occurs "outward"—a term's range of meaning is expanded (safety, for instance, does not only refer to physical but also emotional threats) as well

---

20. Heb 12:27.

21. Haidt and Lukianoff, *Coddling*, 20–52. They actually note three great untruths, but only one is noteworthy for the purposes of this study.

22. Haidt and Lukianoff, *Coddling*, 20, 32.

23. Haslam, "Concept Creep," 1–17.

INTRODUCTION

as "downward" (lesser inconveniences are now also viewed as leaving a person unsafe). To illustrate, when Oberlin College released a memo in 2014 urging professors to use trigger warnings and the correct pronouns when referring to students, they stated that those who fail to do so "prevents or impairs their safety in the classroom."[24] Society has changed what it means to keep a person safe and what should be deemed as dangerous. No longer is it enough to set up systems intended to prevent the kind of bodily harm that might land a person in the hospital. We now deem a person unsafe if their subjective assessment of their own emotional state of equilibrium is disrupted by anything outside of the person. The correct action, according to the powers that be, is to remove this disruption, regardless of logic or truth.

Haslam's study on concept creep reveals that in the field of psychology the category of trauma has undergone a similar shift.[25] In the early versions of the *Diagnostic and Statistical Manual of Mental Disorders* (DSM)[26] trauma was used by psychiatrists "only to describe a physical agent causing physical damage, as in the case of what we now call *traumatic brain injury*."[27] However, in the 2000 version of the DSM, the meaning of trauma shifted to include anything "*experienced by an individual* as physically or emotionally harmful . . . with lasting adverse effects on the individual's functioning and mental, physical, social, emotional, or spiritual well-being."[28] The meaning of trauma shifted from being only a designation of physical, abnormal activity that would affect all people in a damaging way to including any subjective experiences determined harmful by the subject.[29] Therefore, there is no longer an objective matrix through which to determine whether trauma is real or only perceived.[30]

As with trauma, so it is with danger. Haidt and Lukianoff show how in the internet generation, suffering and danger are no longer defined as physical phenomena but include anything that can be emotionally disturbing.[31]

---

24. Quoted in Haidt and Lukianoff, *Coddling*, 25.
25. Haslam, "Concept Creep."
26. American Psychiatric Association, "History of the DSM."
27. Haidt and Lukianoff, *Coddling*, 25 (emphasis original).
28. Substance Abuse and Mental Health Services Administration, quoted in Haidt and Lukianoff, *Coddling*, 26 (emphasis original).
29. Haslam, "Concept Creep."
30. Haslam, "Concept Creep."
31. Haidt and Lukianoff, *Coddling*, 24–31; see also, Tweng, *iGen*.

Furthermore, the notion exists that all threats to a person, whether emotional or physical, should be removed.[32] This has resulted in what we now call the "safe space" movement on college campuses all over America and the UK. At its essence, campuses are safe spaces when any idea that makes a person feel uncomfortable needs to be censored. Gone are the days where students sign up for a university education with the expectation that their ideas and mindsets will be challenged and changed. Even grading has been deemed an oppressive practice by some in the United States due to its alleged promotion of inequality and oppression of minority groups.[33] Students, rather than receiving a D or an F, should be given an opportunity to take the test/assignment again; if they fail to complete the assignment or fail the final exam they are given an "incomplete."[34] A further reason, according to Patricia Russel, an advisor to various school districts in the USA, is that giving a student a D or an F grade can cause "*significant psychological repercussions.*"[35] In the same vein, both the University of California and Harvard University will no longer consider SAT scores during the admission process.[36]

These trends indicate that humans are regarded as inherently fragile to the point where they should be guarded from all unsavory experiences. They are not expected to survive, let alone thrive, in environments where they encounter any kind of pushback. Is this a helpful view of human nature? Nassim Nicholas Taleb, in his book *Antifragile*,[37] labels this view as inherently counterproductive by showing that it is precisely during uncontrollable and threatening moments where humanity has the largest opportunity for progress.[38] We require stressors, unforeseen changes, and challenges in order to learn and to adapt.[39] Not only are we able to survive these moments, but they drive us to dig deeper, so to speak, and result in

---

32. Haidt and Lukianoff, *Coddling*, 24–31; see also, Tweng, *iGen*.
33. Cost, "Critics Lambast Coddling Schools."
34. Cost, "Critics Lambast Coddling Schools."
35. Quoted in Cost, "Critics Lambast Coddling Schools," para. 19 (emphasis added).
36. Cost, "Critics Lambast Coddling Schools"; Ali, "Harvard Ditching Standardized Testing Requirements."
37. Taleb, *Antifragile*.
38. Taleb, *Antifragile*, 5.
39. Taleb, *Antifragile*, 5.

INTRODUCTION

exponential growth. Just as muscle atrophy is unavoidable when someone is bedridden, those who are sheltered from stressors end up weak.[40]

In the same vein, Haidt and Lukianoff state that the avoidance of triggers does not prevent PTSD.[41] Rather, the fact that someone is triggered is simply an indication that the person suffers from PTSD. When the person receives true healing, the trigger loses its power.[42] Likewise, when people are triggered emotionally it should not move us to eliminate the trigger but rather to ask why it leaves the person overwhelmed. Richard McNally, director of clinical training at the University of Harvard's Department of Psychology, notes:

> Trigger warnings are counter-therapeutic because they encourage avoidance of reminders of trauma, and avoidance maintains PTSD. Severe emotional reactions triggered by course material are a signal that students need to prioritize their mental health and obtain evidence-based, cognitive-behavioral therapies that will help them overcome PTSD. These therapies involve gradual, systematic exposure to traumatic memories until their capacity to trigger distress diminishes."[43]

Rather than avoiding these triggers, people should be encouraged to face them since this is the only way to overcome them. To do otherwise is to empower abnormal behavioral tendencies in people.

The dominant culture in the West is teaching people to close themselves off to all things that they find disagreeable. In fact, they are to militantly oppose and discredit such views.[44] However, society's avoidance of suffering with an evangelistic fervor is ironically what will cause it to suffer even more. On both physical and psychological levels, discomfort proves to be essential in building strength and resilience. If one removes all of these stressors, basic bodily and societal functions are seriously hampered.

---

40. Taleb, *Antifragile*, 5.
41. Haidt and Lukianoff, *Coddling*, 29.
42. Haidt and Lukianoff, *Coddling*, 29.
43. McNally, "If You Need," para. 5. McNally shows how triggers are actually beneficial to PTSD patients instead of destructive.
44. This militant opposition has been termed cancel culture; in other words, any idea that disagrees with the popular metanarrative should be rejected and quieted. We see this happen in examples like the Christian baker who was sued for refusing to bake a cake for a homosexual couple. See Slevin, "Christian Baker Sued Again." This even occurs with secular voices like J. K. Rowling, who spoke out against transgenderism (Sachdeva, "Harry Potter Fans").

Why has society responded so favorably towards this heightened and skewed emphasis on safety? One might assume that people have just become oversensitive, that an increase in affluence and relative security in many parts of the world have left us somewhat delicate. Carl Trueman believes that it runs much deeper than this. He summarizes:

> While hostile commentators berate this tendency as that caused by the hypersensitivity of a generation of "snowflakes," it is actually the result of the slow but steady psychologizing of the self and the triumph of inward-directed therapeutic categories over traditional outward-directed educational philosophies. That which hinders my outward expression of my inner feelings—that which challenges or attempts to falsify my psychological beliefs about myself and thus to disturb my sense of inner well-being—is by definition harmful and to be rejected. And that means that traditional institutions must be transformed to conform to the psychological self, not vice versa."[45]

People are undergoing a radical change in how they construct reality. They make sense of the world not by observing how society is ordered and then conforming to it, but rather they look inward to what they perceive themselves to be and then try to bend societal norms and constructs accordingly. To illustrate, a statement like "I am a woman trapped in a man's body," would not have been commonplace a few decades ago. People would have observed other men and women around them, and then adjusted their own expression to fit into society. Today, this statement could cause a person to be ushered onto the cover of *Time* as a cultural hero. What would have been a nonsensical idea has become a viable, even admirable, form of self-expression.

THE NATURE OF THE SELF AND THE SOCIAL IMAGINARY[46]

It is helpful here to reflect on what philosopher Charles Taylor calls the *social imaginary*—how people make sense of their surroundings.[47] The social imaginary consists not so much of a set of conscious rules but rather a set of

---

45. Trueman, *Rise and Triumph*, 47–48.
46. I am indebted to Carl Trueman's volume for the helpful insights in constructing this section. See Trueman, *Rise and Triumph*, 27–71.
47. Taylor, *Modern Social Imaginaries*, 2.

INTRODUCTION

accepted intuitions about reality, a worldview one might call it. As with all worldview constructs, it can be hard to pinpoint since it exists subliminally.[48] However, although it isn't overt, it has a powerful effect on how society functions.[49]

Taylor, in his book *A Secular Age*, describes how the social imaginary has shifted in recent years from *mimesis* to *poiesis*.[50] Mimesis refers to the process of imitating that which exists in the external world. A *mimetic* society regards the outside world as having intrinsic meaning which is to be discovered and conformed to.[51] Thus, the meaning of life is found outside of the individual. In a Christian sense, one's life purpose is not discovered by looking within, but rather by engaging with God's call that exists outside of oneself. The apostle Paul, for instance, did not spend time looking inward to try and figure out what he enjoyed, what his strengths and weakness were, or how God made him in order to determine how he might best, and with the most enjoyment, serve the Lord. He received an external call from God, both in a generic sense (to submit to Christ as the Son of God and to be conformed to the image of Christ—Acts 9; Rom 8:29) and in a specific sense (as an apostle to the gentiles, e.g., Gal 1:15–16). God's will, and the needs of those around him, determined what he needed to focus his energy on.

A *poietic* society, by contrast, "sees the world as so much raw material out of which meaning and purpose can be created by the individual."[52] The world does not possess intrinsic meaning, nor is there an objective truth to be discovered. The individual is called to impose meaning on the raw material in a way that best suits their self-expression, and those around them are called to affirm and celebrate their self-expression. This change in how we view reality has allowed a redefinition of what it means to be a person or a "self." Our personhood is no longer something that is defined by a communal, external reality; rather, the modern conception of the self has made a decisive, inward shift.[53] Self-creation, Trueman observes, becomes "a routine part of our modern social imaginary."[54] I can (and should!) create

---

48. Taylor, *Modern Social Imaginaries*, 2.
49. Taylor, *Modern Social Imaginaries*, 2.
50. Taylor, *Secular Age*, 97–99.
51. Taylor, *Secular Age*, 97–99.
52. Trueman, *Rise and Triumph*, 39; Taylor, *Secular Age*, 97–99.
53. Taylor, *Sources of the Self*, x.
54. Trueman, *Rise and Triumph*, 42.

Called to Suffer

or re-create myself into anything that I feel best expresses by inward self. For example, if I feel like a woman trapped in a man's body, I can use surgical means to create a new self. Authenticity to who I imagine myself to be is the highest purpose of life, and expressing this inner reality becomes a crucial part of human existence.

This correlates with what sociologist Philip Rieff calls the psychological man.[55] The psychological man refers to people who no longer find their identity in external activities but rather through an inward search for psychological happiness.[56] Thus, for the modern person ultimate virtue is found through an inward focus.[57] Nothing outside of the individual self has the right to determine "who I am." Taylor calls this expressive individualism a "culture of authenticity," and describes it as follows:

> I mean the understanding of life which emerges with the Romantic expressivism of the late-eighteenth century, that each one of us has his/her own way of realizing our humanity, and that it is important to find and live out one's own, as against surrendering to conformity with a model imposed on us from outside, by society, or the previous generation, or religious or political authority.[58]

The individual must not only express his own inner self but must resist all attempts from external factors to impinge on this expression. Parents, government, even pastors no longer retain the right to tell you who you are, or what you are supposed to do. This is a reversal of epic proportions.

Maybe this is best seen in the field of psychology. Historically, the therapist's role was to help the patient grasp the nature of the community in which he belonged.[59] In the religious world of the Middle Ages, the therapist/priest trained individuals in the various practices, rituals, and beliefs of the church so that the person could participate in the life of the community.[60] These things were aimed to promote commitment to the community, which has always been conceived of as prior to, and of greater importance than, the individual.[61]

---

55. Rieff, "Reflections," 3–10.

56. Rieff, "Reflections," 3–10.

57. Rieff, "Reflections," 3–10; Taylor, *Secular Age*, 474–75; see also, Truman, *Rise and Triumph*, 44–48, for a helpful analysis.

58. Taylor, *Secular Age*, 475.

59. Rieff, *Triumph of the Therapeutic*, 57; Trueman, *Rise and Triumph*, 47.

60. Rieff, *Triumph of the Therapeutic*, 57; Trueman, *Rise and Triumph*, 47.

61. Rieff, *Triumph of the Therapeutic*, 57; Trueman, *Rise and Triumph*, 47.

Introduction

Trueman summarizes this shift well:

> In short, the basic thrust of much modern thinking serves to shatter the idea of the individual as one whose best interests are served by being educated to conform to the canons and protocols of society. And that is the intellectual foundation . . . whereby therapy ceases to serve the purpose of socializing an individual. Instead, it seeks to protect the individual from the kind of harmful neuroses that society itself creates through its smothering of the individual's ability simply to be herself.[62]

In the past, institutions were bigger than the individual, and as the individual participated in these institutions and conformed to them, he/she found meaning.[63] Notice that it was based on the belief that individual flourishing is locked up in communal flourishing. People found "purpose and well-being by being committed to something outside themselves."[64] The psychological, expressive, and authentic individual reverses this age-old order. Institutions must now serve the individual and their inner sense of purpose and well-being. Trueman contends: "institutions cease to be places for the formation of individuals via their schooling in the various practices and disciplines that allow them to take their place in society. Instead, they become platforms for performance, where individuals are allowed to be their authentic selves precisely because they are able to give expression to who they are 'inside.'"[65] Society has shifted from viewing institutions as having a primary role in the shaping of character. Rather, these institutions must provide the individual with a platform or tools to express and display themselves before the world.[66] Consequently, even the contemporary discourse on ethics and morality has broken down, because contemporary society envisions all moral truth claims as expressions of emotional preference.[67] Institutions, then, are harmful and oppressive if they seek to impose any external molds or forms onto the person. Only institutions which allow me to express or perform who I really am inside are worth keeping around.

Why is this shift in how we make sense of the world important in our reflection on the role of suffering in Christian formation? In short,

---

62. Trueman, *Rise and Triumph*, 48.
63. Trueman, *Rise and Triumph*, 48.
64. Trueman, *Rise and Triumph*, 48–49.
65. Trueman, *Rise and Triumph*, 49.
66. Levin, *Time to Build*, 33–34.
67. MacIntyre, *After Virtue*, 23.

because suffering involves living through something that we would rather avoid if we had the choice. Even Jesus prays for the cup to pass from him when he encounters his ultimate trial (Matt 26:39). The reality is that the Christian life involves a process of slowly, and often painfully, letting go of ourselves—our needs, goals, and desires. God promises that this brings life—those who deny themselves and lose their lives will find life (Matt 16:24–26). But if we approach life from the stance that ultimate meaning is found by expressing that which lines up with our inner sense of self we will struggle to embrace the not-so-pleasant turns that God might bring across our paths. Teleology, or the idea that humans are created in the image of God and that God determines our telos (our purpose or ultimate end), becomes an unpalatable lens through which to view the world. A God who stands outside of us and who has full authority to define what is acceptable and what is expected of us becomes offensive. A life that is supposed to be lived with the ultimate end of glorifying him and displaying his nature to the world becomes nonsensical. Suffering, or anything that can inconvenience our pursuit of authenticity, becomes something that needs to be avoided or denounced as oppressive.

SELF-EXPRESSION AS THE ULTIMATE CHRISTIAN GOAL

Unfortunately, the language of self-expression has become so intertwined with contemporary Christian ideas that many have been duped into viewing authenticity as the highest virtue of the Christian life. In fact, in many ways some Christian leaders have acquiesced to this philosophical metanarrative, albeit with a Jesus sticker on the front. As an example, Carl Lentz, in his book *Own the Moment*,[68] proposes that the world would be a better place if people just owned the moment. By doing this we could make a difference in other people's lives, while also enjoying our own lives more fully. In the chapter called "If Jesus had Instagram," Lentz mentions the cross of Christ.[69] However, the cross is presented not as an example of sacrificial love for others, nor as an object of Christian suffering that results in formation (as Heb 5:7–9 indicates), but rather as something that Jesus embraced so we don't have to.[70] It doesn't point to the call to suffer for

---

68. Lentz, *Own the Moment*.
69. Lentz, *Own the Moment*, 111.
70. Lentz, *Own the Moment*, 111–14.

Introduction

others but rather to the fulfilment of a glamorous purpose.[71] This purpose, however, is not something that is received from external sources, i.e., from God. Rather, Lentz asks:

> Do you love where your career is headed? Are you happy with the trail you leave behind in this life? . . . If you answered no to any of these questions, it's not too late. It starts by seeking the truth. You may have to dig deep into who you *were* to actually find out who you *are* and who you can *become*.[72]

The truth here, for Lentz, is not the truth that God has called us in Christ Jesus to be conformed to his image. Rather, it is an inner truth. A person's identity is found as we dig deeper into ourselves. Moreover, what precipitates this inward search is again not a confrontation with the revelation of God's calling but an unhappiness with my current state of life. Lentz, in fact, never connects one's purpose in life with the call to be conformed to Christ's image. Instead, he proposes that everyone, regardless of their religious affiliation, can fulfill their purpose[73] by just taking a long hard look at themselves and deciding to own the moment.[74] This leaves one with the impression that Lentz's gospel is no more than an adage on self-help with a superficial veneer of Christian language. It is, then, not surprising to discover that, according to Lentz, suffering is not from God and it can never be embraced as a positive thing.[75] In fact, for Lentz, if a person can imagine something and believe it for long enough, then he can have whatever he desires and become whatever he wants to be.[76]

This presentation of Christianity by writers like Lentz, Osteen, and others is built around an understanding of personhood where authentic self-creation is the ultimate goal. Unfortunately, a Christianity that is

---

71. Lentz, *Own the Moment*, 123.

72. Lentz, *Own the Moment*, 123 (emphasis original).

73. Lentz's proposal seems to indicate that our purpose comes from within ourselves.

74. Even when he makes a moving appeal for Christ right at the end of the book, he proceeds to collapse it into a form of humanism. Thus, it fails to connect the cross with something Christians have to embrace, unless it means I can't sleep with my girlfriend, and as a result it fails to connect the redemption of our world and our relationships with the work of Christ.

75. Positive suffering is suffering that is embraced, because one deems it to be a necessary part of the Christian life. Positive suffering is deemed necessary for both our formation and eternal salvation. Passive suffering is something that is accepted as part of life and maybe even beneficial, but should be avoided if possible.

76. Lentz, *Own the Moment*, 267.

rooted in self-determination is inherently flawed since it exalts humanity to the position of creator. Married with the inclination to construct reality according to one's own inner desires, it becomes a death trap for anyone who wishes to venture onto the road of Christian formation. We would all do well to accept that God determines what is real, necessary, helpful, and good.

It is outside the scope of this book to explore every aspect of this backdrop in detail.[77] Rather, this book focuses on specifically bringing a helpful corrective to the notion that all suffering is against God's plan. It hopes to help the reader navigate the inevitable trials that life brings so that they might be embraced as agents of formation with greater ease. It hopes to help the reader see that suffering is one of the greatest blessings God can send into your life, even though it might not feel that way. As Hebrews 12:11 says, "For the moment all discipline seems painful rather than pleasant, but later it yields the peaceful fruit of righteousness to those who have been trained by it."

In order to convey a robust theology of suffering as necessary for Christian formation this book now turns to the letter of 1 Peter.

---

77. For a thorough critique of the health, wealth, and prosperity movement, see Jones and Woodbridge, *Health, Wealth, and Happiness.*

Chapter 1

Introduction to the Topic of Suffering in 1 Peter

THE IDEA THAT SUFFERING produces formation is not new.[1, 2, 3] However, in many texts on Christian spiritual formation, suffering is omitted.[4] These books make scant mention of suffering but never treat it as a topic in its own right. Contrarily, the New Testament reflects on suffering quite extensively. First Peter presents one of the longest discourses on the topic of suffering, more so than any other epistle in the New Testament.[5] A cursory reading of 1 Peter presents the following occurrences of suffering grouped together in five broad categories:

---

1. Hall, "Suffering as Formation," 1.

2. All Greek New Testament quotations, unless otherwise noted, are from: K. Aland et al., *Novum Testamentum Graece*.

3. All English Bible quotations unless otherwise noted, are from the *English Standard Version*.

4. Chandler, *Christian Spiritual Formation*; Earley and Dempsey, *Spiritual Formation Is*; Pettit, *Foundations of Spiritual Formation*; Miller, *Spiritual Formation of Leaders*.

5. Hall, "Suffering as Formation," 70.

Table 1. Occurrences of Suffering in 1 Peter

Christ's Suffering	Necessity of Suffering	Two Types of Suffering	Purpose of Suffering	The Response to Suffering
Christ's suffering sets an example to be followed (2:21–24) Christ suffers for sins (3:18)	Suffering is necessary and will be followed by glory (1:6) Suffering is necessary because it completes the believer (5:9–11)	***Suffering for doing good:*** Suffering for good behavior is gracious in God's sight (2:19) Suffering for righteousness is blessed (3:14–16) Better to suffer for doing good than evil (3:17) If you suffer as a Christian, glorify God (4:16) Suffering according to God's will (4:19) ***Suffering for doing evil:*** Suffering for evil behavior is just desserts and has no value (2:20) Do not suffer as an evildoer or murderer for this is just desserts and has no value (4:15) Suffering as God's judgment (4:17)	Suffering purifies the faith of the believer (1:7) Trial enables the believer to obtain the goal of his faith, i.e., salvation (1:9) Suffering is following in Christ's footsteps, i.e., we become like him (2:21) It facilitates the believer's cessation from sin (4:1) The believer participates in Christ's suffering, i.e., it facilitates fellowship between the believer and Christ (4:13)	Bless those who curse (3:8–9) Have the same mindset as Christ towards suffering (4:1) Do not be surprised at the suffering (4:12) Rejoice in the suffering (4:16) Entrust yourself to a faithful creator (4:19)

Furthermore, a careful reading of 1 Peter presents a topical structure that shows how the letter is structured around the topic of suffering:

1. Suffering is necessary and will be followed by glory (1:6–9)

Introduction to the Topic of Suffering in 1 Peter

   a. These trials purify the believers (1:7)

2. These trials allow them to obtain the goal of their faith: the salvation of their souls (1:9)

3. Two types of suffering (2:19–20)

   a. Suffering for good behavior is gracious (2:19)

   b. Suffering for evil behavior is just desserts and has no value (2:20)

4. Christ has set the example through his suffering (2:21–24)

   a. Bless those who curse and revile (3:8–9)

   b. Suffering for righteousness is blessed (3:14–16)

   c. Better to suffer for doing good than evil (3:17)

   d. For Christ also suffered for our sins (3:18)

5. Therefore, because Christ suffered, believers are to have his same mindset (4:1)

   a. He who has suffered has ceased from sin (4:1)

   b. Do not be surprised at the suffering (4:12)

   c. Your suffering is participation in Christ's suffering (4:12–13)

   d. Do not suffer as an evildoer or murderer; this is just desserts and has no value (4:15)

   e. If you suffer as a Christian, glorify God (4:16)

   f. Suffer according to God's will (4:19)

6. Suffering is necessary and will be followed by glory (5:9–11)

At this point, it is necessary to mention a few things regarding the authorship, context, provenance, and audience of this letter. This study addresses these issues in full in the next chapter, so if the reader wants additional support, it is given there. However, these conclusions will inevitably shape the way one reads the text. Therefore, they are summarized below specifically as it relates to the topic of suffering.

Called to Suffer

Throughout the history of the church, the author of 1 Peter has always been claimed to be Peter the apostle,[6,7] who after coming to Rome[8] was martyred[9] there under Nero (AD 54–68).[10,11] This man who did not shrink away from his Christian duty, because of suffering, but in fact chose the road of suffering by going to Rome, "the belly of the beast." There he proclaimed the good news that Jesus Christ is Lord with boldness and paid the ultimate price for it. Indeed, according to Bockmuehl it is the audience's shared memory of Peter's suffering in Rome that gives this letter its pastoral weight and which guards it against misinterpretation.[12] Thus, Peter, a man who shortly after penning this letter gave his life for the Christian faith, stands behind this letter and encourages the Christians in Asia Minor to emulate the way of Christ, like he did, even at great personal cost. And all this knowing that they too would very likely have to pay the ultimate price for their allegiance to Christ. Peter presents Christ's death as the model, proceeds to emulate this model in his own life through his death, and finally expects his readers to do likewise.

---

6. Jobes, *1 Peter*, 14–19; Marshall, *1 Peter*, 21–24; Van Rensburg, "Code of Conduct," 476; Witherington III, *Letters and Homilies*, 53; Grudem, *1 Peter*, 37; McKnight, *1 Peter*, 29; Forbes, *Exegetical Guide*, 1–2; Michaels, *1 Peter*, lxvi–lxvii; Thiede, *From Galilee to Rome*, 177.

7. For the alternate view that Peter did not write the letter, see Achtemeier and Epp, *1 Peter*, 43; Beare, *First Epistle of Peter*, 47–48; Bechtler, *Following in His Steps*, 46; Boring, *1 Peter*, 30; Elliott, *1 Peter*, 118–30; Goppelt, *Commentary on 1 Peter*, 51; Horrell, *Epworth Commentaries*, 2; Schutter, *Hermeneutic and Composition*, 17–18; Le Roux, *Ethics in 1 Peter*, 15–21.

8. This is taken to be fact by Papias, Irenaeus, and Clement of Alexandria (see: Eusebius, *Ecclesiastical History*, 2.15; 3.11, 3.39, 15; 5.8.2–3; 6.14.5–7; also *1 Clem.* 5.1–4).

9. Peter's presence in Rome and his subsequent martyrdom is doubted or flatly denied by Boring, *1 Peter*, 30; Le Roux, *Ethics in 1 Peter*, 133; Goulder, "Did Peter Ever Go to Rome?," 377–97; Foakes-Jackson, *Peter*, vii.

10. In agreement with Witherington III, *Letters and Homilies*, 37–39, this study dates the letter to between AD 61 and 64. Scholars who deny Petrine authorship have various dates ranging from AD 70–105. See Bechtler, *Following in His Steps*, 46; Achtemeier and Epp, *1 Peter*, 42; Beare, *First Epistle of Peter*, 47–48; Elliott, *1 Peter*, 118–30.

11. *1 Clem.* 5.4; Eusebius, *Ecclesiastical History*, 2.25.4–8 citing Tertullian, Dionysius of Corinth and Gaius.

12. Bockmuehl, *Remembered Peter*, 90.

Introduction to the Topic of Suffering in 1 Peter

Now, turning to the question of the *Sitz im Leben* (Life situation)[13] in 1 Peter. All scholars agree that the audience[14] is experiencing slander, false accusations, and abuse for their beliefs.[15] Achtemeier notes that it is clear from the letter that the audience is suffering, and this suffering is widespread among Christians.[16] In the Mediterranean world of the first century, the state used religion in order to control the people as well as to prevent any official rebellion against Rome.[17] This religion expressed itself in the imperial cult, which is essentially, though not exclusively, the worship of the emperor.[18] Christians' rejection of the imperial cult would have been deemed highly inappropriate behavior.[19] Achtemeier and others show that there is no official policy for the persecution of Christians until late in the third century under Emperor Decius.[20] However, after the fire in Rome, Nero needed a scapegoat and proceeded to blame the Christians.[21]

---

13. All non-English words, phrases, and sentences have been given English counterparts for this edition. Where there are multiple options regarding interpretation all options will be given and then exegetical decisions will be made in the section that follows.

14. All scholars agree that the audience is somewhat mixed. However, they do not agree as to whether gentiles or Jews are the dominant group. For gentiles as dominant see, Elliott, *Home for the Homeless*, 64; Achtemeier and Epp, *1 Peter*, 51; Green, *1 Peter*, 5; Boring, *1 Peter*, 43; Hiebert, *1 Peter*, 16; Michaels, *1 Peter*, xlvi; Skaggs, *Pentecostal Commentary*, 9; Horrell, *Epworth Commentaries*, 48. For Jews as dominant, see Boring, *1 Peter*, 24; Witherington III, *Letters and Homilies*, 25–39; Starke, *Cities of God*, 78. Eusebius, Calvin, Wesley, and the church fathers took the audience to be primarily, if not entirely, consisting of Jewish Christians (see Witherington III, *Letters and Homilies*, 34).

15. Bechtler, *Following in His Steps*, 83–104; Achtemeier and Epp, *1 Peter*, 29; Donelson, *I & II Peter and Jude*, 11–12; Le Roux, *Ethics in 1 Peter*, 56–57; Kelly, *Epistles of Peter and Jude*, 189; Marshall, *1 Peter*, 24; Jobes, *1 Peter*, 45; Senior, *1 Peter*, 7.

16. Achtemeier and Epp, *1 Peter*, 34.

17. Magie, *Roman Rule in Asia Minor*, 1:572; Price, *Rituals and Power*, 179; Horrell, *1 Peter*, 55. See also Price, *Rituals and Power*, 59 for a chart of all the imperial temples in Asia Minor.

18. Magie, *Roman Rule in Asia Minor*, 1:572.

19. Schutter, *Hermeneutic and Composition*, 11; Bechtler, *Following in His Steps*, 84; Goppelt, *Commentary on 1 Peter*, 40; Benko, *Pagan Rome*, 1–29; Ste Croix, "Why Were the Early Christians Persecuted?," 24–31; Frend, *Martyrdom and Persecution*, 77–93; Wilken, *Christians as the Romans Saw Them*, 63–64.

20. Achtemeier and Epp, *1 Peter*, 29–36; Le Roux, *Ethics in 1 Peter*, 58; Elliott, *1 Peter*, 103. This, however, misses the point of the discussion completely. The question one has to ask is not whether there is some official document stating that this should happen, but whether this was happening officially or otherwise. The data is clear on this: Christians were being put to death for the faith.

21. Tacitus, "Annals," 15.44.

Tacitus recounts the violent nature of this persecution: some Christians were fed to wild beasts in the arena; others were nailed to crosses; still others were dipped in wax and set alight to serve as lamps in Nero's garden.[22] Suetonius, however, asserts that Nero's persecution of the Christians was not merely for the fire, but because he deemed their religion to be "A novel and malicious superstition."[23] Clearly, Nero is killing Christians (at least some of them) merely for bearing the name "χριστιανός" (Christian).[24] Furthermore, Pliny, the imperial governor in Pontus and Bithynia, killed Christians if they would not recant their Christian faith and pay homage to Caesar.[25] Local citizens could bring Christians before civic magistrates and this could lead to their death.[26] Therefore, Christians' proclamation that Christ is Lord, and, as a result, Caesar is not, was a life-threatening one. This was a tumultuous time in the empire. Persecution was a daily reality, and its nature was deadly. This is the real-life situation of Peter's audience. He writes to them, one suffering Christian to another, and hopes to encourage them and to help them to understand why they are suffering in this way. This study shows that Peter intends to help his readers understand the necessity, nature, source, and purpose of their suffering.

Out of the forty occurrences of the verb, "πάσχω" (I suffer) in the New Testament, eight of them are in 1 Peter (2:19, 20, 23; 3:14, 17; 4:15, 16, 19). The noun "πάθος" (suffering) and its cognates occur eight times in the letter (1:11; 2:21; 4:1 (2x), 13; 5:1, 9, 10). This does not include the occurrences of the following words and their cognates, all of which are related to suffering, persecution, and trials: "πειρασμός" (testing), "δοκιμάζω" (I test), "καταλαλέω" (slander), "φόβος" (fear/intimidation), "λυπέω" (I grieve/insult), "πυρόω" (fiery ordeal/crucible), and "κρίμα" (judgment).[27] Skaggs notes twenty-five occurrences of these various terms throughout the letter.[28] Out of the 105 verses in the entire letter, twenty-six of them

---

22. Tacitus, "Annals," 15.44.
23. Suetonius, "Life of Augustus," 16.
24. 1 Pet 4:16; Donelson, *I & II Peter and Jude*, 13.
25. Pliny the Younger, "Letters of Pliny the Younger"; Ste Croix, "Why Were the Early Christians Persecuted?—A Rejoinder," 28–33.
26. Le Roux, *Ethics in 1 Peter*, 51.
27. Skaggs, *Pentecostal Commentary*, 14.
28. Skaggs, *Pentecostal Commentary*, 14.

mention suffering in some shape or form.²⁹ The following table shows all the words in 1 Peter related to suffering:

Table 2. Words used for suffering in 1 Peter

Verse	Text	Specific Word
1:6	"ἐν ᾧ ἀγαλλιᾶσθε, ὀλίγον ἄρτι, εἰ δέον ἐστίν, λυπηθέντας ἐν ποικίλοις πειρασμοῖς" "In this you rejoice, though now for a little while, if necessary, you have been grieved by various trials"	λυπηθέντας & πειρασμοῖς
1:7	"ἵνα τὸ δοκίμιον ὑμῶν τῆς πίστεως πολυτιμότερον χρυσίου τοῦ ἀπολλυμένου, διὰ πυρὸς δὲ δοκιμαζομένου εὑρεθῇ εἰς ἔπαινον καὶ δόξαν καὶ τιμὴν ἐν ἀποκαλύψει Ἰησοῦ Χριστοῦ" "so that the tested genuineness of your faith—more precious than gold that perishes though it is tested by fire—may be found to result in praise and glory and honor at the revelation of Jesus Christ."	δοκίμιον & δοκιμαζομένου & πυρὸς
1:11	ἐραυνῶντες εἰς τίνα ἢ ποῖον καιρὸν ἐδήλου τὸ ἐν αὐτοῖς πνεῦμα Χριστοῦ προμαρτυρόμενον τὰ εἰς Χριστὸν παθήματα καὶ τὰς μετὰ ταῦτα δόξας. "inquiring what person or time the Spirit of Christ in them was indicating when he predicted the sufferings of Christ and the subsequent glories."	παθήματα
2:12	"τὴν ἀναστροφὴν ὑμῶν ᶠἐν τοῖς ἔθνεσιν ἔχοντες καλήν, ἵνα ἐν ᾧ καταλαλοῦσιν ὑμῶν ὡς κακοποιῶν ἐκ τῶν καλῶν ἔργων ἐποπτεύοντες δοξάσωσιν τὸν θεὸν ἐν ἡμέρᾳ ἐπισκοπῆς." "Keep your conduct among the gentiles honorable, so that when they speak against you as evildoers, they may see your good deeds and glorify God on the day of visitation."	καταλαλοῦσιν
2:14	"εἴτε ἡγεμόσιν ὡς δι' αὐτοῦ πεμπομένοις εἰς ἐκδίκησιν κακοποιῶν, ἔπαινον δὲ ἀγαθοποιῶν" "or to governors as sent by him to punish those who do evil and to praise those who do good."	ἐκδίκησιν

---

29. Skaggs, *Pentecostal Commentary*, 14. Only mentions 21.

Called to Suffer

Verse	Text	Specific Word
2:19	"τοῦτο γὰρ χάρις, εἰ διὰ συνείδησιν θεοῦ ὑποφέρει τις λύπας πάσχων ἀδίκως." "For this is a gracious thing, when, mindful of God, one endures sorrows while suffering unjustly."	λύπας & πάσχων
2:20	"ποῖον γὰρ κλέος, εἰ ἁμαρτάνοντες καὶ κολαφιζόμενοι ὑπομενεῖτε; ἀλλ᾽ εἰ ἀγαθοποιοῦντες καὶ πάσχοντες ὑπομενεῖτε, τοῦτο χάρις παρὰ θεῷ." "For what credit is it if, when you sin and are beaten for it, you endure? But if when you do good and suffer for it you endure, this is a gracious thing in the sight of God."	κολαφιζόμενοι & πάσχοντες
2:21	"εἰς τοῦτο γὰρ ἐκλήθητε, ὅτι καὶ Χριστὸς ἔπαθεν ὑπὲρ ὑμῶν ὑμῖν ὑπολιμπάνων ὑπογραμμόν" "For to this you have been called, because Christ also suffered for you, leaving you an example, so that you might follow in his steps."	ἔπαθεν
2:23	"ὃς λοιδορούμενος οὐκ ἀντελοιδόρει, πάσχων οὐκ ἠπείλει, παρεδίδου δὲ τῷ κρίνοντι δικαίως ἵνα ἐπακολουθήσητε τοῖς ἴχνεσιν αὐτοῦ" "When he was reviled, he did not revile in return; when he suffered, he did not threaten, but continued entrusting himself to him who judges justly."	λοιδορούμενος & πάσχων
3:7	"ὡς Σάρρα ὑπήκουσεν τῷ Ἀβραὰμ κύριον αὐτὸν καλοῦσα ἧς ἐγενήθητε τέκνα ἀγαθοποιοῦσαι καὶ μὴ φοβούμεναι μηδεμίαν πτόησιν." "Likewise, husbands, live with your wives in an understanding way, showing honor to the woman as the weaker vessel, since they are heirs with you of the grace of life, so that your prayers may not be hindered."	φοβούμεναι & πτόησιν
3:13	"Καὶ τίς ὁ κακώσων ὑμᾶς, ἐὰν τοῦ ἀγαθοῦ ζηλωταὶ γένησθε" "Now who is there to harm you if you are zealous for what is good?"	κακώσων
3:14	"ἀλλ᾽ εἰ καὶ πάσχοιτε διὰ δικαιοσύνην, μακάριοι. τὸν δὲ φόβον αὐτῶν μὴ φοβηθῆτε μηδὲ ταραχθῆτε" "But even if you should suffer for righteousness' sake, you will be blessed. Have no fear of them, nor be troubled"	πάσχοιτε & φόβον & φοβηθῆτε & ταραχθῆτε

Introduction to the Topic of Suffering in 1 Peter

Verse	Text	Specific Word
3:16	"ἀλλὰ μετὰ πραΰτητος καὶ φόβου, συνείδησιν ἔχοντες ἀγαθήν, ἵνα ἐν ᾧ καταλαλεῖσθε καταισχυνθῶσιν οἱ ἐπηρεάζοντες ὑμῶν τὴν ἀγαθὴν ἐν Χριστῷ ἀναστροφήν." "having a good conscience, so that, when you are slandered, those who revile your good behavior in Christ may be put to shame."	καταλαλεῖσθε & ἐπηρεάζοντες
3:17	"κρεῖττον γὰρ ἀγαθοποιοῦντας, εἰ θέλοι τὸ θέλημα τοῦ θεοῦ, πάσχειν ἢ κακοποιοῦντας." "For it is better to suffer for doing good, if that should be God's will, than for doing evil."	πάσχειν
4:1	"Χριστοῦ οὖν παθόντος σαρκὶ καὶ ὑμεῖς τὴν αὐτὴν ἔννοιαν ὁπλίσασθε, ὅτι ὁ παθὼν σαρκὶ πέπαυται ἁμαρτίας" "Since therefore Christ suffered in the flesh, arm yourselves with the same way of thinking, for whoever has suffered in the flesh has ceased from sin"	πάσχειν
4:4	"ἐν ᾧ ξενίζονται μὴ συντρεχόντων ὑμῶν εἰς τὴν αὐτὴν τῆς ἀσωτίας ἀνάχυσιν βλασφημοῦντες" "With respect to this they are surprised when you do not join them in the same flood of debauchery, and they malign you"	βλασφημοῦντες
4:12	"Ἀγαπητοί, μὴ ξενίζεσθε τῇ ἐν ὑμῖν πυρώσει πρὸς πειρασμὸν ὑμῖν γινομένῃ ὡς ξένου ὑμῖν συμβαίνοντος" "Beloved, do not be surprised at the fiery trial when it comes upon you to test you, as though something strange were happening to you."	πυρώσει & πειρασμὸν
4:13	"ἀλλὰ καθὸ κοινωνεῖτε τοῖς τοῦ Χριστοῦ παθήμασιν, χαίρετε, ἵνα καὶ ἐν τῇ ἀποκαλύψει τῆς δόξης αὐτοῦ χαρῆτε ἀγαλλιώμενοι." "But rejoice insofar as you share Christ's sufferings, that you may also rejoice and be glad when his glory is revealed."	παθήμασιν
4:14	"εἰ ὀνειδίζεσθε ἐν ὀνόματι Χριστοῦ, μακάριοι, ὅτι τὸ τῆς δόξης καὶ τὸ τοῦ θεοῦ πνεῦμα ἐφ᾽ ὑμᾶς ἀναπαύεται" "If you are insulted for the name of Christ, you are blessed, because the Spirit of glory and of God rests upon you."	ὀνειδίζεσθε

Verse	Text	Specific Word
4:15	"μὴ γάρ τις ὑμῶν πασχέτω ὡς φονεὺς ἢ κλέπτης ἢ κακοποιὸς ἢ ὡς ἀλλοτριεπίσκοπος·" "But let none of you suffer as a murderer or a thief or an evildoer or as a meddler."	πασχέτω
4:16	"εἰ δὲ ὡς χριστιανός, μὴ αἰσχυνέσθω, δοξαζέτω δὲ τὸν θεὸν ἐν τῷ μέρει τούτῳ" "Yet if anyone suffers as a Christian, let him not be ashamed, but let him glorify God in that name."	πασχέτω (implied from verse 15)
4:17	ὅτι ὁ καιρὸς τοῦ ἄρξασθαι τὸ κρίμα ἀπὸ τοῦ οἴκου τοῦ θεοῦ· εἰ δὲ πρῶτον ἀφ' ἡμῶν, τί τὸ τέλος τῶν ἀπειθούντων τῷ τοῦ θεοῦ εὐαγγελίῳ" "For it is time for judgment to begin at the household of God; and if it begins with us, what will be the outcome for those who do not obey the gospel of God?"	κρίμα
4:19	"ὥστε καὶ οἱ πάσχοντες κατὰ τὸ θέλημα τοῦ θεοῦ πιστῷ κτίστῃ παρατιθέσθωσαν τὰς ψυχὰς αὐτῶν ἐν ἀγαθοποιΐᾳ" "Therefore let those who suffer according to God's will entrust their souls to a faithful Creator while doing good."	πάσχοντες
5:1	"Πρεσβυτέρους τοὺς ἐν ὑμῖν παρακαλῶ ὁ συμπρεσβύτερος καὶ μάρτυς τῶν τοῦ Χριστοῦ παθημάτων, ὁ καὶ τῆς μελλούσης ἀποκαλύπτεσθαι δόξης κοινωνός" "So I exhort the elders among you, as a fellow elder and a witness of the sufferings of Christ, as well as a partaker in the glory that is going to be revealed."	παθημάτων
5:9	"ᾧ ἀντίστητε στερεοὶ τῇ πίστει εἰδότες τὰ αὐτὰ τῶν παθημάτων τῇ ἐν κόσμῳ ὑμῶν ἀδελφότητι ἐπιτελεῖσθαι" "Resist him, firm in your faith, knowing that the same kinds of suffering are being experienced by your brotherhood throughout the world."	παθημάτων

Introduction to the Topic of Suffering in 1 Peter

Verse	Text	Specific Word
5:10	"ὁ δὲ θεὸς πάσης χάριτος, ὁ καλέσας ὑμᾶς εἰς τὴν αἰώνιον αὐτοῦ δόξαν ἐν Χριστῷ ὀλίγον παθόντας αὐτὸς καταρτίσει, στηρίξει, σθενώσει, θεμελιώσει" "And after you have suffered a little while, the God of all grace, who has called you to his eternal glory in Christ, will himself restore, confirm, strengthen, and establish you."	παθόντας

Therefore, it is safe to say that suffering is a significant topic in 1 Peter. The purpose of this study is to investigate how 1 Peter views suffering:

a. Does 1 Peter view suffering as necessary for Christian formation? What is the possible meaning of "εἰ δέον ἐστίν" (if/since it is necessary)?[30] Why does he exhort his readers "μὴ ξενίζεσθε . . . πυρώσει πρὸς πειρασμὸν ὑμῖν γινομένῃ" (do not be surprised at the fiery trial that is coming upon you)?[31] What does Peter mean when he says that the believers are "κοινωνεῖτε τοῖς τοῦ Χριστοῦ παθήμασιν" (sharing in the sufferings of Christ)?[32]

b. Furthermore, what is the source of this suffering? When Peter exhorts the believers, he says "οἱ πάσχοντες κατὰ τὸ θέλημα τοῦ θεοῦ" (the one who suffers according to the will of God).[33] Does this mean that there is a specific way in which the believers are to suffer, which is "κατὰ τὸ θέλημα τοῦ θεοῦ" (according to the will of God)? Conversely, does it imply that it is God who sends this suffering to the believers? Could it be that both are in view?

c. What is the nature of the believer's suffering? Peter uses words like καταλαλέω (speak against/slander), φόβος (fear/intimidation), and λυπέω (grieve/inflict pain), which seem to indicate that believers are suffering from social ostracism and verbal abuse. However, one also finds words like πάσχω (I suffer), πάθος (suffering), πειρασμός (test/trial), δοκιμάζω (I test/examine), πυρόω (fiery trial), and κρίμα (judgment), which leads one to ask whether there was more to their suffering than mere verbal abuse.

---

30. 1 Pet 1:6.
31. 1 Pet 4:13.
32. 1 Pet 4:13.
33. 1 Pet 4:19.

d. Finally, what is the purpose of the believer's suffering? Whether suffering is necessary or not, and whether it forms part of God's will for his people or not does not negate the fact that it is a reality, for Peter, his audience, and our world today. Therefore, one has to ask the question: Why do people suffer? Furthermore, is suffering a good thing, a bad thing, or a bit of both? Does it function as a means through which people are transformed, or destroyed? The following section presents a brief introduction to the exegetical basis for these questions. This study provides further support for the assertions made below in the next chapter.

First Peter 1:6 reads "ἐν ᾧ ἀγαλλιᾶσθε, ὀλίγον ἄρτι, εἰ δέον ἐστίν, λυπηθέντας ἐν ποικίλοις πειρασμοῖς" (In this you rejoice, though now for a little while, if/since necessary, you have been grieved by various trials). Scholars translate the phrase "εἰ δέον ἐστίν" (if/since it is necessary) in a variety of ways.[34] A literal translation of this phrase presents the following two options "if it is necessary"[35] or "since it is necessary."[36] Clearly, one's choice will have a significant impact on the meaning of the phrase. Marshall, Witherington III, Beare, and others translate this phrase as a hypothetical conditional.[37] In other words, they translate "εἰ" (if/since) as "if," thereby emphasizing the conditional and hypothetical nature of the audience's suffering.[38] Davids agrees that suffering, although unavoidable in this world, is not necessary, nor can anyone attribute its presence in the life of the believer to God.[39] A similar translation is in the ESV: "In this you rejoice, though now for a little while, if necessary, you have been grieved by various trials."[40] However, there is another side to this story. Achtemeier, Forbes, Best, and others[41] translate "εἰ δέον ἐστίν" (if/since it is necessary) quite differently. Contra Beare, Achtemeier denotes that "εἰ" (if/since) when used in the New Testament usually points to a conditional

---

34. See footnote 13–17.

35. My translation.

36. My translation.

37. Marshall, *1 Peter*, 40; Witherington III, *Letters and Homilies*, 80–81; Beare, *First Epistle of Peter*, 86; Senior, *1 Peter*, 32.

38. Beare, *First Epistle of Peter*, 86; Witherington III, *Letters and Homilies*, 78.

39. Davids, *First Epistle of Peter*, 55–56.

40. Emphasis mine.

41. Achtemeier and Epp, *1 Peter*, 100–101; Best, *1 Peter*, 78; Forbes, *Exegetical Guide*, 23–34; Hiebert, *1 Peter*, 66–67; Johnstone, *First Epistle of Peter*, 63–66.

Introduction to the Topic of Suffering in 1 Peter

of fact.[42] In this context, it therefore denotes the present reality and necessity of the audience's suffering. Indeed, the presence of "ἐστίν" (it is) affirms this translation and renders "εἰ" as "since."[43] Thus, the statement denotes the inevitability of the trial, as well as its necessity.

This study proposes that the correct translation of "εἰ δέον ἐστίν" is "since it is necessary" as proposed by Achtemeier and others. However, this study acknowledges that it is not possible to conclusively prove this interpretation based on 1 Peter 1:6 alone. Therefore, this study endeavors to analyze various other portions within the letter of 1 Peter to support the translation chosen above.

A second point of contention among scholars arises in 1 Peter 4:19: "ὥστε καὶ οἱ πάσχοντες κατὰ τὸ θέλημα τοῦ θεοῦ πιστῷ κτίστῃ παρατιθέσθωσαν τὰς ψυχὰς αὐτῶν ἐν ἀγαθοποιΐᾳ" (Therefore let those who suffer according to God's will entrust their souls to a faithful Creator while doing good), specifically the phrase "οἱ πάσχοντες κατὰ τὸ θέλημα τοῦ θεοῦ" (the one who suffers according to the will of God). This phrase raises all sorts of questions about whether God desires believers to suffer or if he merely allows them to do so, and even more, whether suffering is part of God's plan at all.

On the one hand, Achtemeier, Senior, and Davids assert that this phrase does not imply that the believer suffers because it is God's will for him to do so.[44] Instead, these scholars propose that the phrase enjoins that those who "suffer according to God's will" are those who suffer like God would want them to suffer.[45] There is a clear allusion here to Jesus' suffering as portrayed in 1 Peter 2:23 where Peter enjoins his readers to suffer like Christ did.[46] This connection then solidifies that the phrase does not speak to whether it is God's "will" for believers to suffer, but rather relates to how believers should suffer.

On the other hand, Marshall, Donelson, Goppelt, and others agree with the observations of Achtemeier, Jobes, Davids, and Senior[47] that this

---

42. Achtemeier and Epp, *1 Peter*, 100–101.

43. Johnstone, *First Epistle of Peter*, 63–66.

44. Achtemeier and Epp, *1 Peter*, 318–19; Senior, *1 Peter*, 132–33; Davids, *First Epistle of Peter*, 173–74.

45. Achtemeier and Epp, *1 Peter*, 318–19; Senior, *1 Peter*, 132–33; Davids, *First Epistle of Peter*, 173–74.

46. Green, *1 Peter*, 151.

47. Achtemeier and Epp, *1 Peter*, 318–19; Jobes, *1 Peter*, 295–96; Senior, *1 Peter*, 132–33; Davids, *First Epistle of Peter*, 173–74.

phrase pertains to how believers suffer.[48] However, Forbes, along with these scholars, maintains that this phrase does not only refer to how God wills the believer to suffer.[49] Indeed, they assert that the believers are suffering because God wants them to.[50] According to Marshall, the believers' suffering can be likened to Christ's suffering, in the sense that both happen "according to God's will."[51] This study agrees that suffering, for Peter, happens because God has willed it to happen. In the same way as God willed Christ to suffer in the way that he did.

These two exegetical problems then serve as a starting point in order to understand why the apostle Peter, a man martyred for his faith, would write this letter about suffering, and what he saw to be the purpose of that suffering. This study asks the following questions: Firstly, why does Peter deem suffering to be necessary for the believer? Secondly, if God is the source of the suffering, what is the purpose of the suffering? This study will return to these questions after reviewing the relevant literature on the topic in the next chapter.

---

48. Marshall, *1 Peter*, 157–58; Donelson, *I & II Peter and Jude*, 139–40; Goppelt, *Commentary on 1 Peter*, 330–32; Forbes, *Exegetical Guide*, 163; Witherington III, *Letters and Homilies*, 217–18; Stibbs, *First Epistle General of Peter*, 164.

49. Marshall, *1 Peter*, 157–58; Donelson, *I & II Peter and Jude*, 139–40; Goppelt, *Commentary on 1 Peter*, 330–32; Forbes, *Exegetical Guide*, 163; Witherington III, *Letters and Homilies*, 217–18; Stibbs, *First Epistle General of Peter*, 164.

50. Marshall, *1 Peter*, 157–58; Donelson, *I & II Peter and Jude*, 139–40; Goppelt, *Commentary on 1 Peter*, 330–32; Forbes, *Exegetical Guide*, 163; Witherington III, *Letters and Homilies*, 217–18; Stibbs, *First Epistle General of Peter*, 164.

51. Marshall, *1 Peter*, 157–58.

CHAPTER 2

Literature Review

AUTHORSHIP

THROUGHOUT THE HISTORY OF the church the author of 1 Peter has always been claimed to be Peter the apostle[1] who, after coming to Rome,[2] was martyred there under Nero.[3] However, this seems to have fallen out of fashion amongst some interpreters of the past century.[4] This study proceeds to summarize and evaluate the options against and in favor of Petrine authorship.

Pseudepigraphal Author

The argument against Petrine authorship rests on three legs. The first objection, according to Elliott, Achtemeier, and others, asserts that the Greek

---

1. Jobes, *1 Peter*, 14–19; Marshall, *1 Peter*, 21–24; Van Rensburg, "Code of Conduct," 476; Witherington III, *Letters and Homilies*, 53; Grudem, *1 Peter*, 37; McKnight, *1 Peter*, 29; Forbes, *Exegetical Guide*, 1–2; Michaels, *1 Peter*, lxvi–lxvii; Thiede, *From Galilee to Rome*, 177.

2. This is taken to be fact by Papias, Irenaeus, and Clement of Alexandria (see Eusebius, *Ecclesiastical History*, 2.15; 3.11, 3.39, 15; 5.8.2–3; 6.14.5–7; also *1 Clem.* 5.1–4.

3. *1 Clem.* 5.4; Eusebius, *Ecclesiastical History*, 2.25.4–8, citing Tertullian, Dionysius of Corinth and Gaius.

4. Achtemeier and Epp, *1 Peter*, 43; Beare, *First Epistle of Peter*, 47–48; Bechtler, *Following in His Steps*, 46; Boring, *1 Peter*, 30; Elliott, *1 Peter*, 118–30; Goppelt, *Commentary on 1 Peter*, 51; Horrell, *1 Peter*, 2; Schutter, *Hermeneutic and Composition*, 17–18; Le Roux, *Ethics in 1 Peter* 15–21.

syntax is way too sophisticated to have been written by a Galilean fisherman.[5] They propose that because the rulers refer to Peter as unschooled in Acts 4:13, he could by no means have accomplished this feat. The second objection leans on the first, assuming that Peter was only proficient in Aramaic; therefore, he would not have inserted the allusions to the teachings of Jesus in Greek, but in Aramaic, as he would have heard them the first time, and thus would have had to provide a fresh translation into Greek. Therefore, according to Le Roux, because these allusions to the sayings of Jesus rely on the so-called "Gospel Tradition" and do not appear in an independently translated form they could not have been written by Peter.[6] Moreover, the numerous quotations from the Old Testament in this letter are from the LXX.[7] They continue that if Peter wrote this letter, the quotations would have come from the Hebrew and Aramaic Targums, with which someone from Galilee would have been familiar.[8] Another objection raised against Petrine authorship is the clear dependence that the letter has on Pauline writings, therefore, it could not have been written by Peter, because he would have exhibited his own theology and not Paul's.[9] These scholars conclude, therefore, that the tradition we have is not in keeping with the historical apostle from the New Testament.[10] Bechtler asserts furthermore that the cipher "Babylon" for Rome is something that only arises after AD 70, thus after the death of Peter.[11] Thus, they conclude that all this evidence taken together overpowers the traditional understanding that Peter wrote the letter.[12] This study now turns to the alternative author that these scholars propose.

---

5. Elliott, *1 Peter*, 120; Achtemeier and Epp, *1 Peter*, 1; Horrell, *1 Peter*, 2; Le Roux, *Ethics in 1 Peter*, 5.

6. Le Roux, *Ethics in 1 Peter*, 7.

7. Elliott, *1 Peter*, 120; Best, *1 Peter*, 49–50; Achtemeier and Epp, *1 Peter*, 1; Boring, *1 Peter*, 31; Horrell, *1 Peter*, 21.

8. Elliott, *1 Peter*, 120; Best, *1 Peter*, 49–50; Achtemeier and Epp, *1 Peter*, 1; Boring, *1 Peter*, 31; Horrell, *1 Peter*, 21.

9. Brown and Meier, *Antioch and Rome*, 135–36; This is an extremely convoluted argument that comes from a history of religions approach.

10. Brown and Meier, *Antioch and Rome*, 135–36; cf. Le Roux, *Ethics in 1 Peter*, 10.

11. Bechtler, *Following in His Steps*, 45.

12. Bechtler, *Following in His Steps*, 47; Le Roux, *Ethics in 1 Peter* 7; Elliott, *1 Peter*, 120; Best, *1 Peter*, 49–50; Achtemeier and Epp, *1 Peter*, 1; Boring, *1 Peter*, 31; Horrell, *1 Peter*, 21.

Literature Review

Achtemeier states that because Petrine authorship has been refuted the author must be pseudonymous.[13] Although there are many options for who the pseudoauthor is, there is very little agreement.[14] Danker continues that pseudonymity was a widespread practice in the ancient world and was morally neutral.[15] This practice was employed often in biblical literature in order to give the text authority.[16] In antiquity, a student would attribute his writings to the master from which he learned them.[17] Therefore, it is clear that pseudowriters attributed their writing to the name of the apostle in whose tradition they stand in order to use that tradition authoritatively at a later stage.[18] In the same vein, Elliott argues that the letter comes from a "Petrine Circle" in Rome.[19] This circle of Petrine disciples then wrote this letter in the name of Peter. They would have preserved and developed the traditions of the apostle and were then transmitting it across the empire.[20] Scholars argue that this group would have seen themselves as continuing the traditions of the apostle Peter, and they owed their existence to the legacy of Peter in Rome.[21] Elliott and Le Roux provide the following support for the probability of such a circle. Missionaries never operated alone as can be seen in the book of Acts.[22] Moreover, they continue that from a sociological perspective it is also more likely that there was a circle around Peter because shared experiences and thoughts defined religions.[23] Furthermore, the letter mentions Mark and Silvanus because they are known to the audience to be associated with Peter.[24] The association of these two Petrine disciples would have given authority to the letter.[25] They used both their own missionary lives as bearing witness to Christ and that of the tradition of Peter being in Rome and being martyred there as encouragement for the

---

13. Achtemeier and Epp, *1 Peter*, 2.
14. Le Roux, *Ethics in 1 Peter*, 14.
15. Danker, *Invitation to the New Testament*, 4:129.
16. Danker, *Invitation to the New Testament*, 4:129.
17. Achtemeier and Epp, *1 Peter*, 40.
18. Le Roux, *Ethics in 1 Peter*, 14.
19. Elliott, *1 Peter*, 95; cf. Le Roux, *Ethics in 1 Peter* 15.
20. Le Roux, *Ethics in 1 Peter*, 15.
21. Le Roux, *Ethics in 1 Peter*, 15; Elliott, *1 Peter*, 95.
22. Elliott, *Home for the Homeless*, 273. See also Le Roux, *Ethics in 1 Peter*, 16–17.
23. Elliott, *1 Peter*, 128.
24. Elliott, *1 Peter*, 128.
25. Le Roux, *Ethics in 1 Peter*, 18.

addressees.[26] This study now turns to the argument for Petrine authorship. This study first answers the objections of the pseudepigraphal view and then proposes an alternative.

Peter as Author

First, the argument that the Greek is too good to have been written by a Galilean fisherman has been successfully refuted as early as 1991 by Marshall.[27] According to Turner and Jobes, scholars have highly exaggerated the excellence of the Greek grammar in 1 Peter.[28] Both scholars assert that the Semitic style of the Greek is clear, and the letter has a superficial and incomplete veneer of "good" Greek.[29] Jobes has also shown that the quality and prevalence of Greek in Galilee was a lot higher than previously proposed.[30] Moreover, this study asks the question: Why do scholars assume that Peter remained an unschooled fisherman throughout his entire life? After thirty-odd years of ministry in a deeply hellenized context is it not possible that Peter might have learned a thing or two about Greek syntax and vocabulary? Moreover, although Peter was the apostle to the Jews,[31] one must not make the mistake of thinking that these are all Aramaic- or Hebrew-speaking Jews.[32] As Witherington III contends, the hellenization of Jews outside of Judea was far more widespread than anyone would like to acknowledge.[33] In fact, Jews would have been indiscernible from their gentile neighbors outside of the synagogue.[34] Therefore, one could easily make the case that his command of the LXX was a necessity if he was to reach the Jews at all. These Jews would have been most familiar with the LXX, thus making Peter's use of it indispensable.

---

26. Le Roux, *Ethics in 1 Peter*, 17.
27. Marshall, *1 Peter*, 22.
28. Turner, "Style," 121–31; Jobes, *1 Peter*, 325–38.
29. Turner, "Style," 121–31; Jobes, *1 Peter*, 325–38.
30. Jobes, *1 Peter*, 325–38.
31. Le Roux, *Ethics in 1 Peter*, 10; cf. Gal 2:8.
32. Witherington III makes a compelling case, as will be argued below, that the Hellenization of the Jews was far greater than most scholars tend to admit (see Witherington III, *Letters and Homilies*, 22–39).
33. Witherington III, *Letters and Homilies*, 26.
34. Starke, *Cities of God*, 78.

Secondly, Bauckham has sufficiently refuted the assertion that the term "Babylon" as a cipher for Rome was only recognized post-AD 70.[35] Rather, it is highly plausible for this term to have carried this connotation before AD 70.[36] Consequently, for this to be the case, this term must have been in use before the destruction of the temple. Thus, it proves to be a moot point in the argument against Petrine authorship.

Thirdly, as to the objection that Peter uses the common gospel tradition. The authors noted above have not provided any evidence for the fact that any document containing this gospel tradition ever existed. Thiessen, in addressing the hypothetical document Q, says, "I refuse to write about something I do not believe existed."[37] Consequently, until they can provide said evidence their argument is based on a figment of their imagination. The presence of these traditions is more simply explained by the fact that if the author was indeed an eyewitness to Jesus, he would have been one of the main proponents of that tradition.

Fourth, Jobes sufficiently refutes the proposed overlap between Paul and 1 Peter.[38] Jobes asserts that if this book was so Pauline, then it would have been attributed to Paul and not to Peter.[39] Moreover, if Paul and Peter are testifying in their letters about the story of Jesus and his significance for the lives of their audiences, surely there would be obvious overlap between the gospel tradition and Paul and Peter's words in this letter without requiring literary dependence.[40] In fact, one could only make the case for literary dependence if Jesus Christ of Nazareth was not a real person and never existed. However, because he was a real person, and these apostles are bearing witness to his life, death, and resurrection, similarities should be expected.

---

35. Bauckham, "Martyrdom of Peter," 539–95.
36. Bauckham, "Martyrdom of Peter," 543.
37. Thiessen, *Jesus and the Forces of Death*, 6.
38. Jobes, *1 Peter*, 11–13.
39. Jobes, *1 Peter*, 11–13. One scholar has made the case that it is indeed Paul who wrote this letter (Boring, *1 Peter*, 42).
40. This argument for a "gospel tradition" and the distinctiveness in Paul and Peter's theology is clearly something that emanates from the history of religions approach. These scholars propose that Paul and Peter, Antioch and Rome, AD 30–60 and AD 70–110 all have distinctive characteristics as the religion of Christianity emanates from society. However, the parallels between Paul and Peter are evident, and if it is the case that two different people wrote them at the same time, then we must ask the question: What really happened in the life of Jesus that this religion appears out of nowhere and has a distinct, unified witness across places and people?

The objection that we neither have historical evidence close enough to the time of authorship that points to Peter as the author, and nor do we have "historically verifiable"[41] evidence that Peter went to Rome, or that he was martyred there, is an argument that collapses on itself. Clement of Rome and Ignatius of Antioch do point to the fact that Peter was martyred for the faith.[42] Ignatius does seem to assert that this happened in Rome as well.[43] These witnesses are from AD 95 and AD 110, respectively, which seems pretty early to this author. Moreover, Tertullian, Dionysius, Gaius, Papias, Irenaeus, and Clement of Alexandria affirm that this is indeed the case, as quoted by Eusebius.[44] We have no evidence of an *alternative tradition* from church history that says Peter did not write this letter, or that Peter was not martyred in Rome.[45] It seems that scholars proposing pseudepigraphal authorship are arguing from silence instead of fact. Moreover, the letter's self-attestation as being from the apostle Peter must be allowed to bear some weight.[46] If we cannot accept the authorial self-designation as true, why would we deem anything else in this letter to be true? Furthermore, Dankers' assertion that pseudepigraphal documents were widely disseminated and accepted as standard practice is a lie.[47] Witherington III and Jobes show that while wisdom literature accepted pseudepigraphal authorship, this was not the case for personal correspondences like a letter.[48] Jobes continues that the claim that apostolic authority is given to a letter just because it infers apostolic authorship is not verifiable.[49] Historically, the Epistle to the Laodiceans and 3 Corinthians enjoyed acceptance while

---

41. Goulder, "Did Peter Ever Go to Rome?," 377–97; cf. Le Roux, *Ethics in 1 Peter*, 19.

42. *1 Clem.* 5.4, although he does not explicitly say that this happens in Rome the letter he is writing comes from Rome, and it is likely that he is using the examples of Peter and Paul because they were martyred in Rome (Ignatius to the Romans, 4.3, in Lightfoot, *Apostolic Fathers, Part II*, 206).

43. Ignatius to the Romans, 4.3, in Lightfoot, *Apostolic Fathers, Part II*, 206.

44. This is taken to be fact by Papias, Irenaeus, and Clement of Alexandria see Eusebius, *Ecclesiastical History*, 2.25.4–8 citing Tertullian, Dionysius of Corinth and Gaius.

45. Neither is there an alternative tradition that proposes that someone else wrote the letter. If this letter was Pauline or written by someone else, it is reasonable to expect that there would be at least some sources in the first and second centuries that mention it.

46. 1 Pet 1:1

47. See above.

48. Jobes, *1 Peter*, 15; Witherington III, *Letters and Homilies*, 38.

49. Jobes, *1 Peter*, 15.

their authorship was deemed to be by Paul.[50] However, these letters were rejected, as soon as their pseudonymous authorship became evident.[51] The pseudonymous author was not congratulated for his effort of "passing on the Pauline tradition" but was censured by the church for it.[52] Witherington III continues that 1 Peter was accepted by the early church unanimously, while they rejected other documents also supposedly penned by him, i.e., Apocalypse of Peter, Gospel of Peter, and Acts of Peter.[53] The reception of 1 Peter by the early church as authentic was widespread and early.[54] First Peter and 1 John are the only two documents whose authenticity was undisputed by both the Eastern and Western church.[55] Clearly the case for Petrine authorship is stronger than the one against it.

As it pertains to the presence of a Petrine circle in Rome, Elliott's assertion that the New Testament shows that missionaries never worked alone is hardly evidence for a Petrine circle.[56] Moreover, Elliott's appeals to the sociological conventions of religion in the first century are mere speculation, and certainly not evidence of a Petrine circle either.[57] This study also finds that Le Roux is severely inconsistent as she denies that the tradition of Peter in Rome has any historical value, and then proceeds to use that tradition to justify a Petrine circle in Rome.[58]

Furthermore, it is ironic that these scholars reject Petrine authorship as historically proposed by church tradition, and then they proceed to propose an author for which they have even less historically verifiable evidence. There is not one patristic author that notes the existence of a Petrine school. Nor is there one patristic author that asserts 1 Peter was not written by the apostle Peter.[59] Nor is there an alternative tradition that says Peter did not die in Rome. The authors who suggest a Petrine school or another author

---

50. Guthrie, *New Testament Introduction*, 675–77.

51. Guthrie, *New Testament Introduction*, 675–77.

52. Jobes, *1 Peter*, 15.

53. Witherington III, *Letters and Homilies*, 38.

54. Selwyn, *First Epistle of St. Peter*, 38.

55. Witherington III, *Letters and Homilies*, 39.

56. Elliott, *Home for the Homeless*, 273.

57. Elliott, *1 Peter*, 128.

58. Le Roux, *Ethics in 1 Peter*, 17. Moreover, she uses this tradition as the basis for the meaning of the entire letter.

59. Just because 1 Clement, Ignatius, and Polycarp do not mention the author by name is not evidence that it is someone else.

are just grabbing at straws. Contra Boring, the evidence against pseudonymous authorship is convincing.[60] Therefore, this study concludes that the only position with any evidence at all, both internally and externally, is the position that the apostle Peter wrote this letter from Rome.

PETER'S MARTYRDOM: TRUTH OR TRADITION?

For scholars doubting Peter's martyrdom in Rome the critical question one needs to ask is: Did Peter ever set foot in Rome?[61] The later tradition merely assumes Peter's presence in Rome, i.e., Irenaeus and Ignatius.[62] Goulder agrees and asserts that it is the patronizing instincts of the church in Rome that facilitated this tradition of Peter in Rome.[63] The evidence from Clement, Ignatius, Apocalypse of Peter, and Ascension of Isaiah provide no new insights other than reiterating the already-established tradition.[64] According to Green, this tradition of Peter in Rome served a political agenda in order to establish and enlarge the authority of the church in Rome.[65] For some, there is just no historical evidence to prove that Peter was ever in Rome.[66] Le Roux contends that the earliest attestation we have to Peter's martyrdom in Rome is from AD 180–190 in the *Acta Petri*.[67] Consequently, one should not interpret the account of Peter bearing witness in Rome as testifying by blood.[68] The euphemistic language from 1 Clement 5.4.7 suggests nothing of a violent death.[69] Le Roux acknowledges that the Acts of

---

60. Boring, *1 Peter*, 30.

61. Goulder, "Did Peter Ever Go to Rome?," 377–97; Le Roux, *Ethics in 1 Peter*, 133.

62. Goulder, "Did Peter Ever Go to Rome?," 377–97; cf. Le Roux, *Ethics in 1 Peter*, 134.

63. Goulder, "Did Peter Ever Go to Rome?," 377–97; cf. Le Roux, *Ethics in 1 Peter*, 134.

64. Goulder, "Did Peter Ever Go to Rome?," 383.

65. Green, *Christianity in Ancient Rome*, 45.

66. Foakes-Jackson, *Peter*, vii. However, Foakes-Jackson continues that although the physical evidence seems scarce one cannot but be struck by the unanimous teaching of the church, both in the east and in the west, that Peter was indeed in Rome and that he was martyred there. Thus, Foakes-Jackson concludes "To the candid historian it seems far more perverse to deny that St. Peter was actually at Rome than to affirm that he was the founder of its church."

67. Le Roux, *Ethics in 1 Peter*, 9.

68. Le Roux, *Ethics in 1 Peter*, 134.

69. Le Roux, *Ethics in 1 Peter*, 134.

Peter provide an account of Peter's martyrdom in Rome.[70] However, this is merely a later compilation of the historically uncertifiable tradition that this was so.[71] This evidence leaves these scholars unconvinced.

Bockmuehl makes a crucial observation in *The Remembered Peter* that the individual and communal memory of the early church offers us an interpreted appropriation of the past that contain experiential and cultural links to the actual events.[72] Clement of Alexandria described the tradition that he received regarding the apostolic origins "not as a 'story' but a true account . . . passed on and guarded in memory."[73] Bockmuehl continues that the concern in the early church was for the "living" memory of the apostles.[74] This memory turns out to be extremely widespread in the second- and third-generational sources, according to Bockmuehl.[75] Bockmuehl finds this memory in Papias, Polycarp, Ignatius, Justin Martyr, and Irenaeus, to only name a few.[76] In his work, *Against Heresies*, Irenaeus places a high premium on Scripture and the tradition of interpretation that he has received from the apostles.[77] Bauckham has done an in-depth analysis of the early Christian evidence for Peter's death in Rome.[78] This study will only present some of his findings, but the article can be consulted for the finer points of his argument. First, Ignatius of Antioch, Letter to the Smyrneaens:

Ἐγὼ γὰρ καὶ μετὰ τὴν ἀνάστασιν ἐν σαρκὶ αὐτὸν οἶδα, καὶ πιστεύω ὄντα. Καὶ ὅτε πρὸς τοὺς περὶ Πέτρον ἦλθεν, ἔφη αὐτοῖς· Λάβετε,

---

70. Le Roux, *Ethics in 1 Peter*, 136.

71. Le Roux, *Ethics in 1 Peter*, 136. Again, this study finds Le Roux to be severely inconsistent on this point. In the same section she covers the historical account of the martyrdom of Paul in the *Acts of Paul*, and lo and behold she concludes that it is historically probable that Paul was martyred in Rome, even though the *Acts of Paul and Peter* both originate around the same time and are conveying the same thing, a tradition.

72. Bockmuehl, *Remembered Peter*, 119–20.

73. Eusebius, *Ecclesiastical History*, 3.23.5.

74. Bockmuehl, *Remembered Peter*, 119.

75. Bockmuehl, *Remembered Peter*, 120.

76. Bockmuehl, *Remembered Peter*, 120.

77. Irenaeus, *Adversus Haereses*, 3.1–5. Note how Irenaeus here intermingles Scripture and ecclesiology for the correct interpretation.

78. Bauckham, "Martyrdom of Peter," 539–95. In this article, Bauckham analyzes fourteen pre-AD 200 sources and shows comprehensively that the collective memory of the early church was that Peter was martyred in Rome. Bockmuehl, *Remembered Peter*, 127 adds another six pre-AD 200 sources that attest to this fact.

ψηλαφήσατέ με, καὶ ἴδετε, ὅτι οὐκ εἰμὶ δαιμόνιον ἀσώματον. Καὶ εὐθὺς [αὐτοῦ ἥψαντο, καὶ] ἐπίστευσαν, [κρατηθέντες τῇ σαρκὶ αὐτοῦ καὶ τῷ πνεύματι.] Διὰ τοῦτο καὶ θανάτου κατεφρόνησαν, [ηὑρέθησαν δὲ ὑπὲρ θάνατον.] Μετὰ δὲ τὴν ἀνάστασιν συνέφαγεν αὐτοῖς καὶ συνέπιεν [ὡς σαρκικός, καίπερ πνευματικῶς ἡνωμένος τῷ Πατρί.[79]

For I know and believe that he was in the flesh even after the resurrection; and when he came to Peter and his company, he said to them, *Lay hold and handle me, and see that I am not a demon without body*. And straightway they touched him, and they believed, being joined unto his flesh and his blood. Wherefore also they despised death, nay they were found superior to death. And after his resurrection he [both] ate with them and drank with them as one in the flesh, though spiritually he was united with the Father.[80]

Bauckham notes that that expression "θανατου καταφρονειν" (despise death) was a standard one.[81] Moreover, it was commonly used to refer to the heroism of soldiers, but in Christianity and Judaism it was also used to refer to the attitude of a martyr.[82] Thus, Bauckham asserts that when Ignatius uses it, it must have been martyrological.[83] Furthermore, for Bauckham, it seems strange that Peter is mentioned here explicitly if his martyrdom was not "common knowledge."[84] The memory of Peter as an apostolic martyr underpins his writings and guards it against misinterpretation.[85] The context, therefore, demands that it was common knowledge that Peter died as a martyr.[86] Bockmuehl continues that in Ignatius's letter to the Romans 4.3:

Οὐχ ὡς Πέτρος καὶ Παῦλος διατάσσομαι ὑμῖν· ἐκεῖνοι ἀπόστολοι, ἐγὼ κατάκριτος· ἐκεῖνοι ἐλεύθεροι, ἐγὼ δὲ μέχρι νῦν δοῦλος. Ἀλλ' ἐὰν πάθω, ἀπελεύθερος Ἰησοῦ, καὶ ἀναστήσομαι ἐν αὐτῷ ἐλεύθερος[87]

---

79. Ignatius of Antioch, *Corpus Ignatianum*, 105.
80. Lightfoot, *Apostolic Fathers, Part II*, 67–68 (emphasis original).
81. Bauckham, "Martyrdom of Peter," 563.
82. Bauckham, "Martyrdom of Peter," 563.
83. Bauckham, "Martyrdom of Peter," 563.
84. Bauckham, "Martyrdom of Peter," 563.
85. Bockmuehl, *Remembered Peter*, 90.
86. Bockmuehl, *Remembered Peter*, 90.
87. Ignatius of Antioch, *Corpus Ignatianum*, 47

I do not enjoin you, as Peter and Paul did. They were apostles, I am a convict; they were free, but I am a slave to this very hour. Yet if I shall suffer, then am I a freed-man of Jesus Christ, and I shall rise free in him. Now I am learning in my bonds to put away every desire.[88]

Ignatius takes for granted the fact that they will remember Peter's ministry in Rome.[89] Furthermore, no writer has suggested that Peter instructed the church in Rome through a letter.[90] Therefore, this study concludes that the collective memory of the church in Rome must be present because he was there.[91] It is interesting to note here contra Le Roux, Zwierlein, and Bottrich,[92] that Ignatius sees his impending martyrdom as the method through which he will become free like the apostle Peter. Schoedel and Fischer conclude that it is evident that Ignatius is here appealing to a local memory in the Roman church of the "personal" presence, ministry, and martyrdom of the apostle Peter.[93] On the objection that "μαρτυρέω" (I witness) did not mean martyrdom, a couple of things must be further noted. First Clement 5:2–7:

> Διὰ ζῆλον καὶ φθόνον οἱ μέγιστοι καὶ δικαιότατοι στῦλοι ἐδιώχθησαν καὶ ἕως θανάτου ἤθλησαν. Λάβωμεν πρὸ ὀφθαλμῶν ἡμῶν τοὺς ἀγαθοὺς ἀποστόλους· Πέτρον, ὃς διὰ ζῆλον ἄδικον οὐχ ἕνα οὐδὲ δύο ἀλλὰ πλείονας ὑπήνεγκεν πόνους, καὶ οὕτω μαρτυρήσας ἐπορεύθη εἰς τὸν ὀφειλόμενον τόπον τῆς δόξης. διὰ ζῆλον καὶ ἔριν Παῦλος ὑπομονῆς βραβεῖον ὑπέδειξεν, ἑπτάκις δεσμὰ φορέσας, φυγαδευθείς, λιθασθείς, κῆρυξ γενόμενος ἔν τε τῇ ἀνατολῇ καὶ ἐν τῇ δύσει, τὸ γενναῖον τῆς πίστεως αὐτοῦ κλέος ἔλαβεν, δικαιοσύνην διδάξας ὅλον τὸν κόσμον καὶ ἐπὶ τὸ τέρμα τῆς δύσεως ἐλθών· καὶ μαρτυρήσας ἐπὶ τῶν ἡγουμένων, οὕτως ἀπηλλάγη τοῦ κόσμου καὶ εἰς τὸν ἅγιον τόπον ἐπορεύθη, ὑπομονῆς γενόμενος μέγιστος ὑπογραμμός.[94]
>
> By reason of jealousy and envy the greatest and most righteous pillars of the church were persecuted, and contended even unto

---

88. Lightfoot, *Apostolic Fathers, Part II*, 560.
89. Bockmuehl, *Remembered Peter*, 91.
90. Bockmuehl, *Remembered Peter*, 91.
91. Bockmuehl, *Remembered Peter*, 91.
92. Quoted in Le Roux, *Ethics in 1 Peter*, 8–9.
93. Schoedel, *Hermeneia*, 176–77; Fischer, quoted in Bockmuehl, *Remembered Peter*, 91.
94. Lightfoot, *Apostolic Fathers, Part I*, 23.

death. Let us set before our eyes the good apostles. There was Peter who by reason of unrighteous jealousy endured not one nor two but many labours, and thus having borne his testimony went to his appointed place of glory. By reason of jealousy and strife Paul by his example pointed out the prize of patient endurance. After that he had been seven times in bonds, had been driven into exile, had been stoned, had preached in the East and in the West, he won the noble renown which was the reward of his faith, having taught righteousness unto the whole world and having reached the farthest bounds of the West; and when he had borne his testimony before the rulers, so he departed from the world and went unto the holy place, having been found a notable pattern of patient endurance.[95]

Bockmuehl observes that the aorist participle used of Peter's passing here points to their "definitive" witness.[96] Furthermore, it implies their death as can be seen in the heading in verse 2 "ἕως θανάτου ἤθλησαν" (to compete unto death).[97] The phrase "ἐπορεύθη εἰς τὸν ὀφειλόμενον τόπον" (to go unto one's own place) as found in verses 4 and 7 is a euphemism referring to one's death that is used similarly in other Christian texts.[98] This study admits that the term "μαρτυρέω" (I testify/bear witness) remains a nontechnical term in itself. However, the "μαρτυρήσας" (I bear witness/testify) of the apostles in this text clearly signifies the "mode and means" by which they passed from this world to glory, asserts Bockmuehl.[99] Thus the terms "suffering, "witness," and "death are a seamless whole . . . ."[100] Thus, it seems reasonable to conclude that "μαρτυρέω" already had the meaning of martyrdom in the early 90s AD Moreover, the collective memory of the community in Rome connected bearing witness with martyrdom. At least it seems this is how Ignatius views it, and he assumes that the church in Rome will see it the same way.

Second, The Ascension of Isaiah 4:2–3:

τος αὐτοῦ ἐ(ν εἴδει) ἀνθρώπου βασιλέως ἀνόμου μητραλώου
ὅστις αὐτὸς ὁ βασιλεὺς οὗτος τὴν φυτ(ε)ίαν ἣν φυτεύσουσιν οἱ

---

95. Lightfoot, *Apostolic Fathers, Part I*, 273–74.
96. Bockmuehl, *Remembered Peter*, 126.
97. Bockmuehl, *Remembered Peter*, 126.
98. Bockmuehl, *Remembered Peter*, 126; Acts 1:25 refers to Judas's demise mentioned in 1:18 with the exact phrase "πορευθῆναι εἰς τὸν τόπον τὸν ἴδιον."
99. Bockmuehl, *Remembered Peter*, 127.
100. Bockmuehl, *Remembered Peter*, 127.

δώδεκα ἀπόστολοι τοῦ ἀγαπητοῦ διώξε(ι) καὶ (τ)ῶν δώδεκα (εἷς) ταῖς χερσὶν αὐτοῦ (π)αραδοθήσεται[101]

After it is consummated, Beliar the great ruler, the king of this world, will descend, who hath ruled it since it came into being; yea, he will descend from his firmament in the likeness of a man, a lawless king, the slayer of his mother: who himself (even) this king. Will persecute the plant which the Twelve apostles of the Beloved have planted. Of the Twelve one will be delivered into his hands[102]

Bauckham shows conclusively that this text uses Beliar as a pseudonym for Emperor Nero.[103] Thus, "(εἷς) ταῖς χερσὶν αὐτοῦ (π)αραδοθήσεται" (to be delivered into his hands) cannot mean anything other than martyrdom.[104] Moreover, he shows that this description of Nero as coming to put to death one of the Twelve is an explicitly Christian one.[105] Finally, because there is no competing tradition regarding an apostle's martyrdom under Nero's reign in Rome, it must be referring to the apostle Peter.[106] Finally, the Apocalypse of Peter 14:4–6:

"καὶ πορεύου εἰς πόλιν ἄρχουσιν δύσεως, καὶ πίε τὸ ποτήριον ὅ ἐπηγγειλάμην σοι ἐν χεροῖν τοῦ ἐν Ἅιδου, ἵνα ἀρχὴν λάβῃ αὐτοῦ ἡ ἀφάνεια καὶ σὺ δεκτὸς τῆς ἐπαγγελίας . . ."[107]

"And go to the city which rules over the West and drink the cup which I have promised you at the hands of the son of him who is in Hades, so that his destruction may receive a beginning. And you . . . of the promise . . ."[108]

Here Bauckham notes that the expression "πίε τὸ ποτήριον" (drink the cup) is an explicitly martyrological one.[109] It is used by Jesus in the Gospels to the sons of Zebedee when referring to his own fate.[110] This analysis by

---

101. Penner and Heiser, *Old Testament Greek Pseudepigrapha*.
102. Kirby, "Ascension of Isaiah."
103. Penner and Heiser, *Old Testament Greek Pseudepigrapha*, 567.
104. Penner and Heiser, *Old Testament Greek Pseudepigrapha*, 568.
105. Penner and Heiser, *Old Testament Greek Pseudepigrapha*, 567.
106. Penner and Heiser, *Old Testament Greek Pseudepigrapha*, 567.
107. Text from Bauckham, "Martyrdom of Peter," 571.
108. Bauckham, "Martyrdom of Peter," 571.
109. Bauckham, "Martyrdom of Peter," 572.
110. Bauckham, "Martyrdom of Peter," 572; Matt 20:22–23.

Bauckham provides some substantial evidence to the common tradition in the early church that Peter's martyrdom occurred in Rome.

In conclusion, then Bockmuehl notes that there is a wide range of sources which situate Peter and his subsequent martyrdom in Rome.[111] More importantly though, there are no sources that situate it elsewhere.[112] There is no competing tradition during this period or subsequently for that matter, whether "East or West, orthodox or heretical, Jewish, pagan or Christian."[113] There is not even a whisper of another narrative than the one that seems to have been unanimously understood by the early church in both the East and the West. Foakes-Jackson agrees that although the physical evidence seems scarce, one cannot but be struck by the unanimous teaching of the church, both in the East and in the West, that Peter was indeed in Rome and that he was martyred there.[114] Thus, Foakes-Jackson concludes: "To the candid historian it seems far more perverse to deny that St. Peter was actually at Rome than to affirm that he was the founder of its church."[115] Therefore, this study concludes that the burden of proof remains on those who dissent to the commonly held tradition that Peter was in Rome and that he was martyred there under Emperor Nero—a burden which, as has been shown, they are utterly unable to carry.

AUDIENCE

The study now moves forward to the issue of audience. There are generally two groups in which scholars can be placed. All scholars[116] will acknowledge that the audience is mixed at least to a certain extent. Thus, the one group asserts a primarily Jewish audience, while the other group asserts a primarily gentile audience.

---

111. Bockmuehl, *Remembered Peter*, 127.

112. Bockmuehl, *Remembered Peter*, 127.

113. Bockmuehl, *Remembered Peter*, 131–32; The reason why this is significant is the fact that with all other doubtful "traditions," like the burial of Mary or John the Baptist, all have multiple traditions as to where they are buried.

114. Foakes-Jackson, *Peter*, vii.

115. Foakes-Jackson, *Peter*, vii.

116. Elliott, *Home for the Homeless*, 64; Achtemeier and Epp, *1 Peter*, 51; Green, *1 Peter*, 5; Boring, *1 Peter*, 43; Hiebert, *1 Peter*, 16; Michaels, *1 Peter*, xlvi; Skaggs, *Pentecostal Commentary*, 9.

Literature Review

On the one hand, scholars propose a primarily Jewish audience because this letter is so rife with Jewish exilic terms. Elliott has shown that it would be a mistake to view the language of "παροικίας" (stranger/sojourner) in this letter as merely a spiritual designation.[117] This term refers to the explicit social situation of the Christian readers.[118] The use of this term and its cognates in the New Testament (with one possible exception in Ephesians 2:19) refers to actual social conditions.[119] It refers to someone who is a resident alien and has limited legal rights.[120] Witherington III agrees and notes that "παροικίας" does not mean "exile" or "pilgrim," but literally someone who is on the outside looking in.[121] Thus, someone who is not part of the "in-group" of a particular social environment.[122] In the LXX, this term is used to refer to the actual resident alien status that the Jews experienced in Babylon.[123] Thus, Psalm 119:53–54 reads "ἐν τόπῳ παροικίας μου" (in a strange place) and not "a stranger on the earth."[124] This literal expression of exiles in a foreign land is found in the postexilic literature as well.[125] Peter's designation of his readers as "παρεπιδήμοις διασπορᾶς" (sojourners of the diaspora) in 1:1 alludes again to the Jewish understanding of exile. Elliott has shown the virtual synonymity between "παροικίας" (exile/sojourner) and "διασπορᾶς" (diaspora) in the LXX.[126] Witherington III contends that the author is writing from Babylon, the epicenter of the diaspora, because it was the Romans who displaced all these Jews who were now living in Asia Minor.[127] In this vein, Jobes provides an attractive proposal. The audience is referred to as "παρεπιδήμοις διασπορᾶς" and "παροικίας" because Roman colonization policies had displaced them.[128] Colonization had been common practice in the Roman Empire

---

117. Elliott, *Home for the Homeless*, 1–30.
118. Goppelt, *Commentary on 1 Peter*, 286.
119. Goppelt, *Commentary on 1 Peter*, 1–30.
120. Goppelt, *Commentary on 1 Peter*, 1–30
121. Witherington III, *Letters and Homilies*, 24.
122. Witherington III, *Letters and Homilies*, 24.
123. Witherington III, *Letters and Homilies*, 24; Elliott, *Home for the Homeless*, 1–30.
124. Ps 119:53–54 translated in Witherington III, *Letters and Homilies*, 24.
125. Witherington III, *Letters and Homilies*, 24; Ezra 8:35 LXX; Jdt 5:7–10; 1 Esd 5:7.
126. Elliott, *Home for the Homeless*, 30.
127. Witherington III, *Letters and Homilies*, 24.
128. Jobes, *1 Peter*, 28–41. This study will only provide a summary, and those who would like more details can consult Jobes's commentary.

Called to Suffer

since Antiochus III (d. 187 BC).[129] Claudius was the emperor (AD 41–54) who colonized Asia Minor in order to have a stable military presence in an area with borders which were in flux at the time.[130] The way the Romans colonized was by presenting a socioeconomic opportunity to those who would otherwise have remained poor in Rome.[131] Slaves were freed and granted citizenship if they would leave Rome and colonize the new city.[132] Moreover, emperors would often expel people deemed to be troublemakers from Rome to a remote area of the empire, like a new colony.[133] They defined troublemakers as: "Disturbing the public peace; offending accepted morals; engaging in converting native Romans."[134] A common feature in all of the expulsions from Rome in the second, third, and fourth centuries is that the people who were expelled were foreigners.[135] Not only were they foreigners in Rome, but they were deemed to be foreigners in their destination as well.[136] These colonists would often benefit from the confiscation of goods from the local people.[137] Therefore, they were often despised by them as well.[138] Suetonius notes that this is what happened with the Jews in Rome under Claudius: "since the Jews constantly made disturbances at the instigation of Chrestus, he [Claudius] expelled them from Rome."[139] Thus, Jobes asserts that the designation of "παροικίας" (sojourner/exile) and "παρεπιδήμοις διασπορᾶς" (exile of the diaspora) refers to the fact that these readers were expelled from Rome by the emperor because they had broken the three rules mentioned above.[140] In short, they had preached that Jesus is Lord and, by implication, that Caesar is not. Jobes's proposal is one that shows a lot of promise and one that this study affirms. It can shed light on how Peter knew that these people were in these areas even though there is no evidence that he had been there before. If these were Christians

---

129. Jobes, *1 Peter*, 28.
130. Jobes, *1 Peter*, 29.
131. Frank, *Aspects of Social Behavior in Ancient Rome*, 58.
132. Frank, *Aspects of Social Behavior in Ancient Rome*, 58.
133. Frend, *Martyrdom and Persecution*, 108.
134. Jobes, *1 Peter*, 33.
135. Jobes, *1 Peter*, 30.
136. Jobes, *1 Peter*, 31.
137. Jobes, *1 Peter*, 31.
138. Jobes, *1 Peter*, 31.
139. Suetonius, "Life of Claudius," 25.4.
140. Jobes, *1 Peter*, 39–41.

expelled from Rome for whatever reason, it shows a connection between the church in Rome and the audience.

However, this study disagrees with Elliott's conclusion that everyone addressed in the letter is poor and from a lower social class.[141] Jobes, Clowney, and Achtemeier resist the notion that this designation is social and read it instead as a metaphorical explication of their situation.[142] It is reasonable to assume that people from all social classes would have been within the Christian community.[143] This is why Peter addresses slaves, masters, wives, husbands, and the like. It is more than probable that the language can be metaphorical and real at the same time. They are physically on the outside looking in because they are no longer a part of mainstream society due to their confession of Jesus as Lord. Metaphorically, they are exiles because they realize that this world is not their home and that they should live with the eschaton in mind.

Others,[144] however, note that the audience is primarily of gentile origin. They will refer to statements in the letter referring to idolatry, separation from God, and their former ignorance.[145] These scholars find it unlikely that Peter would refer to Jews as ones who had inherited a useless way of life.[146] It is argued, according to Jobes, that one cannot describe diaspora Jews in such a spiritually bankrupt way.[147] Horrell, therefore, asserts that the reason for all the Jewish designations is that he is reapplying this Jewish history to the gentile converts.[148] In short, the Jews' history is now the gentiles' history.

However, on this point, Boring observes that hellenization and the enormous influence it had on the Mediterranean makes it virtually impossible to draw clear lines between "Jew" and "gentile" as mentioned above.[149] Witherington III has shown convincingly that the level of hellenization

---

141. Jobes, *1 Peter*, 36.

142. Jobes, *1 Peter*, 25; Achtemeier, "Newborn Babes and Living Stones," 228; Clowney, *Message of 1 Peter*, 228.

143. Horrell, *1 Peter*, 49.

144. Elliott, *Home for the Homeless*, 64; Achtemeier and Epp, *1 Peter*, 51; Green, *1 Peter*, 5; Boring, *1 Peter*, 43; Hiebert, *1 Peter*, 16; Michaels, *1 Peter*, xlvi; Skaggs, *Pentecostal Commentary*, 9.

145. 1 Pet 1:14, 18; 4:3–5; Skaggs, *Pentecostal Commentary*, 9.

146. Jobes, *1 Peter*, 23; 1 Pet 1:18.

147. Jobes, *1 Peter*, 23; 1 Pet 1:18.

148. Horrell, *1 Peter*, 48.

149. Boring, *1 Peter*, 24.

Called to Suffer

amongst the Jews of the diaspora is a lot more extensive than one would imagine.[150] There is archaeological evidence that shows a synagogue attached to a gymnasium in the middle of the town.[151] There is evidence that Jews had tried to reverse their circumcision in order to compete in the athletic games.[152] Historian Rodney Stark notes that Jews would have been indistinguishable from gentiles unless one went to look for them in the synagogue.[153] These Jews would have participated in the trade guilds and dinner parties held in pagan temples.[154] According to Witherington III, this would have been less of a problem for them than for the Jews living in Judea.[155] Moreover, Peter tells his readers that they are to conduct themselves in a Christian manner among the "ἔθνεσιν."[156] It is hard to believe that Peter would be saying this to gentile Christians.[157] They would never have regarded themselves as among the "gentiles."[158] This is clearly Jewish language.[159] Thus, this study concludes that the audience consists of primarily hellenized Jewish Christian people who are living among an overwhelmingly gentile population. This also is coincidentally how the entire Christian tradition has viewed the audience, except for Augustine and Jerome in the early church and Luther and Tyndale in the 1500s.[160] This view is able to reconcile both the deeply Jewish language, which they would have been familiar with, but also the scathing critiques of their former lives.

---

150. Witherington III, *Letters and Homilies*, 25–39. This study only provides a summary of Witherington III's argument, which can be found in his commentary cited.

151. Witherington III, *Letters and Homilies* 26; The gymnasium would have been a hub of social activity and host to athletic games as well as other social clubs. The presence of the synagogue this close to a gymnasium suggests that Jews of the diaspora were more than comfortable engaging in various gentile social practices.

152. Witherington III, *Letters and Homilies*, 26.

153. Starke, *Cities of God*, 78.

154. Witherington III, *Letters and Homilies*, 26.

155. Witherington III, *Letters and Homilies*, 26.

156. Witherington III, *Letters and Homilies*, 25.

157. Witherington III, *Letters and Homilies*, 25.

158. Witherington III, *Letters and Homilies*, 25.

159. Witherington III, *Letters and Homilies*, 25.

160. Eusebius, Calvin, Wesley, and the church fathers took the audience to be primarily if not entirely consisting of Jewish Christians (see Witherington III, *Letters and Homilies*, 34).

Literature Review

PERSPECTIVES ON SUFFERING

Jewish Perspectives on Suffering

It would be erroneous to assume that there is only one Jewish perspective when it comes to suffering. Moreover, as we look at Judaism more broadly, we find various streams of Judaism presenting a particular understanding of suffering, whereas other streams of Judaism present a different understanding. Robinson brings this to light and identifies six distinct perspectives on human suffering in the Old Testament: 1) retributive: suffering because of their sins; 2) educational: suffering designed to discipline or correct the person; 3) probationary: suffering that purifies and tests the person; 4) revelation: suffering causes a person to deepen in his understanding of God; 5) sacrificial: presents suffering as a sacrifice to God, as in Isaiah 53 and Qumran,[161] and 6) eschatological: the suffering that will precede the end times, or the messianic woes.[162] One can broadly differentiate here, as Croy does, and categorize two types of suffering: punitive (i.e., punishment for wrongdoing or sin) and nonpunitive or pedagogical (i.e., suffering designed to test and form the person).[163] This study proceeds to explicate the various perspectives on suffering within Judaism using this binary lens.

The prophets view Israel's suffering as God's punishment for their sins. Isaiah sees the destruction that the foreign armies will bring upon Israel as punishment from God.[164] Amos sees God's decision to strike Israel with famine, drought, and pestilence in the same light.[165] The book of Habakkuk presents a similar narrative. Israel has been unfaithful, and God is going to raise up the Chaldeans to judge them. Croy notes in this regard that these prophetic announcements are proleptic in that they are warning the people of the dire consequences of their infidelity.[166] Croy makes a compelling case from the book of Job that this punitive suffering was the main view in Judaism.[167] One can see this in how Job's friends respond to his suffering.

---

161. Qumran's Manual of Discipline 8:2–4, as in Vermes, *Dead Sea Scrolls in English*, 72.

162. Robinson, *Suffering Human and Divine*, 31–48.

163. Croy, *Endurance in Suffering*, 82. This study is indebted to Croy for the following analysis. Do refer to his volume for an even deeper analysis.

164. Isa 1:5–9; Croy, *Endurance in Suffering*, 88.

165. Amos 4:6–12; Croy, *Endurance in Suffering*, 88.

166. Croy, *Endurance in Suffering*, 88.

167. Croy, *Endurance in Suffering*, 96.

They constantly tell him to repent of his sin, because his sin is the reason he is suffering.[168] In the wisdom writings, divine discipline is construed as punitive, but also educational. Proverbs 3:11–12 (LXX) "Υἱέ, μὴ ὀλιγώρει παιδείας κυρίου μηδὲ ἐκλύου ὑπ' αὐτοῦ ἐλεγχόμενος, ὃν γὰρ ἀγαπᾷ κύριος παιδεύει, μαστιγοῖ δὲ πάντα υἱὸν ὃν παραδέχεται"[169] (Son, do not despise the discipline of the Lord or grow weak when reproved by him, for the Lord reproves whomever he loves and punishes any son whom he receives[170]) is a clear example of punitive discipline.[171] The word translated "μαστιγοῖ" above means "to whip or flog."[172] This, then, shows how God disciplines his children in order to correct them. As in Proverbs 22:15 (LXX) "ἄνοια ἐξῆπται καρδίας νέου, ῥάβδος δὲ καὶ παιδεία μακρὰν ἀπ' αὐτοῦ" (Folly clings to the heart of the young, but a rod and childhood are far from him), the rod is designed to correct the child from wrongdoing. Thus, we see a conflation of punitive and probative suffering. However, in Sirach 2:1–6 (LXX), this probative view of suffering comes to the fore more clearly:

> TEKNON, εἰ προσέρχῃ δουλεύειν Κυρίῳ Θεῷ, ἑτοίμασον τὴν ψυχήν σου εἰς πειρασμόν· εὔθυνον τὴν καρδίαν σου καὶ καρτέρησον καὶ μὴ σπεύσῃς ἐν καιρῷ ἐπαγωγῆς· κολλήθητι αὐτῷ καὶ μὴ ἀποστῇς, ἵνα αὐξηθῇς ἐπ' ἐσχάτων σου. πᾶν ὃ ἐὰν ἐπαχθῇ σοι, δέξαι καὶ ἐν ἀλλάγμασι ταπεινώσεώς σου μακροθύμησον· ὅτι ἐν πυρὶ δοκιμάζεται χρυσὸς καὶ ἄνθρωποι δεκτοὶ ἐν καμίνῳ ταπεινώσεως. πίστευσον αὐτῷ, καὶ ἀντιλήψεταί σου· εὔθυνον τὰς ὁδούς σου καὶ ἔλπισον ἐπ' αὐτόν.

> Child, if you come to serve the Lord God, prepare your soul for temptation. Make your heart right and be steadfast, and do not hurry in the time of distress. Be joined to him, and do not turn away, so that you might be honored at your last days. Accept everything that would be brought upon you, and when you are changed into a state of humiliation, be patient; because gold is tested in the fire, and acceptable people in the furnace of humiliation. Trust in

---

168. Job 4:1—27:23, and Elihu in 33:9–12.

169. Prov 3:11–12. All quotations from the LXX, unless stated otherwise, are taken from, *Septuaginta: A Reader's Edition*.

170. All English translations of the LXX come from Rick Brannan et al., eds., *The Lexham English Septuagint*.

171. Croy, *Endurance in Suffering*, 89.

172. μαστιγόω fut. μαστιγώσω; 1 aor. ἐμαστίγωσα. Pass.: fut. 3 pl. μαστιγωθήσονται—to beat with a whip or lash, *whip, flog, scourge* Danker, *Greek English Lexicon, 620*.

him, and he will support you; make your ways straight and hope in him.

Skehan observes that in this passage "Ben Sira warns his disciples about the adversity that the Lord allows as a test of whether or not the fear of the Lord is genuine."[173] The person coming to the Lord is to prepare themselves for testing—πειρασμόν. There is, however, no mention of punishment for sins in this passage. Thus, the numerous prohibitions and commands are grounded in the probative suffering through which God is testing the person's character.[174] This probative suffering can be seen in Deuteronomy 8:2–5 (LXX) as well:

> καὶ μνησθήσῃ πᾶσαν τὴν ὁδόν, ἣν ἤγαγέν σε κύριος ὁ θεός σου ἐν τῇ ἐρήμῳ, ὅπως ἂν κακώσῃ σε καὶ ἐκπειράσῃ σε καὶ διαγνωσθῇ τὰ ἐν τῇ καρδίᾳ σου, εἰ φυλάξῃ τὰς ἐντολὰς αὐτοῦ ἢ οὔ. καὶ ἐκάκωσέν σε καὶ ἐλιμαγχόνησέν σε καὶ ἐψώμισέν σε τὸ μαννα, ὃ οὐκ εἴδησαν οἱ πατέρες σου, ἵνα ἀναγγείλῃ σοι ὅτι οὐκ ἐπ' ἄρτῳ μόνῳ ζήσεται ὁ ἄνθρωπος, ἀλλ' ἐπὶ παντὶ ῥήματι τῷ ἐκπορευομένῳ διὰ στόματος θεοῦ ζήσεται ὁ ἄνθρωπος. τὰ ἱμάτιά σου οὐ κατετρίβη ἀπὸ σοῦ, οἱ πόδες σου οὐκ ἐτυλώθησαν, ἰδοὺ τεσσαράκοντα ἔτη. καὶ γνώσῃ τῇ καρδίᾳ σου ὅτι ὡς εἴ τις παιδεύσαι ἄνθρωπος τὸν υἱὸν αὐτοῦ, οὕτως κύριος ὁ θεός σου παιδεύσει σε

> And you shall remember all the ways that the Lord your God led you in the wilderness that he might distress you and test you and to discern in your heart whether you will keep his commands or not. And he distressed you and weakened you by hunger and fed you manna, which your fathers did not see, in order to declare to you that man shall not live on only bread, but on every word going out through the mouth of God man shall live. Your garments were not made old from you, your shoes did not wear out from you, your feet did not become calloused—behold, for forty years! And you shall know in your heart that as a certain man might teach his son, in this way the Lord your God will teach you.

The word translated as "testing" is "εκπειραζω" in the LXX, while the word "disciplines" is "παιδευω." Clearly, then, their suffering is not that the Lord has disciplined them for their sins, but that he might test them to see what is in their hearts. It is suffering that exposes their hearts and refines them.

---

173. Skehan, *Wisdom of Ben Sira*, 150.
174. Croy, *Endurance in Suffering*, 93.

Lindstrom, in his monograph on the Psalms, asserts that there is no explicit connection between disease and sin.[175] The problem with Lindstrom's thesis is that whenever there is an explicit connection between the psalmist's sin and suffering, he attributes those verses to a redactor.[176] Thus, Lindstrom sweeps all the evidence under the rug and then exclaims "Look, there is no evidence." Psalm 38:2–4 (LXX) explicitly connects affliction with the psalmist's sin:

> Κύριε, μὴ τῷ θυμῷ σου ἐλέγξῃς με μηδὲ τῇ ὀργῇ σου παιδεύσῃς με. ὅτι τὰ βέλη σου ἐνεπάγησάν μοι, καὶ ἐπεστήρισας ἐπ' ἐμὲ τὴν χεῖρά σου, ⁴ οὐκ ἔστιν ἴασις ἐν τῇ σαρκί μου ἀπὸ προσώπου τῆς ὀργῆς σου, οὐκ ἔστιν εἰρήνη τοῖς ὀστέοις μου ἀπὸ προσώπου τῶν ἁμαρτιῶν μου.

> O Lord, do not reprove me with your wrath, nor in your anger discipline me. For you planted your arrows in me, and you strengthened your hand against me. And there is no healing in my flesh from the face of your anger. There is no peace for my bones from before my sins.

Moreover, verse 2 asserts that it is the Lord who has given the psalmist this affliction. This is an example of punitive suffering because of the psalmist's sins. However, Psalm 65:10–12 (LXX) portrays a different picture:

> ὅτι ἐδοκίμασας ἡμᾶς, ὁ θεός, ἐπύρωσας ἡμᾶς, ὡς πυροῦται τὸ ἀργύριον, εἰσήγαγες ἡμᾶς εἰς τὴν παγίδα, ἔθου θλίψεις ἐπὶ τὸν νῶτον ἡμῶν. ἐπεβίβασας ἀνθρώπους ἐπὶ τὰς κεφαλὰς ἡμῶν, διήλθομεν διὰ πυρὸς καὶ ὕδατος, καὶ ἐξήγαγες ἡμᾶς εἰς ἀναψυχήν.

> For you tested us, O God, and you purged us as silver is purged. You led us into the trap; you set afflictions before us. You put people upon our heads. We went through fire and water, and you led us into refreshment.

Here we see again that it is God who causes the suffering, or at least allows it, but we see no mention of sin. The metaphor of testing through fire that comes for the sake of purification is explicit in verse 10 (LXX) "ὅτι ἐδοκίμασας ἡμᾶς, ὁ θεός, ἐπύρωσας ἡμᾶς, ὡς πυροῦται τὸ ἀργύριον" (For you tested us, O God, and you purged us as silver is purged.). This is a clear example of probative suffering.

---

175. Lindstrom, *Suffering and Sin*, 445.
176. Lindstrom, *Suffering and Sin*, 70–73, 242–44, 299–300, 329–32.

The evidence presented above is sufficient for this study. Croy has done an in-depth study on the Maccabean literature, Qumran, as well as the rabbinic literature.[177] In 2 and 3 Maccabees, Croy shows the presence of punitive suffering.[178] However, in 4 Maccabees, probative suffering comes to the fore.[179] Qumran also has both types of suffering but includes a unique understanding of expiatory suffering.[180] In the rabbinic literature, Kraemer notes that there is an "almost exclusive insistence that that suffering is punishment for sin."[181] Again, the two clear understandings of suffering come to the fore.

This study concludes therefore that there is a clear understanding of suffering in Jewish literature. On the one hand, it portrays suffering as punitive, which means it is punishment from God for sin. On the other hand, there is probative suffering, where God tests a person's heart through suffering in order to expose what is truly in it. This type of suffering is also used to cleanse the person from wickedness and to train him in the way of godliness.

Greco-Roman Perspectives on Suffering

In the Greco-Roman world, one finds numerous perspectives on the causes of suffering, as well as its purpose. In Homer's *Odyssey*,[182] Zeus makes the following comment:

> ὢ πόποι, οἷον δή νυ θεοὺς βροτοὶ αἰτιόωνται· ἐξ ἡμέων γάρ
> φασι κάκ' ἔμμεναι, οἱ δὲ καὶ αὐτοὶ σφῇσιν ἀτασθαλίῃσιν ὑπὲρ
> μόρον ἄλγε' ἔχουσιν, ὡς καὶ νῦν Αἴγισθος ὑπὲρ μόρον Ἀτρεΐδαο
> γῆμ' ἄλοχον μνηστήν, τὸν δ' ἔκτανε νοστήσαντα, εἰδὼς αἰπὺν
> ὄλεθρον, ἐπεὶ πρό οἱ εἴπομεν ἡμεῖς, Ἑρμείαν πέμψαντες, ἐΰσκοπον
> ἀργεϊφόντην, μήτ' αὐτὸν κτείνειν μήτε μνάασθαι ἄκοιτιν· ἐκ γὰρ
> Ὀρέσταο τίσις ἔσσεται Ἀτρεΐδαο, ὁππότ' ἂν ἡβήσῃ τε καὶ ἧς
> ἱμείρεται αἴης. ὣς ἔφαθ' Ἑρμείας, ἀλλ' οὐ φρένας Αἰγίσθοιο πεῖθ'
> ἀγαθὰ φρονέων· νῦν δ' ἀθρόα πάντ' ἀπέτισεν.

---

177. Croy, *Endurance in Suffering*, 100–129.
178. Croy, *Endurance in Suffering*, 100–105.
179. Croy, *Endurance in Suffering*, 105–6.
180. Croy, *Endurance in Suffering*, 116–24.
181. Kraemer, *Responses to Suffering*, 104–6. He does, however, discuss "The Hint of Alternatives," where some texts seem to imply that suffering is expiatory for others.
182. Homer, *Odyssey*.

> How surprising that men blame the gods, and say their troubles come from us, though they, through their own un-wisdom, find suffering beyond what is fated. Just as Aegisthus, beyond what was fated, took the wife of Agamemnon, son of Atreus, and murdered him when he returned, though he knew the end would be a complete disaster, since we sent Hermes, keen-eyed Slayer of Argus, to warn him not to kill the man, or court his wife, as Orestes would avenge Agamemnon, once he reached manhood and longed for his own land. So Hermes told him, but despite his kind intent he could not move Aegisthus' heart: and Aegisthus has paid the price now for it all.[183]

Here one can see that the reason for Aegisthus's suffering is his actions. This was not brought about by the gods, nor does it seem to have any purpose. However, Aeschylus, in his drama *Persians*,[184] notes a sort of reciprocity:

> οἳ γῆν μολόντες Ἑλλάδ' οὐ θεῶν βρέτη ᾐδοῦντο συλᾶν οὐδὲ πιμπράναι νεώς: βωμοὶ δ' ἄιστοι, δαιμόνων θ' ἱδρύματα πρόρριζα φύρδην ἐξανέστραπται βάθρων. τοιγὰρ κακῶς δράσαντες οὐκ ἐλάσσονα πάσχουσι, τὰ δὲ μέλλουσι, κοὐδέπω κακῶν κρηνὶς ἀπέσβηκ' ἀλλ' ἔτ' ἐκπιδύεται.

> The moment they went to Greece, they forgot their respect to the gods and began to destroy all the statues and images of the gods and set fire to all the temples. They have destroyed altars, and they have upturned from their stands holy edifices, leaving them scattered everywhere on the ground. And so, what ruin they've caused will be, in turn, visited upon them with even greater fury. And the suffering will continue later. The fountain of their suffering is not yet empty.[185]

The Persians' disrespect for the altars of the gods has in turn brought fury on themselves. This type of reciprocity was widespread in popular Greek religion. Burkert is worth quoting at length:

> All the great crises that leave men helpless even when united may be interpreted as caused by the wrath of the Strong Ones, gods and heroes: bad harvests and infertility of the soil, diseases of men and cattle barrenness of women and abnormal offspring, civil wars, and defeat by a foreign army. Conversely, if these powers are

---

183. Homer, *Odyssey*, 1.32–43.
184. Aeschylus, *Persians*.
185. Aeschylus, *Persians*, lines 810–15.

appeased, all kinds of blessing must return, rich harvest, healthy children, and civic order.[186]

The means to avert these calamities was through sacrifice and prayer.[187] These appeals were made to specific deities who, in turn, had specific areas of authority: Poseidon for earthquakes and traveling via the ocean; Apollo for illness; and Demeter for agriculture.[188] In this regard, the earthquake that struck Sparta in 464 BC was due to their violation of the sacred altar of Poseidon, according to Burkert.[189] A similar earthquake in 373 BC was attributed to Poseidon because the Peloponnesians had committed sacrilege against the Ionians who were sacrificing on Poseidon's altar.[190] This then reveals a parallel to the punitive suffering we saw above. This reality would have created extreme anxiety on the part of the people. They were constantly preoccupied with pleasing the gods so as not to incur their judgment.

However, there was also an objection to this kind of punitive suffering. Theognis, a poet from the sixth century BC, is one such example:

> πῶσ δὴ σευ, Κρονίδη, τολμᾶι νόος ἄνδρας ἀλιτρού ἐν ταὐτῆι μοίρηι τόν τε δίκαιον ἔχειν; ἔπης δ' ὄλβον ἔχουσιν ἀπήμονα τοὶ ἀπὸ δειλῶν ἔργων ἴσχυοντες θυμὸν ὅμως πενίην μητέρ' ἀμηχανίησ ἔλαβον τὰ δίκαια φιλεῦντες ...[191]

> How, O son of Kronos, does your mind bear for criminals to have the same fate as the just person? Yet [the wicked] have carefree wealth, and those who keep their hearts from base deeds nevertheless receive poverty, the mother of helplessness, despite their love of justice ...[192]

This is an objection to the idea of retribution for one's deeds. The wicked prosper, and the righteous suffer ills. Theognis does not offer a reflection as to the cause or purpose of this suffering. He merely states that this is the case.

Finally, then, there is the understanding in the Greco-Roman world that suffering is educational. Firstly, there is an understanding that life's

---

186. Burkert, *Greek Religion*, 264. Emphasis added.
187. Croy, *Endurance in Suffering*, 135.
188. Burkert, *Greek Religion*, 264–68; Guthrie, *Greeks and Their Gods*, 27–112.
189. Burkert, *Greek Religion*, 137–38.
190. Croy, *Endurance in Suffering*, 136.
191. Theognis, *Eleg.* 377–78, 383–85; text from Young, *Theognis*, 25.
192. Young, *Theognis*, 25. See also Theognis, *Eleg.*. lines 743–52.

lessons, through a process of trial and error, are educative. Hesiod presents an example of this in *Works and Days*:

> Δίκη δ' ὑπὲρ Ὕβριος ἴσχει ἐς τέλος ἐξελθοῦσα: παθὼν δέ τε νήπιος ἔγνω. αὐτίκα γὰρ τρέχει Ὅρκος ἅμα σκολιῇσι δίκῃσιν. τῆς δὲ Δίκης ῥόθος ἑλκομένης, ᾗ κ' ἄνδρες ἄγωσι δωροφάγοι, σκολιῇς δὲ δίκης κρίνωσι θέμιστας. ἣ δ' ἕπεται κλαίουσα πόλιν καὶ ἤθεα λαῶν, ἠέρα ἑσσαμένη, κακὸν ἀνθρώποισι φέρουσα, οἵ τε μιν ἐξελάσωσι καὶ οὐκ ἰθεῖαν ἔνειμαν.

> But you, Perses, listen to right and do not foster violence; for violence is bad for a poor man. Even the prosperous cannot easily bear its burden but is weighed down under it when he has fallen into delusion. The better path is to go by on the other side towards justice; for Justice beats Outrage when she comes at length to the end of the race. But only when he has suffered does the fool learn this.[193]

There is no mention of divine intervention, nor a divine purpose; merely trial and error which results in formation. Seneca asserts that suffering is an intrinsic part of existence, but continues that one should avoid it if possible.[194] However, Seneca acknowledges the probative value of suffering "Unrelenting misfortune has one advantage: those whom it continually distresses, it eventually toughens . . . it is necessary, that some hardship encounter [the pilot] that will try the soul."[195] Furthermore, in *De Providentia* Seneca posits that it is within God's character to discipline those whom he loves.[196] Seneca goes so far as to relate this to the Spartans' practice of publicly lashing their children.[197] Musonius Rufus, in this vein, asserts that suffering has a probative function "When we know that we are suffering for some good purpose, either to help our friends or to benefit our city, or to defend our wives and children, or, best and most imperative, to become good and just and self-controlled, a state which no man achieves without hardships."[198] These are clear examples of the probative value of suffering.

Aeschylus, however, in *Agamemnon*, asserts that:

> Δίκα δὲ τοῖς μὲν παθοῦσ-ιν μαθεῖν ἐπιρρέπει

193. Hesiod, "Works and Days," lines 218–24.
194. Seneca, *Epistles*, 1:66.19.
195. Seneca, *On Consolation*, "To Helvia," 2.3; "To Marcia," 5.5.
196. Seneca, *Moral Essays*, 1.4.11–12.
197. Seneca, *Moral Essays*, 1.4.11–12.
198. Lutz, "Musonius Rufus," 59.

Literature Review

Justice leans her scale upon us so that we may learn through suffering.[199]

Furthermore, Aeschylus continues with this statement about Zeus:

Ζῆνα δέ τις προφρόνως ἐπινίκια κλάζων τεύξεται φρενῶν τὸ πᾶν: τὸν φρονεῖν βροτοὺς ὁδώ-σαντα, τὸν πάθει μάθος θέντα κυρίως ἔχειν. στάζει δ' ἔν θ' ὕπνῳ πρὸ καρδίας μνησιπήμων πόνος: καὶ παρ' ἄ- κοντας ἦλθε σωφρονεῖν. δαιμόνων δέ που χάρις βίαιος σέλμα σεμνὸν ἡμένων.

But Zeus! Whoever shouts "Zeus is victorious!" will gain wisdom replete. Zeus it was who gave men their knowledge and Zeus who made the rule, "pain is wisdom." For here, into our heart, while we sleep, slowly drips the painful memory and even to those who fight it, that pain, that pain, becomes wisdom. Because it is by force that the gods who sit upon their throne in majesty, give us this gift of wisdom.[200]

"Pain" here is the Greek word "πάθος," which should instead be translated as "that which is endured or experienced, suffering."[201] In this vein, Epictetus notes that hardships are the gods' method of training humans.[202] Epictetus says of Hercules, "Is he not convinced that whatever he suffers, it is Zeus who is exercising him?"[203] These hardships are designed to reveal one's character.[204] One can see the probative purpose of suffering here, but also an explicit connection to the gods as the ones who cause it. However, having noted that this idea of suffering as a means to learn is widespread; it is important to mention that the notion that the gods instigated this suffering purely as probative is extremely rare.

This study concludes that the Greco-Roman world viewed suffering as punitive and probatory. However, even though there are a few examples to the contrary, when the gods were involved in this suffering it was primarily as retribution. There was an understanding that suffering was educational, but rarely was this suffering viewed as the gods educating the people, thus, relegating education to conventional wisdom through trial and error.

---

199. Aeschylus, *Agamemnon*, 250–51.
200. Aeschylus, *Agamemnon*, 174–83.
201. Danker, *Greek-English Lexicon*, 748.
202. Epictetus, *Discourses of Epictetus*, 254.
203. Epictetus, *Discourses of Epictetus*, 254.
204. Epictetus, *Discourses of Epictetus*, 66.

CALLED TO SUFFER

THE NATURE OF THE SUFFERING IN 1 PETER

Now we turn to the exploration of the *Sitz im Leben* (Life situation) in 1 Peter. As noted above, scholars are in agreement regarding the verbal and emotional nature of the suffering experienced by Peter's audience.[205] Achtemeier notes it is clear from the letter that the audience is suffering, and that this suffering is widespread among Christians.[206] However, what is not as clear is whether this suffering includes official or unofficial state persecution or not, as well as whether the state martyred these Christians simply for being Christians. Firstly, however, some background on the religious situation in the Roman world.

Religion and politics in the Roman world were inextricably intertwined.[207] Religion was used to control the people as well as to prevent any official rebellion against Rome.[208] This religion expressed itself in the imperial cult. This was especially true in provinces outside of Rome, like Asia Minor.[209] Achtemeier notes that emperors like Augustus, Tiberius, and Claudius all discouraged ideas of being deemed divine by their people.[210] According to the Roman historian Suetonius, Augustus "always shrank away from the title Lord."[211] He did not even permit his children to call him by that designation.[212] The Greek for "Lord" here is "κύριος," which becomes relevant later on. However, all of these emperors had temples in Asia Minor and had divine honors paid to them by the people of the empire.[213] There is a twofold reason for the imperial cult in Asia Minor. On the one hand, it provided a convenient way for people to show their loyalty to Rome and for Rome to gauge their loyalty; Rome saw loyalty to the imperial cult as loyalty towards Rome and vice versa.[214] Tacitus affirms this in his

---

205. Bechtler, *Following in His Steps*, 83–104; Achtemeier and Epp, *1 Peter*, 29; Donelson, *I & II Peter and Jude*, 11–12; Le Roux, *Ethics in 1 Peter*, 56–57; Kelly, *Epistles of Peter and Jude*, 189; Marshall, *1 Peter*, 24; Jobes, *1 Peter*, 45; Senior, *1 Peter*, 7.

206. Achtemeier and Epp, *1 Peter*, 34.

207. Achtemeier and Epp, *1 Peter*, 33; Sordi, *Christians and the Roman Empire*, 62.

208. Horrell, *1 Peter*, 55.

209. Magie, *Roman Rule in Asia Minor*, 1:470; Price, *Rituals and Power*, 130, 198. See also Price, *Rituals and Power*, 59 for a chart of all the imperial temples in Asia Minor.

210. Achtemeier and Epp, *1 Peter*, 27; Suetonius, "Life of Augustus," 53:1.

211. Suetonius, "Life of Augustus," 53:1.

212. Suetonius, "Life of Augustus," 53:1.

213. Magie, *Roman Rule in Asia Minor*, 1:572; Price, *Rituals and* Power, 179.

214. Magie, *Roman Rule in Asia Minor*, 1:572; Price, *Rituals and* Power, 179.

Annals,[215] noting when the people of Cyzicus in Phrygia neglected the cult of Augustus, Rome charged them with abusing Roman citizens.[216] On the other hand, Price argues that the imperial cult was a way for the provinces to integrate the political reality of subjection under Rome within the context of Ancient Greek culture.[217] The Greek culture provided them with a framework of subjugation expressed in reverence for the gods.[218] Therefore, the imperial cult allowed prominent families to maintain cultural continuity in the midst of an altered political situation.[219] Consequently, the imperial cult flourished as a way to maintain cultural stability by providing a way for these provinces to relate themselves to the Roman Emperor, who was deemed to be the central figure in the empire in terms of their own cultural system i.e., the worship of the gods.[220] This made nonconformity to the imperial cult a serious issue.[221] Nonconformity to the cult would be seen as not only a challenge to the empire but a challenge to the essence of society itself.[222] It threatened to unravel the cultural continuity and political stability that the imperial cult provided.[223] As Price asserts, "The (imperial) cult . . . enhanced the dominance of local elites over the populace, of cities over other cities, and of Greek over indigenous cultures. That is, the cult was a major part of the web of power that formed the fabric of society."[224] This led the elites to exert a good amount of social pressure on people who would not conform to the social norm, and as a result jeopardize the elites' political situation as well as their standing with Rome. Furthermore, it was believed that nonconformity could result in divine disfavor and a worsened economic situation.[225] Christians, as a result, were hated by the general populace, because of their profoundly anti-social behavior.[226] Keeping this

---

215. Tacitus, "Annals," 4.36–37.
216. Tacitus, "Annals," 4.36–37.
217. Price, *Rituals and Power*.
218. Price, *Rituals and Power*.
219. Price, *Rituals and Power*.
220. Price, *Rituals and Power*, 118, 206, 225.
221. Horrell, *1 Peter*, 55.
222. Horrell, *1 Peter*, 57.
223. Horrell, *1 Peter*, 54–57.
224. Price, *Rituals and Power*, 248.
225. Sordi, *Christians and the Roman Empire*, 5, 203.
226. Schutter, *Hermeneutic and Composition*, 11; Bechtler, *Following in His Steps*, 84.

cultural situation in mind, this study now turns to the nature of suffering in 1 Peter.

As mentioned above, all scholars agree that Christians were slandered and abused socially for their nonconformity to society.[227] Achtemeier and others have shown that there is no official policy for the persecution of Christians until late in the third century under Emperor Decius.[228] The range of terms in 1 Peter refers mostly to verbal shaming.[229] Terms like "καταλαλοῦσιν" (speak against/slander),[230] "λοιδορούμενος" (revile),[231] "ἀντελοιδόρει" (revile),[232] "ἐπηρεάζοντε," (threaten/abuse),[233] and "ὀνειδίζεσθε" (insult/reproach/mock)[234] all seem to affirm this conclusion. Also, as noted above, all scholars agree that these terms point to the reality of verbal abuse and social shaming.[235] Le Roux adds the term "κακώσων" (mistreat/harm)[236] to this list and affirms that the abuse is verbal rather than physical.[237] There is no sign of confrontation with Rome in the letter, and instead, Elliott contends that it reflects "a time of toleration and peaceful co-existence."[238] Furthermore, Achtemeier maintains that Nero's persecution of Christians was merely local, and did not spread to the rest of the empire.[239] The sheer number of Christians in Bithynia discount any claims that it was illegal to be a Christian at this time.[240] This is in agreement with the official Roman position of leniency and tolerance towards other religions.[241] Elliott concludes that:

227. See footnote 205–06.

228. Achtemeier and Epp, *1 Peter*, 29–36; Le Roux, *Ethics in 1 Peter*, 58; Elliott, *1 Peter*, 103.

229. Donelson, *I & II Peter and Jude*, 11–12.

230. 1 Pet 2:12.

231. 1 Pet 2:23.

232. 1 Pet 2:23.

233. 1 Pet 3:16.

234. 1 Pet 4:14.

235. Bechtler, *Following in His Steps*, 19. See his review of the relevant literature.

236. 1 Pet 3:13.

237. Le Roux, *Ethics in 1 Peter*, 56–57.

238. Elliott, *Home for the Homeless*, 80–81, 86.

239. Achtemeier and Epp, *1 Peter*, 29–30.

240. Best, *1 Peter*, 41.

241. Le Roux, *Ethics in 1 Peter*, 55.

the situation entails intense verbal abuse and incessant maligning and reproach... But with no mention in one Peter of local arrests, trials, or executions, there is no basis for claiming that at the time of one Peter Christianity had been officially prescribed by Roman authorities that being labeled a Christian implied being charged as a criminal.[242]

This, coupled with the fact that there is no evidence of official persecution by the Roman state, leads these scholars to conclude that the Christians were not in any physical danger, nor were Christians formally tried and martyred.

It is true that a fundamental principle in Roman religions was what Goppelt calls "conforming tolerance, i.e., reciprocal acceptance."[243] Therefore, when Peter says "τοῦ κυρίου ἡμῶν Ἰησοῦ Χριστοῦ" (Jesus Christ our Lord),[244] and "κύριον δὲ τὸν Χριστὸν ἁγιάσατε ἐν ταῖς καρδίαις ὑμῶν" (Set apart Christ the Lord in your hearts),[245] he is making an extraordinary claim. Peter claims that Christ is Lord, and this, by implication, means that Caesar is not. This assertion that Christianity is the only religion at the exclusion of all others, especially the imperial cult, violated the most fundamental of Roman religious principles: tolerance and acceptance.[246] This, coupled with the fact that Christianity lacked an ancient heritage—which all traditional religions possessed—made it look fanciful in the eyes of the Romans.[247] Contra the argument above, this led to formal court proceedings.

Bechtler notes that the word "ἀπολογίαν"[248] "ultimately derives from the juridical sphere and is often used as a technical term to denote a legal defense."[249] Furthermore, although this might not point to capital trials before the governor, the language "is at least compatible with petty prosecution before civic magistrates."[250] Le Roux and Horrell affirm that local citizens could bring Christians before civic magistrates and this could lead

---

242. Elliott, *1 Peter*, 794.
243. Goppelt, *Commentary on 1 Peter*, 40.
244. 1 Pet 1:3, my translation.
245. 1 Pet 3:15, my translation.
246. Goppelt, *Commentary on 1 Peter*, 40; Benko, *Pagan Rome*, 1–29; Ste Croix, "Why Were the Early Christians Persecuted?," 24–31; Frend, *Martyrdom and Persecution*, 77–93; Wilken, *Christians as the Romans Saw Them*, 63–64.
247. Wilken, *Christians as the Romans Saw Them*, 63.
248. 1 Pet 3:15.
249. Bechtler, *Following in His Steps*, 90.
250. Kelly, *Epistles of Peter and Jude*, 29.

to their deaths.²⁵¹ It would have been natural for magistrates to intervene if these accusations escalated to a certain point.²⁵² Moreover, from Pliny's letter to Trajan, there is clear evidence that local authorities put Christians to death as early as the 80s.²⁵³ This, however, is not evidence that this was not happening long before that time. Although Pliny's letter cannot be used to date the letter, it does prove that Christians were indeed prosecuted and put to death.²⁵⁴ Achtemeier, Best, Le Roux, and others remain obsessed with the fact that no official Roman policy mandated the persecution of Christians.²⁵⁵ However, that completely misses the point of the discussion. The question is not whether there was some official document stipulating that Christians had to be persecuted by the state. The question is whether the Roman and local authorities put Christians to death for their faith, and the answer is an emphatic yes.

As noted above, Nero, according to Tacitus, violently persecuted the Christian community in Rome because he deemed their belief in Christ a "novel and malicious superstition."²⁵⁶ Contra Elliott, Le Roux, and Best, Horrell notes that after this outburst by Nero against the Christians it would have been deemed illegal to be one, whether in Rome or the provinces.²⁵⁷ Pliny killed Christians if they would not recant their Christian faith and pay homage to Caesar.²⁵⁸ Christians were put to death because a refusal to worship the imperial cult was a violation of the *Pax Romana (Roman Peace)*.²⁵⁹ This study disagrees with Best, and asks: Why would Pliny force them to recant under threat of death if it was perfectly legal to be a Christian?²⁶⁰ Moreover, this study asks how Le Roux comes to the observation that the correspondence between Pliny and Trajan "attests to a leniency and

---

251. Le Roux, *Ethics in 1 Peter*, 51; Horrell, *1 Peter*, 58.

252. Le Roux, *Ethics in 1 Peter*, 51.

253. Pliny the Younger, "Letters of Pliny the Younger"; Ste Croix, "Why Were the Early Christians Persecuted?—A Rejoinder," 28–33.

254. Michaels, *1 Peter*, lxvi.

255. Achtemeier and Epp, *1 Peter*, 29–36; Le Roux, *Ethics in 1 Peter*, 58; Best, *1 Peter*, 41; Bechtler, *Following in His Steps*, 83–86.

256. 1 Pet 4:16; Donelson, *I & II Peter and Jude*, 13.

257. Horrell, *1 Peter*, 57–59.

258. Pliny the Younger, "Letters of Pliny the Younger."

259. Horrell, *1 Peter*, 58–59.

260. Best, *1 Peter*, 41.

toleration regarding the official Roman position towards the Christians."[261] This observation is diametrically opposed to the evidence that this study has provided.

This study concludes that local and Roman magistrates throughout the empire put Christians to death. This happened for various reasons, but primarily because of their Christian faith, which by this time was certainly deemed illegal. This leads to the final section of the literature review: What is the purpose of composition?

PURPOSE OF COMPOSITION

The situation described above was indeed a grim one. Christianity was certainly not winning any popularity contests. There was a real danger that Christians would apostatize, or at the very least become greatly discouraged. The question regarding why Peter writes this letter is one of utmost importance.

To refresh, Wendland observes the following problems present in the community: 1) physical and psychological pressure, 2) social ostracism and exclusion, 3) potential pull from their former way of life, 4) a surrounding, seductive non-Christian worldview, 5) tensions and inconsistent behavior among Christians, 6) doubt regarding the reliability of God's promises and the future, and 7) Satan's constant, deadly temptations and trials.[262] First Peter 5:12 says "Διὰ Σιλουανοῦ ὑμῖν τοῦ πιστοῦ ἀδελφοῦ, ὡς λογίζομαι, δι' ὀλίγων ἔγραψα παρακαλῶν καὶ ἐπιμαρτυρῶν ταύτην εἶναι ἀληθῆ χάριν τοῦ θεοῦ εἰς ἣν στῆτε," (By Silvanus, a faithful brother as I regard him, I have written briefly to you, exhorting and declaring that this is the true grace of God. Stand firm in it) which denotes the purpose of the letter as urging his readers to stand fast in the true grace of God.[263] Scholars propose a variety of solutions when probed by the question of the purpose of 1 Peter. Balch proposes that Peter is urging his readers to assimilate into society to avoid unnecessary suffering.[264] Lohse asserts that the author's aim is to strengthen and comfort the believers by providing them with an eschatological hope.[265] Horrell asserts that "The author's main concern was to instruct and

---

261. Le Roux, *Ethics in 1 Peter*, 55.
262. Ernst Wendland, "'Stand Fast!'" 66.
263. My paraphrase.
264. Balch, *Let Wives Be Submissive*, 81.
265. Lohse, "Parenesis and Kerygma in 1 Peter," 42.

encourage Christians who, because of their faith, were experiencing hostility, prosecution, and suffering."[266] Peter then uses Christ as the example he desires all his readers to emulate while they are enduring suffering.[267] Finally, Dryden proposes that the paraenesis of the letter is to encourage the moral development and character formation of the audience.[268] Thus, suffering is not an end in itself, nor is it merely to be endured. It is designed to facilitate character formation within the believers.

Balch, in his controversial monograph *Let Wives Be Submissive*, asserts that Peter is trying to instruct his readers to behave in a way that will reduce social tension that is resulting in their persecution.[269] The *Haustafel* (household code) is something Peter brought over from the Greco-Roman society.[270] The *Haustafel* then serves as a proper code of conduct for the believers, which helps the readers to conform to the social norms of the Greco-Roman world.[271] In so doing, they will curb their social distinctiveness and thus lessen their persecution.[272] The purpose then is to get the readers to assimilate the values of Greco-Roman society to the point that their persecution ceases.[273] Elliott and Achtemeier have convincingly refuted this thesis as running counter to the thrust of the letter.[274] Achtemeier exclaims, Iif one gains any impression from the whole of First Peter, it would have to be that the farthest thing from the author's mind is accommodation to Hellenistic culture; 4:1–4 ought to make that clear enough."[275] Elliott notes that the letter enjoins the readers to stop conforming to their former passions.[276] The readers should resist the devil and sever certain social ties, i.e., the imperial cult.[277] Elliott continues that "It was precisely a tempta-

266. Horrell, *Epworth Commentaries*, 11.
267. Richard, "Functional Christology in First Peter," 20.
268. Dryden, *Theology and Ethics in 1 Peter*, 40.
269. Balch, *Let Wives Be Submissive*, 81. See Achtemeier, "Newborn Babes and Living Stones," 219, and Elliott, *1 Peter*, 63–64 for a full treatment of the controversy of this book.
270. Balch, *Let Wives Be Submissive*, 65–81.
271. Balch, *Let Wives Be Submissive*, 65–81.
272. Balch, *Let Wives Be Submissive*, 65–81.
273. Balch, *Let Wives Be Submissive*, 65–81.
274. Elliott, *1 Peter*, 63–64; Elliott, "1 Peter," 61–78; Achtemeier, "Newborn Babes and Living Stones," 220–22.
275. Achtemeier, Achtemeier, "Newborn Babes and Living Stones," 219.
276. Elliott, "1 Peter," 66.
277. Elliott, "1 Peter," 66.

tion to assimilate so as to avoid further suffering that the letter intended to counteract."[278] Peter is seeking to provide a distinctive communal identity which promotes internal cohesion and a persuasive rationale for continued hope and endurance.[279] This study affirms that Peter was not enjoining his readers to assimilate but was encouraging them to remain steadfast in the midst of their suffering.

Donelson, Thuren, Hiebert, and others[280] assert that Peter seeks to encourage his audience to remain faithful to Christ in the midst of suffering. Further, there are two types of people in the audience.[281] There are those "tempted to lie low in order to avoid suffering, and to assimilate to the society."[282] Also, there are those who want to act as revolutionaries and fight back against those who oppress them.[283] Neither of these are in keeping with the example of Christ (2:21–24; 4:19). The audience should seek holiness and resist the temptation to return to their previous life.[284] Davids proposes that Peter exhorts his readers to this life of holiness by getting them to hold on to the "living hope."[285] The metanarrative of hope, inheritance, and future salvation frames the entire discourse.[286] Davids shows that the entire epistle has an apocalyptic focus, i.e., judgment is beginning (4:17), the end is at hand (4:7), the suffering they are experiencing is the messianic woes.[287] Therefore, this metanarrative is eschatological.[288] *Eschatology is the framework, and holiness is the goal*.[289] For Peter, then, keeping the end in mind is the key to endurance in suffering.

---

278. Elliott, "1 Peter," 72–73.

279. Elliott, "1 Peter," 72–73.

280. Donelson, *I & II Peter and Jude,* 19; Hiebert, *1 Peter,* 28; Thuren, *Argument and Theology in 1 Peter,* 20; Hall, "For to This You Have Been Called," 137.

281. Thuren, *Rhetorical Strategy,* 112.

282. Thuren, *Rhetorical Strategy,* 112. A view which, as noted above, Balch affirms as the goal of the letter. Balch rejects a conversionist approach to Christianity and asserts that they should adopt the surrounding cultures' values and actions in order to reduce their suffering. See Elliott, "1 Peter," 70.

283. Thuren, *Rhetorical Strategy,* 112.

284. Thuren, *Rhetorical Strategy,* 21.

285. Davids, *First Epistle of Peter,* 19; 1 Pet 1:3.

286. Donelson, *I & II Peter and Jude,* 22.

287. Davids, *First Epistle of Peter,* 15–16.

288. Davids, *First Epistle of Peter,* 17.

289. Davids, *First Epistle of Peter,* 17.

Peter follows a two-pronged approach in his paraenesis. Firstly, believers are enjoined to anticipate the return of Christ as "at hand."[290] There is an expectation that they will meet God in the judgment.[291] Michaels affirms that this expectation of the return of God in judgment serves as a motivation for good behavior.[292] Thus, because God is coming back to judge each one according to his works (1:17), good behavior or a right response towards suffering secures the believers in the saving narrative of Jesus.[293] If they suffer in a manner pleasing to God like Jesus their example did, then they too will receive glorification as Jesus did. However, if they do not, the God who is impartial (1:17) will judge them for it.

Secondly, the believers are given hope of an inheritance and future salvation (1:4, 9).[294] Best asserts that it is within this eschatological framework that believers are to interpret their suffering.[295] Their future glory will outweigh their present afflictions.[296] This hope of an inheritance again is connected to their conduct in the midst of trials. Davids pointedly says that a lack of holiness will incur the judgment of God and cause believers to forfeit their inheritance, i.e., future salvation.[297] Belief is just not enough; the believers' actions, i.e., response to suffering, is everything.[298] If the believers can look to the magnitude of the inheritance that they will receive and compare it to the "ὀλίγον . . . λυπηθέντας" (for a little while . . . grieved),[299] this will encourage them to endure.

Dryden asserts that Peter's paraenesis "is directed at reinforcing one's social and emotional commitments to the new path and disparaging one's emotional and social ties to the past . . . thus, it seeks to persuade the neophyte in diverse ways to confirm him in the course he has chosen."[300] Worldview, then, is of utmost importance. Indeed, paraenesis promotes virtue by

---

290. Davids, *First Epistle of Peter*, 19. Thuren, *Argument and Theology*, argues that this is a negative use of motivation, which highlights the fear of punishment.

291. Davids, *First Epistle of Peter*, 19.

292. Michaels, *1 Peter*, 404.

293. Donelson, *I & II Peter and Jude*, 22.

294. This is what Thuren, *Argument and Theology*, calls positive motivation. They are motivated to do good so that they can receive a reward.

295. Best, *1 Peter*, 14.

296. Achtemeier and Epp, *1 Peter*, 68–69.

297. Davids, *First Epistle of Peter*, 17–18.

298. Donelson, *I & II Peter and Jude*, 23.

299. 1 Pet 1:6.

300. Dryden, *Theology and Ethics in 1 Peter*, 24.

"picturing a world in which such conduct is only common sense."[301] This helps the reader not to view the moral instructions individually, but as part of a greater whole.[302] It gives the reader an interpretive framework about the nature of the world and how humans flourish within it.[303] It provides a context from which one can interpret life as a whole.[304] It places the reader within a linear narrative that in turn can help the reader to make sense of what is happening around them.[305] The "τέλος" (goal/completion) of this new world becomes the reference point for everything. Thus, for Peter the metanarrative that he is sketching for his readers will help them to make sense of their suffering and understand its purpose. This metanarrative is essential, because it provides the context for what people believe and how they act, thus being essential in character formation. Peter's paraenesis is designed to get his readers to view their suffering from the eschatological "τέλος" of the "new world" that they find themselves in.

Dryden, therefore, disagrees with Lohse[306] that the main point of the letter is to instill hope in the readers.[307] This is not to downplay the strong eschatological focus of the letter, but to show that eschatology does not work in this way.[308] Eschatological hope most often serves as a motivation for ethical action.[309] Indeed, the paraenesis of the letter is to encourage the moral development and character formation of the audience.[310] Peter is encouraging his readers to leave their gentile ways and to desire "spiritual milk" (2:1–2). The author does not merely want them to survive their suffering, but to embrace it so that it can facilitate growth towards maturity.[311] Indeed, the purpose of this letter is not only to help believers endure suffering, but to teach believers "how to suffer."[312] In Dryden's words "the author interprets the situation of suffering as a means of bringing about

301. Geertz, *Interpretation of Cultures*, 129.
302. Dryden, *Theology and Ethics in 1 Peter*, 31.
303. Dryden, *Theology and Ethics in 1 Peter*, 31.
304. Wilson, *Hope of Glory*, 100.
305. Dryden, *Theology and Ethics in 1 Peter*, 31.
306. Lohse, "Parenesis and Kerygma in 1 Peter," 42.
307. Dryden, *Theology and Ethics in 1 Peter*, 40.
308. Dryden, *Theology and Ethics in 1 Peter*, 41.
309. Piper, "Hope as the Motivation for Love," 212–31.
310. Dryden, *Theology and Ethics in 1 Peter*, 40.
311. Dryden, *Theology and Ethics in 1 Peter*, 45.
312. Le Roux, *Ethics in 1 Peter*, 64.

growth. Persecution is not something to be endured but an opportunity for growth."[313] There were people who would have been tempted to forge allegiances with Romans in powerful positions, or who would have sought to assimilate back into society.[314] However, in agreement with Dryden, Green concludes that suffering "offers not so much an invitation as an exercise in formation in the character and ways of God."[315] Dryden, however, interjects and notes that suffering does not produce growth or formation automatically.[316] In fact, suffering is a lot more likely to produce bitterness and selfishness than character formation.[317] It is only when the believer meets suffering with moral fortitude and a well-formed understanding of its purpose that it can produce character formation.[318] This study shows in the next chapter that Peter's goal is to get his readers to understand this very point.

The purpose of 1 Peter is to get the audience to emulate Christ in everything that they do. Peter asserts that Christ is the model, one who neither retaliates nor assimilates to escape suffering even though it is unjust, and who instead entrusted himself to a faithful Creator (2:21–24). The purpose of suffering, then, is to provide believers with the opportunity to act in a Christlike way even when they are being oppressed unjustly. This is the process of putting off the old way of life (1:14) and putting on the new ways of Christ (4:1). This is the essence of Christian formation.

Having portrayed an overview of the relevant literature, this study now turns to the text of 1 Peter in order to ascertain some insights as it pertains to the necessity, source, nature, and purpose of suffering.

---

313. Dryden, *Theology and Ethics in 1 Peter*, 45
314. Green, *1 Peter*, 3.
315. Green, *1 Peter*, 3.
316. Dryden, *Theology and Ethics in 1 Peter*, 45.
317. Dryden, *Theology and Ethics in 1 Peter*, 46.
318. Dryden, *Theology and Ethics in 1 Peter*, 46.

Chapter 3

Exegetical Analysis

IN THE PREVIOUS CHAPTER, this study has dealt with all the contextual issues that pertain to the four main questions that are being asked in this study: a) is suffering necessary?; b) what is the source of their suffering? [Here a sub-section is included regarding the different reasons for the Christians' suffering, i.e., suffering for doing good, doing evil, and suffering as God's judgment]; c) what is the nature of his audience's suffering?; and d) what is the purpose for suffering as a Christians? Furthermore, how should the Christian believer respond to suffering?

This chapter builds on that contextual knowledge and ventures into an exegetical analysis of 1 Peter. Using the four questions mentioned above this study looks at specific texts as they relate to these various questions in order to glean further insight from the text of 1 Peter itself.

THE NECESSITY OF SUFFERING

The primary verse in question is 1 Peter 1:6 "ἐν ᾧ ἀγαλλιᾶσθε, ὀλίγον ἄρτι, εἰ δέον ἐστίν, λυπηθέντας ἐν ποικίλοις πειρασμοῖς," (In this you rejoice, though now for a little while, if necessary, you have been grieved by various trials) specifically the phrase "εἰ δέον ἐστίν" (if/since it is necessary). Some translations render this phrase "you *may* have to"[1] or "*if* necessary."[2] Certain scholars agree with this rendering and translate this phrase as a

---

1. 1 Pet 1:6 RSV, emphasis mine.
2. 1 Pet 1:6 ESV, emphasis mine.

hypothetical conditional.³ Therefore, "εἰ" is translated as "if," thereby emphasizing the conditional and hypothetical nature of the audience's suffering.⁴ Senior, who acknowledges that suffering is necessary for Christian formation, proceeds to translate this phrase as a hypothetical conditional.⁵ Thus, suffering is not necessary, nor can anyone attribute its presence in the life of the believer to God.⁶ Suffering is merely an unfortunate reality that we live with this side of the eschaton.⁷ Elliott exclaims "suffering is *not a necessity*, as the qualifier 'if it must be' (*ei deon [estin]*) makes clear."⁸ However, this study proposes that this may not be an accurate representation of the meaning of "εἰ."

The Bauer, Danker, Arndt, and Gingrich dictionary defines "εἰ" as a "marker of a condition, existing in fact ... to express a condition thought of as real or to denote assumptions relating to what has already happened."⁹ Furthermore, Achtemeier, Dubis, Stibbs, Kelly, and others assert that when "εἰ" is used in the New Testament it usually points to a condition of fact.¹⁰ Hiebert continues that "εἰ" here is a "First class condition, assuming the reality of the condition ... The addition of ἐστί,¹¹ 'is,' in many manuscripts strengthens that reality."¹² Therefore, Johnstone translates "εἰ δέον ἐστίν" as "since it is necessary."¹³ Furthermore, "εἰ" "adds the note of inevitability

---

3. Marshall, *1 Peter*, 40; Witherington III, *Letters and Homilies*, 80–81; Beare, *First Epistle of Peter*, 86; Senior, *1 Peter*, 32.

4. Beare, *First Epistle of Peter*, 86; Witherington III, *Letters and Homilies*, 78.

5. Senior, *1 Peter*, 32.

6. Davids, *First Epistle of Peter*, 55–56.

7. Davids, *First Epistle of Peter*, 55–56.

8. Elliott, *1 Peter*, 339 (emphasis original).

9. Dinker, *Greek-English Lexicon*, s.v. "εἰ."

10. Achtemeier and Epp, *1 Peter*, 101; Dubis, "Messianic Woes in First Peter," 104; Best, *1 Peter*, 78; Stibbs, *First Epistle General of Peter*, 77; Kelly, *Epistles of Peter and Jude*, 54; Forbes, *Exegetical Guide*, 23–24.

11. As it pertains to the textual variants, Dubis is worth quoting at length: "ἐστίν is omitted by the first hand of ℵ, B and also by minuscules 1505, 2495, and Clement of Alexandria. ἐστίν is read by Π 72, a corrector of ℵ, C, P, Y, 048, as well as minuscules 33 and 1739 and the majority of the Byzantine manuscripts, and also Origen. The weight of the external evidence that favors reading ἐστίν as original. Due to the common ν ending on both ἐστίν and δέον, the ἐστίν may have suffered omission you to homoioteleuton. Hence, ἐστίν is accepted here as original" (Dubis, "Messianic Woes in First Peter," 104n13).

12. Hiebert, *1 Peter*, 82, emphasis original.

13. Johnstone, *First Epistle of Peter*, 63–66.

to such trials," according to Achtemeier.¹⁴ Thus, suffering is a reality and not only a possibility.¹⁵ This translation is strengthened even further by the aorist participle "λυπηθέντας" (be distressed/grieved), which points to the reality that the believers have already suffered and that it is not just a possibility.¹⁶ Furthermore, if Peter was trying to express a hypothetical conditional, he would have likely added another particle like "πως" (somehow/perhaps) to make that point clear.¹⁷ Finally, in 1 Peter 3:14, "ἀλλ' εἰ καὶ πάσχοιτε διὰ δικαιοσύνην, μακάριοι" (But even if you should suffer for righteousness' sake, you will be blessed), Peter does use "εἰ" to make a hypothetical conditional statement, but pairs it with "πάσχοιτε" (to suffer), which is in the optative tense. Wallace makes a strong case that the optative tense is used to express a *"mere possibility* that something will take place."¹⁸ Thus, it is clear that Peter has the linguistic tools to express a hypothetical conditional if he wants to, but precisely in the case of 1:6 chooses not to do so. The evidence for "since" as the correct translation proves overwhelming.

In the phrase "εἰ δέον ἐστίν" (since it is necessary), "δέον" (it is necessary), which is the participial form of "δεῖ," bears "the character of necessity or compulsion."¹⁹ Among the Hellenists, the term expressed logical and scientific necessities.²⁰ Grundmann asserts that it denoted "ethical or even religious obligations."²¹ However, it could also be used as an expression of the will of God.²² It functioned as an expression of natural law, denoting what naturally must take place.²³ Further, for the Hellenists, the authority behind "δεῖ" rested on their belief in fate.²⁴ Whatever had been divinely ordained fell under the umbrella of "δεῖ."²⁵ In the LXX, "δεῖ" maintains the

---

14. Achtemeier and Epp, *1 Peter*, 101. Achtemeier will continue that this denotes "an inevitability in this context most likely of divine origin." This is parsed out in the section on the origin of suffering.

15. Forbes, *Exegetical Guide*, 23–24.

16. Filson, "Partakers with Christ," 404; Michaels, *1 Peter*, 28.

17. Danker, *Greek-English Lexicon*, 278.

18. Wallace, *Greek Grammar*, 480–81, emphasis original.

19. Kittel et al., *Theological Dictionary of the New Testament*; Grundmann, "Δεῖ, Δέον Ἐστί," 2:21–24.

20. Grundmann, "Δεῖ, Δέον Ἐστί."

21. Grundmann, "Δεῖ, Δέον Ἐστί," 2:21.

22. Grundmann, "Δεῖ, Δέον Ἐστί."

23. Grundmann, "Δεῖ, Δέον Ἐστί."

24. Tiedke and Link, "Necessity," 2:281–82.

25. Tiedke and Link, "Necessity," 2:281–82; cf. Danker, *Greek-English Lexicon*, "Δεῖ";

Hellenistic sense of religious and ethical obligation as in the New Testament.[26] However, whereas among the Hellenists "δεῖ" was under the sway of a neutral fate, in the Old Testament and the Rabbis "δεῖ" falls squarely under the will of God.[27] Therefore, when Hellenistic Jews translated the Old Testament into Greek, they used the impersonal/neutral term "δεῖ" but subsumed it under the biblical view of God.[28] This is the view that we find in the New Testament. A brief presentation of "δεῖ" in the New Testament will shed some light on 1 Peter's use of the term.

The word "δεῖ" occurs 102 times in the New Testament.[29] Out of these 102 occurrences, twenty of them occur in direct relation to suffering (Matt 16:21; 24:6; 26:54; Mark 8:31; 13:7; 13:14; Luke 9:22; 13:33; 17:25; 21:9; 22:37; 24:7; 24:26; John 3:14; Acts 9:16; 14:22; 17:3; 23:11; Heb 9:26; 1 Pet 1:6). In the Gospels, Jesus' suffering is presented as "δεῖ." Luke in particular parses out the necessity of Jesus' suffering with over forty occurrences of "δεῖ" in his Gospel and subsequent work, Acts. In Luke 9:22, Jesus says the following:

> εἰπὼν ὅτι δεῖ τὸν υἱὸν τοῦ ἀνθρώπου πολλὰ παθεῖν καὶ ἀποδοκιμασθῆναι ἀπὸ τῶν πρεσβυτέρων καὶ ἀρχιερέων καὶ γραμματέων καὶ ἀποκτανθῆναι καὶ τῇ τρίτῃ ἡμέρᾳ ἐγερθῆναι.

> The Son of Man must suffer many things and be rejected by the elders and chief priests and scribes, and be killed, and on the third day be raised.

Similarly, in Luke 13:33:

> πλὴν δεῖ με σήμερον καὶ αὔριον καὶ τῇ ἐχομένῃ πορεύεσθαι, ὅτι οὐκ ἐνδέχεται προφήτην ἀπολέσθαι ἔξω Ἰερουσαλήμ.

> Nevertheless, I must go on my way today and tomorrow and the day following, for it cannot be that a prophet should perish away from Jerusalem.

In 17:25, Luke again emphasizes the necessity of Jesus' suffering:

> πρῶτον δὲ δεῖ αὐτὸν πολλὰ παθεῖν καὶ ἀποδοκιμασθῆναι ἀπὸ τῆς γενεᾶς ταύτης.

Grundmann, "Δεῖ, Δέον Ἐστί."

26. Grundmann, "Δεῖ, Δέον Ἐστί."

27. Tiedke and Link, "Necessity," 2:282.

28. Grundmann, "Δεῖ, Δέον Ἐστί."

29. Tiedke and Link, "Necessity," 2:282.

Exegetical Analysis

But first he must suffer many things and be rejected by this generation.

In Luke 24:7, the angel at the tomb tells Mary and the others with her:

> λέγων τὸν υἱὸν τοῦ ἀνθρώπου ὅτι δεῖ παραδοθῆναι εἰς χεῖρας ἀνθρώπων ἁμαρτωλῶν καὶ σταυρωθῆναι καὶ τῇ τρίτῃ ἡμέρᾳ ἀναστῆναι.

> Saying that the Son of Man must be delivered into the hands of sinful men and be crucified and on the third day rise.

Furthermore, Jesus, after the resurrection, rebukes the disciples on the road to Emmaus, saying:

> Καὶ αὐτὸς εἶπεν πρὸς αὐτούς· ὦ ἀνόητοι καὶ βραδεῖς τῇ καρδίᾳ τοῦ πιστεύειν ἐπὶ πᾶσιν οἷς ἐλάλησαν οἱ προφῆται· οὐχὶ ταῦτα ἔδει παθεῖν τὸν χριστὸν καὶ εἰσελθεῖν εἰς τὴν δόξαν αὐτοῦ;

> O foolish ones, and slow of heart to believe all that the prophets have spoken! Was it not necessary that the Christ should suffer these things and enter into his glory?

Finally, Paul also refers to Jesus' suffering as necessary in Acts 17:3:

> διανοίγων καὶ παρατιθέμενος ὅτι τὸν χριστὸν ἔδει παθεῖν καὶ ἀναστῆναι ἐκ νεκρῶν καὶ ὅτι οὗτός ἐστιν ὁ χριστὸς [ὁ] Ἰησοῦς ὃν ἐγὼ καταγγέλλω ὑμῖν.

> Explaining and proving that it was necessary for the Christ to suffer and to rise from the dead, and saying, this Jesus, whom I proclaim to you, is the Christ.

Clearly, then, both Jesus and the New Testament authors viewed Jesus' suffering as "δεῖ."

However, not all the occurrences of "δεῖ" in the New Testament refer to the suffering of Jesus. The following texts refer to the suffering of Christians. In the Synoptic Gospels, we find Jesus' eschatological discourses which speak of the tribulations which are to come before the end of the age (Mark 13; Matt 24; Luke 21). In Matthew 24, Jesus says that before the end there will be wars, earthquakes, famines, and persecution of believers.[30] In verse 6, Jesus says:

> "ὁρᾶτε μὴ θροεῖσθε· δεῖ γὰρ γενέσθαι, ἀλλ' οὔπω ἐστὶν τὸ τέλος

---

30. Matt 24:4–8. Interestingly, here Jesus predicts that this persecution entails believers being put to death.

And you will hear of wars and rumors of wars. See that you are not alarmed, for this must take place, but the end is not yet) "for it is necessary for this to take place.[31]

This refers to what scholars call the messianic woes.[32] Luke, in his parallel 21:9, says:

μὴ πτοηθῆτε· δεῖ γὰρ ταῦτα γενέσθαι πρῶτον, ἀλλ' οὐκ εὐθέως τὸ τέλος

And when you hear of wars and tumults, do not be terrified, for these things must first take place, but the end will not be at once.

Luke adds the word "πρῶτον" (first). This leads Dubis to conclude that it reveals a definite progression of events.[33] The messianic woes must be completed, and then the end will come.[34] To bolster this point, God, speaking to Ananias regarding Paul, says the following in Acts 9:16:

ἐγὼ γὰρ ὑποδείξω αὐτῷ ὅσα δεῖ αὐτὸν ὑπὲρ τοῦ ὀνόματός μου παθεῖν.

For I will show him how much he must suffer for the sake of my name.

Paul, then, after being rejected in Antioch (Acts 13:50), almost killed in Iconium (Acts 14:1–6) and stoned in Lystra (Acts 14:6–19), returns to these cities and says the following to the believers there Acts 14:22:

ἐπιστηρίζοντες τὰς ψυχὰς τῶν μαθητῶν, παρακαλοῦντες ἐμμένειν τῇ πίστει καὶ ὅτι διὰ πολλῶν θλίψεων δεῖ ἡμᾶς εἰσελθεῖν εἰς τὴν βασιλείαν τοῦ θεοῦ.

Strengthening the souls of the disciples, encouraging them to continue in the faith, and saying that through many tribulations we must enter the kingdom of God.

Dubis asserts that Paul's experience of suffering shapes his understanding that the suffering that the church is experiencing is necessary in

---

31. My translation.

32. Dubis, "Messianic Woes in First Peter." Dubis has written his whole dissertation on the presence of the messianic woes in First Peter.

33. Dubis, "Messianic Woes in First Peter," 102.

34. This point becomes important in the discussion on "ἐπιτελεῖσθαι" in 1 Peter 5:9. See below.

order for them to enter into the kingdom of God.[35, 36] This sets the stage for how Peter uses the term "δεῖ" in the phrase "εἰ δέον ἐστίν" in 1 Peter 1:6.

Suffering, then, for Peter's audience is a present reality and not only a possibility.[37] Davids, however, denies that suffering is necessary and is adamant about the fact that one cannot and should not attribute the presence of suffering in the life of the believer to God in any way.[38] Davids then prefers the translation of the RSV: "In this you rejoice, though now for a little while you *may* have to suffer various trials."[39] Against Davids, Achtemeier asserts that the presence of "δεῖ" "adds the note of inevitability to such trials."[40] Moreover, it is "an inevitability in this context most likely of divine origin."[41] Best affirms and notes regarding the RSV's translation "may conceals a word, which expresses the divine necessity of their trials."[42] Indeed, Johnstone and Marshall agree that trials come as they are deemed necessary by God.[43] This study concludes that the evidence against "εἰ" as a hypothetical conditional, and the mere possibility of suffering is insurmountable. This study, therefore, proposes that the correct translation of "εἰ δέον ἐστίν" is "since it is necessary."

This conclusion is further strengthened by the presence of "μὴ ξενίζεσθε" in 1 Peter 4:12:

Ἀγαπητοί, μὴ ξενίζεσθε τῇ ἐν ὑμῖν πυρώσει πρὸς πειρασμὸν ὑμῖν γινομένῃ ὡς ξένου ὑμῖν συμβαίνοντος.

---

35. Dubis, "Messianic Woes in First Peter," 103.

36. This coincidentally fits squarely within the thesis of this study. Suffering is necessary, because through it the believer's faith is purified and it is the means through which "κομιζόμενοι τὸ τέλος τῆς πίστεως ὑμῶν σωτηρίαν ψυχῶν," (1 Pet 1:9). Furthermore, Peter says that if the believers suffer with Christ, they will also share in his glory at the resurrection (1 Pet 4:13). This, in turn, implies that if the believers do not share in Christ's sufferings, they will not share in his glory. On this last point see Skaggs, *Pentecostal Commentary*, 19.

37. Forbes, *Exegetical Guide*, 23–34; Michaels, *1 Peter*, 28.

38. Davids, *First Epistle of Peter*, 55–56.

39. 1 Pet 1:6 RSV (emphasis added).

40. Achtemeier and Epp, *1 Peter*, 101.

41. Achtemeier and Epp, *1 Peter*, 101. For scholars who agree with this view, see Goppelt, *Commentary on 1 Peter*, 100; Best, *1 Peter*, 78; Kelly, *Epistles of Peter and Jude*, 54; De Villiers, "Joy in Suffering in 1 Peter," 73.

42. Best, *1 Peter*, 78.

43. Johnstone, *First Epistle of Peter*, 63–66; Marshall, *1 Peter*, 157–58.

> Beloved, do not be surprised at the fiery trial when it comes upon you to test you, as though something strange were happening to you.

The Liddell and Scott dictionary offers the following definition for "ξενίζεσθε" "*surpise, astonish by some strange sight . . . to be puzzled, unable to comprehend.*"[44] This word conveys a strong psychological reaction to the unexpected events.[45] Peter commands[46] his readers, "Do not be surprised"[47] at the "intense affliction and suffering that is coming upon them."[48] Dubis asks the question "On what grounds should believers not be surprised?"[49] This command makes it seem as if the believers should have been prepared for the suffering that they are now experiencing.[50] Indeed, Calvin asserts that Peter expected his readers through an extended meditation on the example of Christ to have been prepared to bear their own cross.[51] Jesus said as much in Mark 13:9–13:

> Βλέπετε δὲ ὑμεῖς ἑαυτούς· παραδώσουσιν ὑμᾶς εἰς συνέδρια καὶ εἰς συναγωγὰς δαρήσεσθε καὶ ἐπὶ ἡγεμόνων καὶ βασιλέων σταθήσεσθε ἕνεκεν ἐμοῦ εἰς μαρτύριον αὐτοῖς·. καὶ εἰς πάντα τὰ ἔθνη πρῶτον δεῖ κηρυχθῆναι τὸ εὐαγγέλιον. καὶ ὅταν ἄγωσιν ὑμᾶς παραδιδόντες, μὴ προμεριμνᾶτε τί λαλήσητε, ἀλλ' ὃ ἐὰν δοθῇ ὑμῖν ἐν ἐκείνῃ τῇ ὥρᾳ τοῦτο λαλεῖτε· οὐ γάρ ἐστε ὑμεῖς οἱ λαλοῦντες ἀλλὰ τὸ πνεῦμα τὸ ἅγιον. Καὶ παραδώσει ἀδελφὸς ἀδελφὸν εἰς θάνατον καὶ πατὴρ τέκνον, καὶ ἐπαναστήσονται τέκνα ἐπὶ γονεῖς καὶ θανατώσουσιν αὐτούς· καὶ ἔσεσθε μισούμενοι ὑπὸ πάντων διὰ τὸ ὄνομά μου. ὁ δὲ ὑπομείνας εἰς τέλος οὗτος σωθήσεται.

> But be on your guard. For they will deliver you over to councils, and you will be beaten in synagogues, and you will stand before governors and kings for my sake, to bear witness before them. And the gospel must first be proclaimed to all nations. And when

---

44. Liddell et al., *Greek-English Lexicon*, 1188 (emphasis original).

45. Danker, *Greek-English Lexicon*, s.v. "ξενίζω."

46. "μὴ ξενίζεσθε" is in the imperative mood, which according to Wallace is most commonly used for commands (Wallace, *Greek Grammar*, 485).

47. My translation.

48. My translation. The justification for this study's translation of "πυρώσει" as "Intense suffering and affliction" is given below under the heading "The Nature of the Believer's Suffering."

49. Dubis, "Messianic Woes in First Peter," 96.

50. Dubis, "Messianic Woes in First Peter," 96.

51. Calvin, *Commentaries on the Catholic Epistles*, 31.

they bring you to trial and deliver you over, do not be anxious beforehand what you are to say, but say whatever is given you in that hour, for it is not you who speak, but the Holy Spirit. And brother will deliver brother over to death, and the father his child, and children will rise against parents and have them put to death. And you will be hated by all for my name's sake. But the one who endures to the end will be saved.

Moreover, Best says that

> they ought to recollect that in the Old Testament members of the people of God suffered when they were faithful to God, that Jesus himself suffered (cf. 2:18–25), that Peter, Paul and many other leaders of the church had suffered, and that the Gospel tradition contained many predictions of that suffering that was to fall on Jesus' followers (e.g., Mt. 5:10–12; Mk 8:34; 13:9–13; Jn 15:18–20).[52]

Davids is worth quoting at length:

> Here the Christians are instructed not to think the same about their persecution by the pagan culture. Unlike the Jews who had for generations been a foreign and culturally distinct minority in the diaspora (and suffered as all such minority suffer) and since the persecution under Antiochus IV Epiphanes (cf. 1 and 2 Maccabees) had had a developed theology of suffering and martyrdom, these gentile converts had no experience of being a cultural minority. Before their conversion they were perfectly at home in their city. And instead of rebelling against God they accepted the gospel message. But now they were experiencing cultural isolation and personal hostility, not what they might have expected as the blessing of God. Well might they have wondered if something had not gone wrong. Thus our author reassures them: persecution is not something strange or foreign to their existence as Christians. What is happening is right in line with Christ's predictions (Matt 5:11–12; 10:34; Mark 13:9–13; John 15:18–20.[53]

Davids hits the nail on the head. Peter's purpose with this letter is to encourage his audience to stay the course even though they are experiencing suffering. Moreover, their suffering is not a sign of divine disfavor

---

52. Best, *1 Peter*, 162.

53. Davids, *First Epistle of Peter*, 164. It is interesting that Davids can reach this conclusion after denying the necessity of suffering in 1:6.

as the Greeks commonly believed.[54] It is clear enough when Peter tells his audience that:

> εἰ δέον ἐστίν . . . μὴ ξενίζεσθε τῇ ἐν ὑμῖν πυρώσει πρὸς πειρασμὸν ὑμῖν γινομένῃ ὡς ξένου ὑμῖν συμβαίνοντος
>
> Since it is necessary . . . Beloved, do not be surprised at the fiery trial when it comes upon you to test you, as though something strange were happening to you.

Peter is merely conveying to these believers what Jesus had conveyed to his disciples. The questions as to why the suffering is necessary and where it comes from are discussed in the following section.[55]

THE SOURCE OF CHRISTIAN SUFFERING

The conversation on Christian suffering has been overshadowed by discussions on theodicy, says Hall.[56] Although the question of how evil and a loving, all-powerful God coexist in this world is a worthy one, it seems to distract the exegete from the assertions of the text itself. Indeed, this question is one that is raised by the people reading the text and does not arise from the text. In fact, the text seems disinterested in answering it at all. Therefore, this study stays within the confines of the text and seeks to understand what Peter deemed to be the source of his audience's suffering. When Peter says in 1 Peter 4:19 "οἱ πάσχοντες κατὰ τὸ θέλημα τοῦ θεοῦ" (Therefore let those who suffer according to God's will), what does he intend to convey? Is Peter asking his readers to suffer in a manner that is according to the will of God, i.e., not returning curse for curse, but blessing etc.?[57] Conversely, is he asking his readers to understand that this suffering originated in God's will, and thus should be endured as obedience to him?[58]

---

54. See Greek perspectives on suffering in chapter 2.

55. Why suffering is necessary will be dealt with under the heading "The Purpose of Suffering" and where the suffering comes from will be discussed under the source of their suffering.

56. Hall, "Suffering as Formation," 69.

57. So, Achtemeier and Epp, *1 Peter*, 318–19; Skaggs, *Pentecostal Commentary*, 68; Davids, *First Epistle of Peter*, 173–74; Senior, *1 Peter*, 132–33.

58. So, Witherington III, *Letters and Homilies*, 217–18; Marshall, *1 Peter*, 157–58; Donelson, *I & II Peter and Jude*, 139–40; Kistemaker, *New Testament Commentary*, 182; Stibbs, *First Epistle General of Peter*, 164; Johnstone, *First Epistle of Peter*, 374–75; Hiebert, *1 Peter*, 294–95; Forbes, *Exegetical Guide*, 163; Best, *1 Peter*, 78.

Maybe it is a bit of both? This study parses out these two perspectives and then contrasts the various reasons for suffering in a subsection.

Some scholars propose that the phrase "οἱ πάσχοντες κατὰ τὸ θέλημα τοῦ θεοῦ" (Therefore let those who suffer according to God's will) refers to the way in which Christians suffer.[59] Senior notes that this phrase "refers to the unique character of Christians suffering."[60] It is not suffering that comes justly as punishment for something done wrong but suffering that comes because one is a Christian.[61] This suffering is "not haphazard but is in accord with God's will . . ."[62] However, Achtemeier says this

> is shown not so much because the divine will favors suffering as because such suffering will inevitably result from following God's ways rather than those of secular society . . . It also assures the Christians that such suffering is not due to human arbitrariness, or a sign that God has abandoned them; rather it is the result of activity pleasing to God, and so is in accord with the divine will.[63]

Green concurs that those suffering "κατὰ τὸ θέλημα τοῦ θεοῦ" (according to the will of God) are those who suffer for being Christians, and not for doing a crime.[64] There is an evident parallel between 4:19 and Jesus' "mode" of suffering in 2:21–24.[65] Like Jesus, the believer is not to retaliate or curse, but they are to bless and entrust themselves to God, like Jesus did. To reiterate Davids's sentiments, one is not to ascribe the presence of suffering in the life of the Christian to God in any way.[66] It is interesting that all of the scholars mentioned in this section will acknowledge that the believer's suffering falls under the sovereignty of God, meaning that their suffering is not a sign that God has abandoned them, nor a sign that they are merely at the mercy of their persecutors.[67] And yet these scholars remain adamant

59. Davids, *First Epistle of Peter*, 173–74; Senior, *1 Peter*, 132–33; Green, *1 Peter*, 151.
60. Senior, *1 Peter*, 133.
61. Senior, *1 Peter*, 133; McKnight, *1 Peter*, 75
62. Achtemeier and Epp, *1 Peter*, 318.
63. Achtemeier and Epp, *1 Peter*, 318.
64. Green, *1 Peter*, 151.
65. Green, *1 Peter*, 151; Witherington III, *Letters and Homilies*, 217–18.
66. Davids, *First Epistle of Peter*, 56.
67. This notion leaves one with an interesting conundrum. Whilst these scholars acknowledge God's sovereignty over evil and suffering they deny that God sends it. However, they will acknowledge that God uses this suffering for his glory and the good of those who serve him (i.e., Rom 8). This will lead some to say that God does not send the suffering, he merely allows it to happen. Although this solves the theodicy problem for

that the suffering does not "come from God" in any way. Therefore, for these scholars, to suffer "κατὰ τὸ θέλημα τοῦ θεοῦ" (according to the will of God) refers to the way in which the believer suffers.

Kistemaker, Forbes, Best, Hiebert, and others agree that to suffer "κατὰ τὸ θέλημα τοῦ θεοῦ" is to do so in the manner that God wants his people to suffer, that is as a Christian and not an evildoer.[68] Witherington III and Jobes furthermore agree with Green that there is a clear allusion to Jesus' suffering in 2:21–24,[69] thus emphasizing the mode in which Jesus suffered and calling on them to emulate that mode of suffering.[70] Indeed, Schreiner notes, "Those who suffer according to God's will are those who share in Christ's sufferings (v. 12), who are insulted in Christ's name (v. 14), and who suffer as Christians rather than for doing something evil (vv. 15–16)."[71] However, Schreiner continues that "The reference to God's will here as in 3:17 indicates that all suffering passes through his hands (cf. 3:17), that nothing strikes a believer apart from God's loving and sovereign control. When suffering strikes, believers should 'commit themselves to their faithful Creator.'"[72] Peter seeks to assure his readers that their suffering is in accord with the divine will for their lives.[73] Therefore, they should

---

these scholars and popular pastors like Joel Osteen (*Next Level Thinking*) and Carl Lentz (*Own The Moment*), it really does not hang together logically. If God is all-powerful and really does not want evil or persecution to come into believers' lives, then why does he not just stop it? To say that God is not responsible for the evils that befall us makes even less sense. If a person sees another person with a gun walking into a store to shoot someone and that person has all the tools he needs to stop this person, but does nothing, is this person not responsible for what happened? This person did not make the man go in and shoot someone, but given the opportunity and the means to stop the man this person chose not to. That sounds even worse than committing it, because now this person is not only responsible for allowing it, they seem indifferent to the lives and actions of the people around them. Is that the God of the New Testament? A God who is so indifferent to what happens to his people that he just allows suffering to happen, because that's just the way this sinful world is? There must be a better way and Peter shows us that way.

68. Kistemaker, *New Testament Commentary*, 182; Marshall, *1 Peter*, 157–58; Donelson, *I & II Peter and Jude*, 139–40; Stibbs, *First Epistle General of Peter*, 164; Johnstone, *First Epistle of Peter*, 374–75; Hiebert, *1 Peter*, 294–95; Forbes, *Exegetical Guide*, 163; Best, *1 Peter*, 78; Jobes, *1 Peter*, 295; Witherington III, *Letters and Homilies*, 217–18; Dubis, "Messianic Woes in First Peter," 176–77.

69. Witherington III, *Letters and Homilies*, 217–18; Jobes, *1 Peter*, 295.

70. Witherington III, *Letters and Homilies*, 217–18; Jobes, *1 Peter*, 295.

71. Schreiner, *1, 2 Peter, Jude*, 229.

72. Schreiner, *1, 2 Peter, Jude*, 229.

73. Hiebert, *1 Peter*, 294.

not "be discouraged or grow faint and weary in their Christian course."[74] Forbes asserts emphatically that it is unnecessary here to choose between one of these options, because they are both present in the text.[75] However, this study finds Green, Senior, Davids, and others' assertion that the "οἱ πάσχοντες κατὰ τὸ θέλημα τοῦ θεοῦ" (Therefore let those who suffer according to God's will) refers to the way in which Christians suffer to be quite problematic,[76] primarily because they affirm that the way in which believers suffer is in God's will, but the suffering itself is not. As noted above, there is an explicit link between this phrase and Jesus' suffering in 2:21–24.[77] Therefore, it seems to this study that these scholars are implying that the way in which Jesus suffered, i.e., not reviling, or cursing, but entrusting himself to God, fell within God's will, but his actual suffering did not fall within God's will. This runs contrary to Jesus' own understanding of his suffering as "δεῖ" and the subsequent evidence provided in the section above. Furthermore, the only way in which we can truly "follow in Christ's footsteps" is if our suffering and his suffering are similar, i.e., deemed necessary by God and in accordance with his will. Best continues that "it is in God's hands and not man's whether they take place or not, just as it was in God's hands that the Messiah had to suffer."[78] Likewise, God is the one who sends suffering into the lives of believers.[79] To conclude, Schreiner says "Christ modeled what Peter enjoined, for when he was suffering, he entrusted himself to God."[80] Thus, Jesus, while suffering "κατὰ τὸ θέλημα τοῦ θεοῦ," not only suffered in the way in which God wanted him to suffer by entrusting himself to a faithful Creator, but could entrust himself to God because he knew that it was God who was sending this suffering on his path. Jesus' prayer in Gethsemane says it so clearly:

> λέγων· πάτερ, εἰ βούλει παρένεγκε τοῦτο τὸ ποτήριον ἀπ' ἐμοῦ· πλὴν μὴ τὸ θέλημά μου ἀλλὰ τὸ σὸν γινέσθω.

---

74. Lillie, *Lectures*, 298.

75. Forbes, *Exegetical Guide*, 163.

76. Skaggs, *Pentecostal Commentary*, 68; Davids, *First Epistle of Peter*, 173–74; Senior, *1 Peter*, 132–33; Green, *1 Peter*, 151.

77. Green, *1 Peter*, 151.

78. Best, *1 Peter*, 78.

79. The reasons are explored in the subsection "Reasons for Suffering."

80. Schreiner, *1, 2 Peter, Jude*, 229.

saying, "Father, if you are willing, remove this cup from me. Nevertheless, not my will, but yours, be done."[81]

Clearly, the suffering itself is according to God's will. Therefore, because suffering is "κατὰ τὸ θέλημα τοῦ θεοῦ" (according to the will of God), believers can take solace that they are not at the mercy of some random, impersonal, and evil force like the "δεῖ" of the Hellenists, but they are under the care of a God who for their holistic formation sends suffering so that they might be pure and undefiled before him. Here it is fitting to include an excursus on the various reasons for the audience's suffering.

Reasons for Suffering

As mentioned in chapter 2,[82] the previous section, and what is seemingly clear throughout 1 Peter, believers suffer for mainly two reasons. Firstly, they suffer as Christians because of their good behavior (2:19; 3:14–17; 4:16, 19), which is commendable before God (2:20).[83] Secondly, there are those among them that suffer for doing evil (2:20; 4:15), which in turn is not commendable before God and the punishment they receive is deserved.[84] However, there is also a third reason for the believers' suffering; it is the start of God's judgment. First Peter 4:17 reads:

> ὅτι ὁ καιρὸς τοῦ ἄρξασθαι τὸ κρίμα ἀπὸ τοῦ οἴκου τοῦ θεοῦ· εἰ δὲ πρῶτον ἀφ' ἡμῶν, τί τὸ τέλος τῶν ἀπειθούντων τῷ τοῦ θεοῦ εὐαγγελίῳ.
>
> For it is time for judgment to begin at the household of God; and if it begins with us, what will be the outcome for those who do not obey the gospel of God?

On this front, there is agreement among scholars that this judgment refers to the suffering that believers are experiencing.[85] However, there is

---

81. Luke 22:42.

82. See Table 1.

83. Suffering for good behavior is gracious in God's sight (2:19); suffering for righteousness is blessed (3:14–16); better to suffer for doing good than evil (3:17); if you suffer as a Christian, glorify God (4:16); suffering according to God's will (4:19).

84. Suffering for evil behavior is just desserts and has no value (2:20); do not suffer as an evildoer or murderer for this is just desserts and has no value (4:15)

85. Achtemeier and Epp, *1 Peter*, 315–16; Beare, *First Epistle of Peter*, 194; Elliott, *1 Peter*, 775, 797–98; Goppelt, *Commentary on 1 Peter*, 311; Schutter, *Hermeneutic and*

disagreement as to how one is to interpret this judgment. First, however, this study turns to the issue of which Old Testament texts lie behind Peter's expression of judgment, beginning with the house of God.

Johnson proposes that there are two texts that inform Peter's imagery in 1 Peter 4:17. Firstly, Zechariah 13:9 (LXX), which reads:

> καὶ διάξω τὸ τρίτον διὰ πυρὸς καὶ πυρώσω αὐτούς, ὡς πυροῦται τὸ ἀργύριον, καὶ δοκιμῶ αὐτούς, ὡς δοκιμάζεται τὸ χρυσίον, αὐτὸς ἐπικαλέσεται τὸ ὄνομά μου, κἀγὼ ἐπακούσομαι αὐτῷ καὶ ἐρῶ Λαός μου οὗτός ἐστιν, καὶ αὐτὸς ἐρεῖ Κύριος ὁ θεός μου.

> And I will carry over the third part through fire, and I will make them red-hot like silver tried by fire, and I will test them like gold that has been tested. He will call on my name, and I will hear him, and I will say, 'This is my people,' and he will say, 'The Lord is my God.'

Secondly, Malachi 3:1–3 (LXX), which reads:

> ἰδοὺ ἐγὼ ἐξαποστέλλω τὸν ἄγγελόν μου, καὶ ἐπιβλέψεται ὁδὸν πρὸ προσώπου μου, καὶ ἐξαίφνης ἥξει εἰς τὸν ναὸν ἑαυτοῦ κύριος, ὃν ὑμεῖς ζητεῖτε, καὶ ὁ ἄγγελος τῆς διαθήκης, ὃν ὑμεῖς θέλετε, ἰδοὺ ἔρχεται, λέγει κύριος παντοκράτωρ. καὶ τίς ὑπομενεῖ ἡμέραν εἰσόδου αὐτοῦ; ἢ τίς ὑποστήσεται ἐν τῇ ὀπτασίᾳ αὐτοῦ; διότι αὐτὸς εἰσπορεύεται ὡς πῦρ χωνευτηρίου καὶ ὡς πόα πλυνόντων. καὶ καθιεῖται χωνεύων καὶ καθαρίζων ὡς τὸ ἀργύριον καὶ ὡς τὸ χρυσίον, καὶ καθαρίσει τοὺς υἱοὺς Λευι καὶ χεεῖ αὐτοὺς ὡς τὸ χρυσίον καὶ ὡς τὸ ἀργύριον, καὶ ἔσονται τῷ κυρίῳ προσάγοντες θυσίαν ἐν δικαιοσύνῃ.

> "Behold, I send my messenger, and he will observe the way before my face. And immediately, the Lord, whom you seek, will come

---

Composition, 155; Best, *1 Peter*, 162–65; Jobes, *1 Peter*, 290–92; Green, *1 Peter*, 153–54; Dubis, "Messianic Woes in First Peter," 142–45; Donelson, *I & II Peter and Jude*, 138–39; Kelly, *Epistles of Peter and Jude*, 193; Davids, *First Epistle of Peter*, 171–72; Senior, *1 Peter*, 131–32; Witherington III, *Letters and Homilies*, 216–17; Skaggs, *Pentecostal Commentary*, 66–68; Scott, "'Sufferings of Christ,'" 234–40; James Moffatt, *General Epistles*, 101; Selwyn, *First Epistle of St. Peter*, 128; Sander, "ΠΥΡΩΣΙΣ and the First Epistle of Peter 4:12," 50; Leaney, *Letters of Peter and Jude*, 64; Watson, "Implications of Christology," 198–99; Hillyer, "First Peter and the Feast of Tabernacles," 39–70; Borchert, "Conduct of Christians," 451–62; De Villiers, "Joy in Suffering in 1 Peter," 64–86, esp. 81; Webb, "Apocalyptic Perspective of First Peter," 266–67; Michaels, *1 Peter*, 260–61, 270; Martin, *Metaphor and Composition in 1 Peter*, 240–45; Miller, *On This Rock*, 145–47; Parker, "Eschatology of 1 Peter," 27–32, esp. 28–31; Krodel, "1 Peter," 42–83; Porter, "Tribulation, Messianic Woes," 1179–83.

into his own temple. And the messenger of the covenant, whom you desire, behold, he comes," says the Lord Almighty. "But who will endure the day of his entrance, or who will stand in his appearance? Because he enters as a fire of a furnace and as a kind of cleansing. He will sit, smeltering and cleansing, as if it were silver and as if it were gold; and he will purify the children of Levi and pour them out just like gold and like silver, and they will become those who bring to the Lord a sacrifice in righteousness."

Both assert that God is coming as a refiner's fire.[86] These two passages, according to Johnson, "provide the pattern for the escalation of eschatological judgment as it moves out from the house of God to those outside the covenant."[87] Schutter,[88] however, argues that the text behind 1 Peter 4:17 is Ezekiel 9:5–6 (LXX) which reads:

καὶ τούτοις εἶπεν ἀκούοντός μου Πορεύεσθε ὀπίσω αὐτοῦ εἰς τὴν πόλιν καὶ κόπτετε καὶ μὴ φείδεσθε τοῖς ὀφθαλμοῖς ὑμῶν καὶ μὴ ἐλεήσητε, πρεσβύτερον καὶ νεανίσκον καὶ παρθένον καὶ νήπια καὶ γυναῖκας ἀποκτείνατε εἰς ἐξάλειψιν, ἐπὶ δὲ πάντας, ἐφ' οὓς ἐστιν τὸ σημεῖον, μὴ ἐγγίσητε, καὶ ἀπὸ τῶν ἁγίων μου ἄρξασθε. καὶ ἤρξαντο ἀπὸ τῶν ἀνδρῶν τῶν πρεσβυτέρων, οἳ ἦσαν ἔσω ἐν τῷ οἴκῳ.

And he said to these people, with me listening, "Go after him into the city and slaughter, and have no pity in your eyes, and show no mercy. Kill utterly elder and youth and virgin and infant and woman. But you shall not approach any upon whom is the sign. Begin at my holy *places*." And they began with the old men who were inside in the house.

The lexical affinity of Ezekiel 9:5–6 with the prepositional phrase "κρίμα ἀπὸ τοῦ οἴκου τοῦ θεοῦ" (judgement from the house of God) in 1 Peter 4:17 makes it the obvious option.[89] Finally, though, against Schutter and Johnson, Jobes argues convincingly that neither of these texts stand behind Peter's assertions.[90] Whenever Peter has used passages from the Old Testament elsewhere, i.e., Psalm 33 (LXX) in 3:10–12, and Isaiah 53 in

86. Johnson, "Fire in God's House," 285–94.
87. Johnson, "Fire in God's House," 285–94.
88. Schutter, *Hermeneutic and Composition* 276–84.
89. Schutter, *Hermeneutic and Composition*. It is interesting that Schutter does not include the presence of the imperative "ἄρξασθε" as a lexical correlation as well.
90. Jobes, *1 Peter*, 292; Witherington III, *Letters and Homilies*, 217n506; Green, *1 Peter*, 153–55.

2:19–24, he preserves the original context.⁹¹ However, none of the contexts of the passages in Zechariah, Malachi, or Ezekiel fit Peter's use of judgment.⁹² These texts pronounce God's judgment on Israel for violating the covenant, i.e., sinning.⁹³ Jobes exclaims:

> Peter here is saying exactly the opposite. Peter's readers are suffering because they are living for Christ and not because God has abandoned them as in (Ezek. 9) or is punishing their sins as in (Jer. 25) . . . Moreover, the lack of precise lexical correspondence to any one of these passages suggests that Peter is not referring to any of them but is drawing on a familiar tradition in Judaism to make a somewhat different point for his Christian readers. That is, the suffering that Peter's readers are experiencing is an integral part of God's eschatological judgment, which all human beings must face . . .⁹⁴

Davids concurs with Jobes that this theme of purifying judgment beginning with God's house was especially developed in the intertestamental period.⁹⁵ Second Baruch states "Therefore, he did not spare his own son's first . . . Therefore they were once punished that they might be forgiven."⁹⁶ Also, the Testament of Benjamin:

> καὶ κρινεῖ κύριος ἐν πρώτοις τὸν Ἰσραὴλ περὶ τῆς εἰς αὐτὸν ἀδικίας, ὅτι παραγενάμενον θεὸν ἐν σαρκὶ ἐλευθερωτὴν οὐκ ἐπίστευσαν.⁹⁷

> For the Lord first judges Israel for the wrong she has committed and then he shall do the same for all the nations.⁹⁸

The early church then picks up on this already-developed theology in Judaism and interprets their own persecution and suffering through that lens.⁹⁹ This, then, is what scholars call the "messianic woes."¹⁰⁰ The

---

91. Jobes, *1 Peter*, 292.
92. Jobes, *1 Peter*, 292.
93. Jobes, *1 Peter*, 292.
94. Jobes, *1 Peter*, 292.
95. Davids, *First Epistle of Peter*, 171. Also, known as the Second Temple period
96. Charles, "2 Baruch," 13:9–10. This section in 2 Baruch is only available in Syriac, therefore this study relies on a translation.
97. Jonge, *Testament of the Twelve Patriarchs*, 177.
98. Platt, "Testament of Benjamin 10:8–9," in *Forgotten Books of Eden*.
99. Davids, *First Epistle of Peter*, 171.
100. Lillie, *Lectures*, 298.

messianic woes refer to a period of intense suffering and chaos that are expected to accompany the end of the age, usually brought to a close by the return of the Messiah.[101] However, the aforementioned disagreement arises as to whether the suffering in 1 Peter 4:17 refer to the messianic woes or not. Furthermore, if one interprets this reference as the messianic woes, there are still two further interpretive possibilities. Should the woes be read as a harbinger to the end, or as part of the final judgment?

Dubis argues that one is able to read every verse in 1 Peter 4:12–19 within the framework of the messianic woes.[102] Pobee, Dubis, Russell, and others present the following points as they pertain to the trials and tribulations of the woes: 1) they are temporally close to the return of the Messiah; 2) they are characterized by apostasy, famines, wars, and strife within families; 3) there is an escalation of immorality; 4) the righteous are persecuted; 5) there is an eschatological sifting, i.e., a separation of the righteous from the unrighteous; 6) it highlights the sovereignty of God over all suffering locating it within his will; and 7) it urges the people affected to trust in God and his providential care for them.[103] Daniel 12:1 (LXX) expands this thought pretty dramatically:

> καὶ κατὰ τὴν ὥραν ἐκείνην παρελεύσεται Μιχαηλ ὁ ἄγγελος ὁ μέγας ὁ ἑστηκὼς ἐπὶ τοὺς υἱοὺς τοῦ λαοῦ σου, ἐκείνη ἡ ἡμέρα θλίψεως, οἵα οὐκ ἐγενήθη ἀφ' οὗ ἐγενήθησαν ἕως τῆς ἡμέρας ἐκείνης, καὶ ἐν ἐκείνῃ τῇ ἡμέρᾳ ὑψωθήσεται πᾶς ὁ λαός, ὃς ἂν εὑρεθῇ ἐγγεγραμμένος ἐν τῷ βιβλίῳ.

> And toward that country, Michael, the great messenger who stands over the sons of your people, will go by. That will be a day of affliction, of a kind that never was from when there were nations until that day. And in that day all the people, whoever may be found inscribed in the book, will be lifted up.

Green asserts:

> It was easy for early Christians to mold it in light of their claim, first, about the suffering and death of Christ are integral to the cosmic battle preceding the End, by which the age of Salvation was given birth, and, second, that the suffering and martyrdom of

---

101. Allison, *End of the Ages Has Come*, 5. Lillie, *Lectures*, 298.

102. Dubis, "Messianic Woes in First Peter," 117–278.

103. Russell, *Method and Message*, 263–84; Pobee, *Persecution and Martyrdom*; Dubis, "Messianic Woes in First Peter"; Green, *1 Peter*, 154.

Christ's followers participate in these "birth pangs." Clearly, this is a perspective that Peter shares.[104]

Furthermore, these "woes" are seen as a participation in the sufferings of Christ.[105] There is a strong case, then, for the suffering in 1 Peter as the start of the messianic woes. The only person to deny the presence of the messianic woes in 1 Peter outright is Klausli.[106] Klausli proposes that the suffering that the believers are experiencing has nothing to do with the messianic woes, and the suffering is instead to be read as God's judgment on believers who are continuing in the life of sin.[107] This study however, finds Klausli's conclusions to be erroneous.[108] Peter, throughout the letter, calls on his audience to not suffer as an evildoer, but as a Christian, or one who does good. In fact, Peter exclaims in 2:20:

ποῖον γὰρ κλέος, εἰ ἁμαρτάνοντες καὶ κολαφιζόμενοι ὑπομενεῖτε; ἀλλ' εἰ ἀγαθοποιοῦντες καὶ πάσχοντες ὑπομενεῖτε, τοῦτο χάρις παρὰ θεῷ.

For what credit is it if, when you sin and are beaten for it, you endure? But if when you do good and suffer for it you endure, this is a gracious thing in the sight of God.

Furthermore, to those who suffer as evildoers he says that it is their just desserts. Even more alarmingly, Peter says that it is of no value to you if you suffer for doing evil. Therefore, this study sides with the majority of scholars who propose that the suffering in 1 Peter is coming on undeserving Christians[109] and are the necessary prelude to the final judgment.

Wand asserts that the presence of the definite article "τὸ κρίμα" (the judgment) paired with the allusions to "prophetic tradition of fiery

---

104. Green, *1 Peter*, 154.

105. Leaney, *Letters of Peter and Jude*, 64. More is said on this in the fourth section of this chapter under the heading "The Purpose of Suffering."

106. Klausli, "Question of the Messianic Woes in 1 Peter," 240–45.

107. Klausli, "Question of the Messianic Woes in 1 Peter," 240–45.

108. This, however, does not mean that suffering cannot function as punishment for sin within God's house. In fact, this study does think that it does but to make that the only purpose of the suffering is not correct.

109. Even further off the mark than Klausli is Lenski, who proposes that the judgment spoken of in 4:17 has nothing to do with the church at all. Neither does it fall on sinning believers in the church. This judgment is to fall on the enemies of the church. It should be evident to the reader by this point that this is not in keeping with the message of 1 Peter at all. (see Lenski, *Interpretation of the Epistles*, 214–15).

eschatological judgment" affirm the fact that the judgment in question is God's judgment.[110] Miller, however, contends that the judgment is not the final judgment.[111] For Miller, this judgment refers to God's judgment meted out in history.[112] However, Miller is the only scholar who makes such a claim and the evidence against this claim proves overwhelming. Against Miller, "ὁ καιρὸς" (the time), when found elsewhere in the New Testament, points to God's final judgment at the end of the age.[113] In 1 Peter 1:11, the prophets inquire when the "καιρὸς" would arrive. The term "καιρὸς" occurs twice elsewhere in 1 Peter, and both instances are eschatological.[114] Thus, this interpretation of "καιρὸς" suits the overall eschatological context of the passage and the letter.[115] As Senior notes, the nearness of the final day and impending judgment are recurring themes throughout the letter.[116] This leads Achtemeier, Beare, Schutter, Goppelt, and others to propose that suffering represents the beginning of God's final judgment.[117] However, one must not mistake this "final judgment" to be somewhere in the future.[118] The presence of the aorist infinitive "ἄρξασθαι" (to begin) points to the fact that this judgment has already begun.[119] This, coupled with "ὁ καιρὸς," according to Jobes, "suggests that 'now,' at the time Peter writes, is the appointed time for God's judgment to begin."[120] The judgment believers are experiencing IS not "so much a harbinger or proleptic participation as it is

---

110. Wand, "Lessons of First Peter," 387–99; Jobes, *1 Peter*, 292; Davids, *First Epistle of Peter*, 171.

111. Miller, *On This Rock*, 321–22. To quote: "The judgment here mentioned is hardly the 'last judgment.'"

112. Miller, *On This Rock*, 321–22.

113. Skaggs, *Pentecostal Commentary*, 66–68; Jobes, *1 Peter*, 292.

114. Dubis, "Messianic Woes in First Peter," 218.

115. Senior, *1 Peter*, 131–32; Dubis, "Messianic Woes in First Peter," 216.

116. Senior, *1 Peter*, 131–32.

117. Achtemeier and Epp, *1 Peter*, 315–16; Beare, *First Epistle of Peter*, 194; Goppelt, *Commentary on 1 Peter*, 311; Schutter, *Hermeneutic and Composition*, 155; Donelson, *I & II Peter and Jude*, 138–39; Dubis, "Messianic Woes in First Peter," 215–16; Kelly, *Epistles of Peter and Jude*, 193.

118. Moffatt, *General Epistles*, 159–60. Moffatt seems divided on the issue "[First Peter] views the sufferings of Christians as the prelude to the final judgment, or rather as the initial scene in the last act of judgment, and trying (the apocalyptic thought of Mark xiii.20) because they involve the possibility of failing under the severe test."

119. Achtemeier and Epp, *1 Peter*, 315.

120. Jobes, *1 Peter*, 292; Webb, "Apocalyptic Perspective of First Peter," 115–16.

EXEGETICAL ANALYSIS

part of it, indeed the beginning of it."[121] The final judgment has broken into the present.[122] This connection of the judgment with the final judgment is further strengthened by the fact that the judgment falls on the unbelievers, which certainly refers to the final judgment. Therefore, even though God's house is being judged now, unbelievers will be judged as well.[123] The judgment has already started with the house of God.[124] Borchert and others emphasize that this judgment, as noted above, is not judgment as punishment, as it is in the Old Testament, but is to be understood as judgment for purification.[125] Indeed, God is beginning the process of judging humanity, i.e., separating the goats from the sheep, and this judgment starts inside his house.[126] To conclude, Beare's imagery is especially vivid: it is "the first act in the great drama of the Last Judgment."[127] This section concludes, then, that to suffer "κατὰ τὸ θέλημα τοῦ θεοῦ" (according to the will of God) is to suffer in the way God wants us to and to suffer what God wants us to suffer. Suffering can be for doing good or, conversely, for doing evil. However, Peter's main point is that this suffering "κατὰ τὸ θέλημα τοῦ θεοῦ" is God's final judgment that has already begun. Its purpose is to purify the house

---

121. Achtemeier and Epp, *1 Peter*, 315–16. Cf. Watson, "Implications of Christology," 198; Donelson, *I & II Peter and Jude*, 138; Kelly, *Epistles of Peter and Jude*, 193. Even though scholars like Jobes, *1 Peter*, 293 contend that the Woes will increase in severity as the second coming approaches. This does not assert that only those sufferings close to Jesus' coming qualify as the messianic woes.

122. Skaggs, *Pentecostal Commentary*, 66–68. Therefore, Jobes, *1 Peter*, 293 makes a compelling case that even though the believers are suffering the messianic woes this does in no way have to point to the fact that the appearance of the Messiah is near, as has been proposed historically.

123. Here the question arises as to whether the judgment that is to fall on unbelievers is also already breaking into this age. Texts like Romans 1:24–30 seem to indicate there is a handing over of unbelievers and sinners to their sinful desires, which is almost like God judging them by giving them what they desire even though it will ultimately kill them.

124. Selwyn, *First Epistle of St. Peter*, 299–300.

125. Borchert, "Conduct of Christians," 454; Witherington III, *Letters and Homilies*, 216–17; Hiebert, *1 Peter*, 291–92; Davids, *First Epistle of Peter*, 171–72; Jobes, *1 Peter*, 293. For some reason, Goppelt, *Commentary on 1 Peter*, 311–12 distinguishes between the messianic woes and the purifying judgment of God and says that this judgment is not the messianic woes. However, as Davids, *First Epistle of Peter*, 171 notes, "given the association of suffering with discipline in the church (Heb. 12:7–11), it is probably incorrect to separate the 'messianic woes' concept from the purification concept."

126. Jobes, *1 Peter*, 293.

127. Beare, *First Epistle of Peter*, 194. Similar metaphors can be found in Selwyn, *First Epistle of St. Peter*, 300; Moffatt, *General Epistles*, 160; Goppelt, *Commentary on 1 Peter*, 330.

of God so that if they suffer with Christ, they may also be raised with him. The penultimate section of this chapter turns to the nature of the suffering experienced by the audience by 1 Peter.

THE PURPOSE OF SUFFERING

In chapter 2, this study provided ample contextual evidence that the suffering experienced by the readers of 1 Peter was not merely verbal abuse and social ostracism as proposed by many scholars. Furthermore, this study shows that suffering comes from God because he deems it necessary. In this section, this study builds on that contextual evidence and seeks to explicate why Peter asserts that suffering is "εἰ δέον ἐστίν." What is the purpose of this suffering? Consequently, this process provides further exegetical evidence as to the nature of the suffering of Peter's readers. This study acknowledges that "καταλαλοῦσιν" (speak against/slander),[128] "λοιδορούμενος" (revile),[129] "ἀντελοιδόρει" (revile),[130] "ἐπηρεάζοντες" (threaten/abuse),[131] and "ὀνειδίζεσθε" (insult/reproach/mock)[132] all point to the reality of verbal abuse and social ostracism.[133] However, words like "πειρασμοῖς" (trials),[134] "δοκίμιον" (to test),[135] "δοκιμαζομένου" (testing),[136] "πυρὸς" (fiery trial/fierce affliction),[137] "πυρώσει" (fiery trial/fierce afflication),[138] and "πάσχων" (suffering)[139] point to something more than verbal abuse. Furthermore, this study ventures into the question of how believers are to respond to this suffering that they are experiencing and what effect their response has on the outcome of that suffering. This section proceeds by utilizing a verse-by-verse exegesis of the relevant passages in 1 Peter that expound on suffering, its nature, purpose, and desired response.

128. 1 Pet 2:12.
129. 1 Pet 2:23.
130. 1 Pet 2:23.
131. 1 Pet 3:16.
132. 1 Pet 4:14
133. See chapter 2 under the heading "The Nature of the Suffering in First Peter."
134. 1 Pet 1:6.
135. 1 Pet 1:7.
136. 1 Pet 1:7.
137. 1 Pet 1:7.
138. 1 Pet 4:12.
139. 1 Pet 2:19.

Exegetical Analysis

First Peter 1:6–9

The passage reads:

> ἐν ᾧ ἀγαλλιᾶσθε, ὀλίγον ἄρτι, εἰ δέον ἐστίν, λυπηθέντας ἐν ποικίλοις πειρασμοῖς, ἵνα τὸ δοκίμιον ὑμῶν τῆς πίστεως πολυτιμότερον χρυσίου τοῦ ἀπολλυμένου, διὰ πυρὸς δὲ δοκιμαζομένου εὑρεθῇ εἰς ἔπαινον καὶ δόξαν καὶ τιμὴν ἐν ἀποκαλύψει Ἰησοῦ Χριστοῦ.

> In this you rejoice, though now for a little while, "*since it is necessary*," you have been grieved by various trials, ⁷ so that the tested genuineness of your faith—more precious than gold that perishes though it is tested by fire—may be found to result in praise and glory and honor at the revelation of Jesus Christ.[140]

This study deals with the first part of verse 6 in the previous section of chapter 3, therefore that is not considered here. The words that are of particular importance for this study are "λυπηθέντας," "πειρασμοῖς," "δοκίμιον," "εὑρεθῇ," and the phrase "εἰς ἔπαινον καὶ δόξαν καὶ τιμὴν ἐν ἀποκαλύψει Ἰησοῦ Χριστοῦ." This study discusses these in turn in what follows.

The participle "λυπηθέντας," (grieved), according to Hiebert, "does not mean the infliction of pain but the inward feeling of distress or grief caused by outward circumstances."[141] Furthermore, it is "to cause severe mental or emotional distress."[142] This study affirms that "λυπηθέντας" and its cognates bear this meaning of inward and emotional pain. However, this is not its only meaning. This agrees with the following definition from the Liddell and Scott dictionary "*grieve, vex, whether in body or mind . . . cause pain or grief . . . to be grieved, distressed.*"[143] Donelson asserts that "λύπη" is the traditional word for grief and pain.[144] This pain, however, can be both physical and spiritual or mental.[145] Peter, therefore, is using probably the most offensive word for suffering that he has at his disposal.[146]

---

140. ESV, removed "if" and inserted quotation.

141. Hiebert, *1 Peter*, 66.

142. Danker, *Greek-English Lexicon*, "λυπέω," 605 (emphasis original, bold has been removed).

143. Liddell et al., *Greek-English Lexicon*, 1065 (emphasis original).

144. Donelson, *I & II Peter and Jude*, 33.

145. Spicq, *Theological Lexicon of the New Testament*, 2:417–22; see also, Donelson, *I & II Peter and Jude*, 33; TDNT, 4:313.

146. Donelson, *I & II Peter and Jude*, 33.

Peter uses this word to highlight the "offensiveness" of the suffering.[147] In ancient Greek philosophy, a conversation about "λύπη" is framed within the conversation of "ἡδονή."[148] This idea of "ἡδονή" (hedonism) is defined as follows "state or condition of experiencing pleasure for any reason, *pleasure, delight, enjoyment, pleasantness.*"[149] Furthermore, the discussion of "λύπη" and "ἡδονή" fall within the Aristotelian investigation of the "ἀγαθόν" (the good).[150] For the Greek philosophers what distinguishes man from beast is his ability to distinguish between what is good and what is evil.[151] Furthermore, the discovery and contemplation of the "ἀγαθόν" is what leads to true joy.[152] Thus, "ἀγαθόν" is set in apposition to "λύπη."[153] Also, in the Platonic understanding, "Hedone (ἡδονή) and Lupe (λύπη) are the basic modes of awareness of existence since they are the ways in which existence understands itself in terms of the world."[154] Therefore, seeing that the goal of life, in the eyes of the Greek philosophers, was to escape "λύπη" and embrace "ἡδονή" through the contemplation of the "ἀγαθόν," Peter's presentation of the gospel would have been a serious problem. What made a philosophy or religion worthy was its capacity to deliver people from "λύπη."[155] Peter's presentation of the gospel, however, did not include deliverance from "λύπη." In fact, Peter declares "λύπη" to be "εἰ δέον ἐστίν."

The Danker dictionary defines "πειρασμός" as "an attempt to learn the nature or character of someth., test, trial."[156] Liddell and Scott add "*make a trial* or *put* a matter *to the* test."[157] As noted in chapter 2, the notion that "fire tests gold, affliction tests strong men,"[158] is widespread within Greek thought. Although this would have been in Peter's audience's minds, would this have been Peter's primary reference point? This study proposes rather

---

147. Donelson, *I & II Peter and Jude*, 33.
148. *TDNT*, 4:313.
149. Danker, *Greek-English Lexicon*, 434, (emphasis original, Bold has been removed).
150. *TDNT*, 4:314.
151. *TDNT*, 4:314.
152. *TDNT*, 4:314.
153. *TDNT*, 4:314.
154. *TDNT*, 4:314; Gadamer, *Plato's Dialectical Ethics*, 55, 105, 107.
155. Donelson, *I & II Peter and Jude*, 33.
156. Danker, *Greek-English Lexicon*, 793 (emphasis original, bold removed).
157. Liddell et al., *Greek-English Lexicon*, 1355 (emphasis original).
158. Seneca, *On Providence*, 5.10.

that Peter would have been more familiar with the Old Testament and intertestamental Jewish understanding of "πειρασμός."

In the Old Testament, as early as the book of Genesis, one finds this notion of God testing human beings. In Genesis 22:1–19, one finds the story of Abraham and Isaac. The story starts with this phrase in Genesis 22:1 (LXX):

> "Καὶ ἐγένετο μετὰ τὰ ῥήματα ταῦτα ὁ θεὸς ἐπείραζεν τὸν Αβρααμ.

> After these things God tested Abraham.

Here God comes to Abraham to test him (ἐπείραζεν)(tested), and Abraham is found faithful. At the height of the story one finds this phrase in Genesis 22:12 (LXX):

> νῦν γὰρ ἔγνων ὅτι φοβῇ τὸν θεὸν σὺ καὶ οὐκ ἐφείσω τοῦ υἱοῦ σου τοῦ ἀγαπητοῦ δι' ἐμέ.

> He said, "Do not lay your hand on the boy or do anything to him, for now I know that you fear God, seeing you have not withheld your son, your only son, from me."

The purpose of God testing Abraham was to see whether he would obey God at the cost of his son. In Exodus 16:4 (LXX), the Lord says the following to Moses:

> εἶπεν δὲ κύριος πρὸς Μωυσῆν Ἰδοὺ ἐγὼ ὕω ὑμῖν ἄρτους ἐκ τοῦ οὐρανοῦ, καὶ ἐξελεύσεται ὁ λαὸς καὶ συλλέξουσιν τὸ τῆς ἡμέρας εἰς ἡμέραν, ὅπως πειράσω αὐτοὺς εἰ πορεύσονται τῷ νόμῳ μου ἢ οὔ.

> Then the Lord said to Moses, "Behold, I am about to rain bread from heaven for you, and the people shall go out and gather a day's portion every day, that I may test them, whether they will walk in my law or not."

Here, again, God is the one who tests Israel, and the purpose is to see whether they will walk in his law. In 2 Chronicles 32:31 (LXX):

> καὶ οὕτως τοῖς πρεσβευταῖς τῶν ἀρχόντων ἀπὸ Βαβυλῶνος τοῖς ἀποσταλεῖσιν πρὸς αὐτὸν πυθέσθαι παρ' αὐτοῦ τὸ τέρας, ὃ ἐγένετο ἐπὶ τῆς γῆς, καὶ ἐγκατέλιπεν αὐτὸν κύριος τοῦ πειράσαι αὐτὸν εἰδέναι τὰ ἐν τῇ καρδίᾳ αὐτοῦ.

> And so in the matter of the envoys of the princes of Babylon, who had been sent to him to inquire about the sign that had been done

in the land, God left him to himself, in order to test him and to know all that was in his heart.

God sends the Babylonian envoy to "test and to know what is in Hezekiah's heart."[159] In Deuteronomy 8:2–5 (LXX), one finds a similar thought:

> καὶ μνησθήσῃ πᾶσαν τὴν ὁδόν, ἣν ἤγαγέν σε κύριος ὁ θεός σου ἐν τῇ ἐρήμῳ, ὅπως ἂν κακώσῃ σε καὶ ἐκπειράσῃ σε καὶ διαγνωσθῇ τὰ ἐν τῇ καρδίᾳ σου, εἰ φυλάξῃ τὰς ἐντολὰς αὐτοῦ ἢ οὔ. καὶ ἐκάκωσέν σε καὶ ἐλιμαγχόνησέν σε καὶ ἐψώμισέν σε τὸ μαννα, ὃ οὐκ εἴδησαν οἱ πατέρες σου, ἵνα ἀναγγείλῃ σοι ὅτι οὐκ ἐπ' ἄρτῳ μόνῳ ζήσεται ὁ ἄνθρωπος, ἀλλ' ἐπὶ παντὶ ῥήματι τῷ ἐκπορευομένῳ διὰ στόματος θεοῦ ζήσεται ὁ ἄνθρωπος. τὰ ἱμάτιά σου οὐ κατετρίβη ἀπὸ σοῦ, οἱ πόδες σου οὐκ ἐτυλώθησαν, ἰδοὺ τεσσαράκοντα ἔτη. καὶ γνώσῃ τῇ καρδίᾳ σου ὅτι ὡς εἴ τις παιδεύσαι ἄνθρωπος τὸν υἱὸν αὐτοῦ, οὕτως κύριος ὁ θεός σου παιδεύσει σε.

> And you shall remember the whole way that the Lord your God has led you these forty years in the wilderness, that he might humble you, testing you to know what was in your heart, whether you would keep his commandments or not. And he humbled you and let you hunger and fed you with manna, which you did not know, nor did your fathers know, that he might make you know that man does not live by bread alone, but man lives by every word that comes from the mouth of the Lord. Your clothing did not wear out on you and your foot did not swell these forty years. Know then in your heart that, as a man disciplines his son, the Lord your God disciplines you.

Here Moses interprets the entire wilderness experience as God's means of testing the Israelites. Again, there is a purpose behind the testing: "So that God might know what is in your (the Israelites') hearts and if you would keep his commandments or not."[160] Furthermore, in verse 5, it is clear that this testing is like a two-pronged sword. On the one hand, it tests their hearts in order to expose what is in it, i.e., to expose whether their faith is truly in God. On the other hand, God is using this testing to discipline his people like a father disciplines a son. It exposes and purges at the same time.[161] Clearly, then, in the Old Testament the idea of God

---

159. My translation.

160. My translation.

161. This second part of purging is dependent on how a person responds to the "discipline." Like Dryden, *Theology and Ethics in 1 Peter*, 34 asserts, formation is not automatic. In fact, suffering is more likely to produce bitterness and selfishness in a person

testing his people in order to know what is in their hearts, and furthermore to correct them as is clear from the Deuteronomy passage, is present and is most likely within Peter's mind when he writes to his audience regarding their "ποικίλοις πειρασμοῖς" (various trials).

Judaism during the intertestamental[162] period develops this idea even further. They, however, emphasize the educative aspect of this testing. The Wisdom of Solomon 3:5–6 (LXX) says:

> καὶ ὀλίγα παιδευθέντες μεγάλα εὐεργετηθήσονται, ὅτι ὁ θεὸς ἐπείρασεν αὐτοὺς καὶ εὗρεν αὐτοὺς ἀξίους ἑαυτοῦ, ὡς χρυσὸν ἐν χωνευτηρίῳ ἐδοκίμασεν αὐτοὺς καὶ ὡς ὁλοκάρπωμα θυσίας προσεδέξατο αὐτούς.

> And having been a little chastised, they shall be greatly rewarded: for God proved them, and found them worthy for himself. As gold in the furnace hath he tried them and received them as a burnt offering.

The Deuteronomistic idea of God disciplining his children through testing "like gold in a furnace"[163] is repeated and expanded. Sirach 2:1–6 (LXX) conveys a similar idea:

> Τέκνον, εἰ προσέρχῃ δουλεύειν κυρίῳ, ἑτοίμασον τὴν ψυχήν σου εἰς πειρασμόν, εὔθυνον τὴν καρδίαν σου καὶ καρτέρησον καὶ μὴ σπεύσῃς ἐν καιρῷ ἐπαγωγῆς, κολλήθητι αὐτῷ καὶ μὴ ἀποστῇς, ἵνα αὐξηθῇς ἐπ᾽ ἐσχάτων σου. πᾶν, ὃ ἐὰν ἐπαχθῇ σοι, δέξαι καὶ ἐν ἀλλάγμασιν ταπεινώσεώς σου μακροθύμησον, ὅτι ἐν πυρὶ δοκιμάζεται χρυσὸς καὶ ἄνθρωποι δεκτοὶ ἐν καμίνῳ ταπεινώσεως. πίστευσον αὐτῷ, καὶ ἀντιλήμψεταί σου, εὔθυνον τὰς ὁδούς σου καὶ ἔλπισον ἐπ᾽ αὐτόν.

> Child, if you come to serve the Lord God, prepare your soul for temptation. Make your heart right and be steadfast, and do not hurry in the time of distress. Be joined to him, and do not turn away, so that you might be honored at your last days. Accept everything that would be brought upon you, and when you are changed

---

than it is to produce holiness. Therefore, knowing what time it is, according to Green, *1 Peter*, 30, is what enables a believer to respond correctly. If one knows this suffering is from God and necessary, one can embrace it for what it is. God's means of purging a person from sin and fashioning him into the image of Christ.

162. The following scholars also see the same connection as noted in this study: Jobes, *1 Peter*, 91–96; Witherington III, *Letters and Homilies*, 81; Dubis, "Messianic Woes in First Peter," 133–36; Davids, *First Epistle of Peter*, 56; *TDNT*, 6:26.

163. My translation.

into a state of humiliation, be patient; because gold is tested in the fire, and acceptable people in the furnace of humiliation. Trust in him, and he will support you; make your ways straight and hope in him.

Serving the Lord does not deliver one from calamities or testing. These tests all serve the same purpose as the fiery furnace does for God: purification. Judith 8:25–27 (LXX) affirms this understanding of testing:

> παρὰ ταῦτα πάντα εὐχαριστήσωμεν κυρίῳ τῷ θεῷ ἡμῶν, ὃς πειράζει ἡμᾶς καθὰ καὶ τοὺς πατέρας ἡμῶν. μνήσθητε ὅσα ἐποίησεν μετὰ Αβρααμ καὶ ὅσα ἐπείρασεν τὸν Ισαακ καὶ ὅσα ἐγένετο τῷ Ιακωβ ἐν Μεσοποταμίᾳ τῆς Συρίας ποιμαίνοντι τὰ πρόβατα Λαβαν τοῦ ἀδελφοῦ τῆς μητρὸς αὐτοῦ . . . ἀλλ' εἰς νουθέτησιν μαστιγοῖ κύριος τοὺς ἐγγίζοντας αὐτῷ.

> Apart from all this, let us give thanks to the Lord our God who tests us just as also our fathers did. Remember all that he did with Abraham and how greatly he tested Isaac and all that happened to Jacob in Mesopotamia of Syria, while tending the sheep of Laban the brother of his mother. For like he did not burn them to affliction of their heart and he did not punish us, but the Lord whips those who draw near to him, for admonition.

Here the writer asserts that God is putting them to the test just as he tested Abraham, Isaac, and Jacob. In the final verse, the writer says that "The Lord whips those who are close to him unto/as an admonition."[164] This then shapes the context within which Peter uses the word "πειρασμός."

Therefore, when Peter says "εἰ δέον ἐστίν, λυπηθέντας ἐν ποικίλοις πειρασμοῖς" (since it is necessary to be grieved by many trials) he builds on this developed tradition that God uses trials in order to test what is in a believer's heart as a means to discipline them to walk in his way. Jobes asserts that these trials are moments in which believers prove their faithfulness to God by correctly responding to them.[165] Like God tested Israel through the wilderness experience, so God is testing believers through many trials. Green builds on this and proposes that these trials present believers with an interesting paradox.[166] These trials have the potential both for glory and

---

164. My translation.
165. Jobes, *1 Peter*, 91–96.
166. Green, *1 Peter*, 30.

tragedy.¹⁶⁷ They can either develop and deepen the spiritual life of the believer, or they can stunt and corrupt it.¹⁶⁸ Indeed, to quote Green:

> 'testing' comprises a crisis of decision, of faithfulness, of outcome, since it is at one and the same time the opportunity for the refiner's fire to carry out its work of purifying faith and the opportunity for diabolic forces to wrestle God's people away from their faith through temptation.¹⁶⁹

The question, however, remains: What is the purpose of this testing? Peter answers that question in 1 Peter 1:7:

> ἵνα τὸ δοκίμιον ὑμῶν τῆς πίστεως πολυτιμότερον χρυσίου τοῦ ἀπολλυμένου, διὰ πυρὸς δὲ δοκιμαζομένου εὑρεθῇ εἰς ἔπαινον καὶ δόξαν καὶ τιμὴν ἐν ἀποκαλύψει Ἰησοῦ Χριστοῦ
>
> so that the tested genuineness of your faith—more precious than gold that perishes though it is tested by fire—may be found to result in praise and glory and honor at the revelation of Jesus Christ.

Wallace asserts that "ἵνα" (so that/in order that) is always more likely to refer to purpose than result.¹⁷⁰ The "ἵνα" clause in verse 7 explains the purpose of what has been said in verse 6. The Danker dictionary defines "δοκίμιον" as "genuineness as result of a test, *genuine, without alloy*."¹⁷¹ Hiebert observes that the papyrological usage of "δοκίμιον" affirms this definition, i.e., "approved."¹⁷² The "ἵνα" clause furthermore proposes that the suffering of believers is not an end in itself as if they should suffer because suffering in itself is a good thing.¹⁷³ The focus of this passage is not suffering but rather what it produces within the believer.¹⁷⁴ The suffering is so that the "τὸ δοκίμιον ὑμῶν τῆς πίστεως" (the tested genuineness of their faith¹⁷⁵) may be revealed. Keener notes:

---

167. Green, *1 Peter*, 30.
168. Green, *1 Peter*, 30.
169. Green, *1 Peter*, 227.
170. Wallace, *Greek Grammar*, 676–77.
171. Danker, *Greek-English Lexicon*, 256.
172. Hiebert, *1 Peter*, 67 (emphasis original).
173. Hiebert, *1 Peter*, 68.
174. Hiebert, *1 Peter*, 68.
175. My translation.

Fire tested and refined metals, just as it tests even more precious faith here. Heating a furnace sufficiently allowed ancients to extract precious metals from ore: lead melts already at 327° C, and its main ore would be heated to 900 or 1000° C to extract silver. Gold remains long after lead, melting only at 1063° C. The gold would remain after most other ore was removed.[176]

Similarly, as the furnace of suffering tests one's faith, so the dross is separated from what is genuine and valuable. This proposal is even further strengthened by the early church's understanding of the nature of testing. The Shepherd of Hermas says the following:

> τὸ δὲ χρυσοῦν μέρος ὑμεῖς ἐστε οἱ ἐκωυγόντες τὸν κόσμον τοῦτον. ὥσπερ γὰρ τὸ χρυσίον δοκιμάζεται διὰ τοῦ πυρὸς καὶ εὔχρηστον γίνεται, οὕτως καὶ ὑμεῖς δοκιμάζεσθε οἱ κατοικοῦντες ἐν αὐτοῖς. οἱ οὖν μείναντες καὶ πυρωθέντες ὑπ' αὐτῶν καθαρισθήσεσθε. ὥσπερ τὸ χρυσίον ἀποβάλλει πᾶσαν λύπην καὶ στενοχωρίαν, καὶ καθαρισθήσεσθε καὶ χρήσιμοι ἔσεσθε εἰς τὴν οἰκοδομὴν τοῦ πύργου.[177]

> For as gold is tested by fire, and thus becomes useful, so are you tested who dwell in it. Those, therefore, who continue stedfast, and are put through the fire, will be purified by means of it. For as gold casts away its dross, so also will ye cast away all sadness and straitness, and will be made pure so as to fit into the building of the tower.

Here, the Shepherd of Hermas asserts just as gold is tested (δοκιμάζεται) by fire, so too believers are tested (δοκιμάζεσθε), and these trials render the believers "pure and useful."[178] Peter continues that the purpose of the suffering is that their faith "εὑρεθῇ εἰς ἔπαινον καὶ δόξαν καὶ τιμὴν ἐν ἀποκαλύψει Ἰησοῦ Χριστοῦ" (might be found unto glory and honor at the revelation of Jesus Christ) through "δοκιμαζομένου." Liddel and Scott define "δοκιμάζω" as "*put them to the test, make trial of them.*"[179] Furthermore, it is "to make a critical examination of someth. to determine genuineness, *put to the test, examine.*"[180] The purpose of the "δοκιμαζομένου" is that their faith might be "εὑρεθῇ" (found) in the desired state. Some scholars propose

---

176. Keener, *1 Peter*, 76.
177. Shepherd of Hermas, "Shepherd_b," s.v. "Ὅρασις δ'" III. 4.
178. My translation.
179. Liddell et al., *Greek-English Lexicon*, 442 (emphasis original).
180. Danker, *Greek-English Lexicon*, 225 (emphasis original).

Exegetical Analysis

that "πολυτιμότερον" (more precious) is the predicate of "εὑρεθῇ."[181] This results in a translation like this: "may be found to be more precious than gold."[182] However, Forbes asserts that the word order of the Greek text makes this rendering unlikely.[183] Forbes and most major translations propose that one should instead take "εὑρεθῇ" (which is in the subjunctive case agreeing with "ἵνα") with "εἰς," which directly follows it and further develops the purpose/result of their suffering.[184] This reading renders the following translation: "may be found to result in praise and glory and honor at the revelation of Jesus Christ."[185] Again, one can see that eschatology is what frames Peter's entire paraenesis.[186] These trials purify believers and ready them for eschatological salvation.[187] These trials are so that they may be found deserving of honor, glory, and praise at the coming of Jesus. The genuine faith that has been approved through fire is precious because it delivers the believers from eschatological judgment.[188] Indeed, Donelson asserts "it is not faith that leads to praise and glory and honor; it is the genuineness of faith."[189] Therefore, Peter adjures his readers to remember "what time it is" so that they can orient themselves correctly towards the eschatological reality that awaits them.[190] This enables them to be faithful during their trials. This is imperative because, as noted above, Skaggs asks the question whether someone would inherit salvation if one does not suffer.[191] Peter seems to venture an answer in 1 Peter 1:9: "κομιζόμενοι τὸ τέλος τῆς πίστεως ὑμῶν σωτηρίαν ψυχῶν" (obtaining the outcome of your faith, the salvation of your souls). The believers, through their suffering and the purification of their faith, are receiving the salvation of their souls.

---

181. Kelly, *Epistles of Peter and Jude*, 54; Selwyn, *First Epistle of St. Peter*, 130; Hort, *First Epistle of St. Peter*, 42.

182. Kelly, *Epistles of Peter and Jude*, 54; Selwyn, *First Epistle of St. Peter*, 130; Hort, *First Epistle of St. Peter*, 42.

183. Forbes, *Exegetical Guide*, 25.

184. Forbes, *Exegetical Guide*, 25; see ESV, NRSV, NKJV, NIV, etc.

185. ESV.

186. Best, *1 Peter*, 77–78.

187. Senior, *1 Peter*, 33.

188. Jobes, *1 Peter*, 95. Here the idea that believers suffer now but unbelievers will suffer later comes to the fore. In 4:18 this is made explicit that it is preferable to suffer now compared to what the unbelievers will face at the end.

189. Donelson, *I & II Peter and Jude*, 33.

190. Green, *1 Peter*, 30.

191. Skaggs, *Pentecostal Commentary*, 20.

Hiebert exclaims that faith that does not endure cannot be claimed to be genuine.[192] Therefore, this study proposes an emphatic "Yes!" to Skaggs's question. If the believer does not suffer correctly, they will not inherit the salvation of their souls. That much seems clear enough from the text itself.

This study shows in the preceding section on 1 Peter 1:6–9 that: 1) "λυπηθέντας" can mean either physical or emotional pain affirming and strengthening the contextual evidence presented in chapter 2; 2) Peter's usage of "πειρασμοῖς" builds on a massive tradition from the Old Testament and intertestamental Judaism [This tradition proposes that it is God who tests his people in various ways in order to expose their true motives, to see whether they are truly committed to following him, and to discipline those who have gone astray]; and 3) the purpose of the various tests/sufferings is to purify their faith so that they might be pure and inherit eschatological salvation. This gives rise to an unsettling observation that if the believer does not suffer correctly, they will not inherit eschatological salvation. In fact, they too will be judged by God at the final judgment.

First Peter 4:12

In reading 1 Peter 4:12:

> Ἀγαπητοί, μὴ ξενίζεσθε τῇ ἐν ὑμῖν πυρώσει πρὸς πειρασμὸν ὑμῖν γινομένῃ ὡς ξένου ὑμῖν συμβαίνοντος

> Beloved, do not be surprised at the fiery trial when it comes upon you to test you, as though something strange were happening to you

One finds a close parallel with 1 Peter 1:6–7:

> ἐν ᾧ ἀγαλλιᾶσθε, ὀλίγον ἄρτι, εἰ δέον ἐστίν, λυπηθέντας ἐν ποικίλοις πειρασμοῖς, ἵνα τὸ δοκίμιον ὑμῶν τῆς πίστεως πολυτιμότερον χρυσίου τοῦ ἀπολλυμένου, διὰ πυρὸς δὲ δοκιμαζομένου εὑρεθῇ εἰς ἔπαινον καὶ δόξαν καὶ τιμὴν ἐν ἀποκαλύψει Ἰησοῦ Χριστοῦ.

> In this you rejoice, though now for a little while, if necessary, you have been grieved by various trials, so that the tested genuineness of your faith—more precious than gold that perishes though it is tested by fire—may be found to result in praise and glory and honor at the revelation of Jesus Christ.

---

192. Hiebert, *1 Peter*, 68–69.

Exegetical Analysis

Repetition of key words like "πυρώσει/πυρὸς" (fiery/severe) and "πειρασμὸν/πειρασμοῖς" (testing/trial) make this connection obvious enough. Furthermore, one finds even further parallels if one is to add 1 Peter 4:13–14, which reads:

> ἀλλὰ καθὸ κοινωνεῖτε τοῖς τοῦ Χριστοῦ παθήμασιν, χαίρετε, ἵνα καὶ ἐν τῇ ἀποκαλύψει τῆς δόξης αὐτοῦ χαρῆτε ἀγαλλιώμενοι. εἰ ὀνειδίζεσθε ἐν ὀνόματι Χριστοῦ, μακάριοι, ὅτι τὸ τῆς δόξης καὶ τὸ τοῦ θεοῦ πνεῦμα ἐφ᾽ ὑμᾶς ἀναπαύεται

> But rejoice insofar as you share Christ's sufferings, that you may also rejoice and be glad when his glory is revealed. If you are insulted for the name of Christ, you are blessed, because the Spirit of glory and of God rests upon you

Furthermore, Peter repeats the command to rejoice ("ἀγαλλιώμενοι/ ἀγαλλιᾶσθε") and the eschatological reference to the revelation of Jesus Christ "ἐν τῇ ἀποκαλύψει τῆς δόξης αὐτοῦ/ἐν ἀποκαλύψει Ἰησοῦ Χριστοῦ" (may be found to result in praise and glory and honor at the revelation of Jesus Christ). It seems as if 1 Peter 1:6–7 functions like a thesis statement, which sums up what is to come, and 1 Peter 4:12–14 functions like an expansion of that thesis.[193] The previous section dealt with "πειρασμὸν" (trial) at length while ignoring "πυρὸς" (fiery/severe). This section only makes slight mention of "πειρασμὸν" insofar as it is deemed relevant with the majority of this section being devoted to "πυρώσει" and its cognates.

The noun "πύρωσις" is a scarce word in the biblical corpus, occurring only three times in New Testament with an additional two uses in the LXX.[194] In extrabiblical use, this term referred to "burning," "baking," a flame from firewood, and the fiery heat of the sun.[195] Josephus uses this word for the destruction that befell Sodom:

> καὶ ὁ θεὸς ἐνσκήπτει βέλος εἰς τὴν πόλιν καὶ σὺν τοῖς οἰκήτορσιν κατεπίμπρα τὴν γῆν ὁμοίᾳ πυρώσει ἀφανίζω[196]

---

193. Now it is clear enough from the text that 4:12–19 contains ideas that are mentioned elsewhere in the letter. Therefore, one could look at 4:12–19 as a summary of the letter as a whole with some expansion of the ideas mentioned above, maybe with the exception of 4:17, which does not seem to have a parallel elsewhere.

194. NT: 1 Pet 4:12, Rev 18:9, 18; LXX: Amos 4:9, Prov 27:21.

195. *TDNT*, s.v. "πύρωσις," 6:929; Dubis, "Messianic Woes in First Peter," 118.

196. Josephus, *Ant.* 1.203.

God then cast a thunderbolt upon the city, and set it on fire, with its inhabitants; and laid waste the country with the like burning.[197]

In the LXX, "πύρωσις" occurs in Amos 4:9:

ἐπάταξα ὑμᾶς ἐν πυρώσει καὶ ἐν ἰκτέρῳ, ἐπληθύνατε κήπους ὑμῶν, ἀμπελῶνας ὑμῶν καὶ συκῶνας ὑμῶν καὶ ἐλαιῶνας ὑμῶν κατέφαγεν ἡ κάμπη, καὶ οὐδ' ὡς ἐπεστρέψατε πρός με, λέγει κύριος.

"I struck you with fevers (πύρωσις) and with jaundice. You multiplied your gardens. The caterpillar devoured your vineyards, and your fig groves and your olive groves, and even so you did not return to me," says the Lord.

Here it denotes God sending blight/scorching winds in order to destroy the crops in Israel. The second reference in the LXX is found in Proverbs 27:21:

δοκίμιον ἀργύρῳ καὶ χρυσῷ πύρωσις, ἀνὴρ δὲ δοκιμάζεται διὰ στόματος ἐγκωμιαζόντων αὐτόν.

The crucible is for silver, and the furnace is for gold, and a man is tested by his praise.

Here the image of the crucible comes to the fore. The idea of fire testing a person, this study contends, is what lies in Peter's mind when he uses it in his letter.[198] The evidence seems sparse, with a mere five occurrences of "πύρωσις" in the canonical text. This study, therefore, relies on its verbal cognate in order to shed light on the meaning of the noun found in 1 Peter.

The verbal cognate of "πύρωσις"—"πυρόω"—occurs six times in the New Testament, with an additional thirty or so mentions in the LXX.[199] Most of the mentions in the LXX fall appear within a metallurgical context. In Psalm 11:6 (LXX):

τὰ λόγια κυρίου λόγια ἀγνά, ἀργύριον πεπυρωμένον δοκίμιον τῇ γῇ κεκαθαρισμένον ἑπταπλασίως

---

197. Josephus, *Works of Flavius Josephus*, 41.

198. Bigg, *Critical and Exegetical Commentary*, 176 suggests that Proverbs 27:21 is tied directly to Peter's usage in 4:12. This, however, remains doubtful as there is not enough lexical overlap to make such a connection.

199. NT: 1 Cor 7:9, 2 Cor 11:29, Eph 6:16, 2 Pet 3:12, Rev 1:15, 3:18; LXX: Ps 11:6, 16:3, 17:30, 25:2, 65:10, 104:19, 118:140, 2 Sam 22:31, Job 22:25, Zech 13:9, Isa 1:25, Jer 9:7, Dan 12:10, etc.

EXEGETICAL ANALYSIS

The oracles of the Lord are pure oracles; as silver tried in the fire, proved in a furnace of earth, purified seven times

Here, it is used as an image of the purity of God's word. In Psalm 17:31 (LXX):

ὁ θεός μου, ἄμωμος ἡ ὁδὸς αὐτοῦ, τὰ λόγια κυρίου πεπυρωμένα, ὑπερασπιστής ἐστιν πάντων τῶν ἐλπιζόντων ἐπ' αὐτόν

As for my God, his way is perfect: the oracles of the Lord are tried in the fire; he is a protector of all that hope in him

Here, it affirms the purity of God's ways. More importantly for this study, "πυρόω" is often used to refer to God's discipline and purification of his people. Job 22:25 (LXX) reads:

ἔσται οὖν σου ὁ παντοκράτωρ βοηθὸς ἀπὸ ἐχθρῶν, καθαρὸν δὲ ἀποδώσει σε ὥσπερ ἀργύριον πεπυρωμένον

Then the Almighty shall be your help from enemies, and he shall restore you pure, like silver that has been tried by fire

Eliphaz makes the case that, coupled with repentance, Job's trials would refine and purify him. In this vein, Psalm 65:10–12 (LXX) reads:

ὅτι ἐδοκίμασας ἡμᾶς, ὁ θεός, ἐπύρωσας ἡμᾶς, ὡς πυροῦται τὸ ἀργύριον, εἰσήγαγες ἡμᾶς εἰς τὴν παγίδα, ἔθου θλίψεις ἐπὶ τὸν νῶτον ἡμῶν. ἐπεβίβασας ἀνθρώπους ἐπὶ τὰς κεφαλὰς ἡμῶν, διήλθομεν διὰ πυρὸς καὶ ὕδατος, καὶ ἐξήγαγες ἡμᾶς εἰς ἀναψυχήν

For you tested us, O God, and you purged us as silver is purged. You led us into the trap; you set afflictions before us. You put people upon our heads. We went through fire and water, and you led us into refreshment.

God is the one who tests Israel by fire in order to render them pure. Furthermore, the psalmist here interprets "the people riding over their heads"[200] as God's means of purifying and testing them.[201] Jeremiah 9:7 (LXX) continues this thought:

διὰ τοῦτο τάδε λέγει κύριος Ἰδοὺ ἐγὼ πυρώσω αὐτοὺς καὶ δοκιμῶ αὐτούς, ὅτι ποιήσω ἀπὸ προσώπου πονηρίας θυγατρὸς λαοῦ μου.

---

200. My translation.

201. Here is a clear connection between the psalmists enemies and the unbelievers who are persecuting Peter's audience.

> Because of this, this is what the Lord says: "Look! I will purge them, and I will test them, for I will act because of the presence of the evil of the daughter of my people."

In Jeremiah's case, it is the Babylonians who will come and destroy Judah. God, however, sees this as his discipline on them, which in turn refines them as a furnace refines gold. In the New Testament, two out of the six occurrences of "πυρόω" also occur in metallurgical contexts. Revelation 1:15 reads:

> καὶ οἱ πόδες αὐτοῦ ὅμοιοι χαλκολιβάνῳ ὡς ἐν καμίνῳ πεπυρωμένης καὶ ἡ φωνὴ αὐτοῦ ὡς φωνὴ ὑδάτων πολλῶν
>
> his [Jesus'] feet were like burnished bronze, refined in a furnace, and his voice was like the roar of many waters.[202]

Also, in Revelation 3:18:

> συμβουλεύω σοι ἀγοράσαι παρ' ἐμοῦ χρυσίον πεπυρωμένον ἐκ πυρὸς ἵνα πλουτήσῃς, καὶ ἱμάτια λευκὰ ἵνα περιβάλῃ καὶ μὴ φανερωθῇ ἡ αἰσχύνη τῆς γυμνότητός σου, καὶ κολλ[ο]ύριον ἐγχρῖσαι τοὺς ὀφθαλμούς σου ἵνα βλέπῃς
>
> I counsel you to buy from me gold refined by fire, so that you may be rich, and white garments so that you may clothe yourself and the shame of your nakedness may not be seen, and salve to anoint your eyes, so that you may see.

Jesus counsels the church in Laodicea to "buy gold from him that has been refined by fire."[203] Sander, however, proposes that "πύρωσις," by the time of Peter's writing, had lost its refinement/purification connotations.[204] Instead, Sander asserts this connotation has given way to the Qumranian technical term for the end-time ordeals, i.e., the messianic woes.[205] Dubis and Campbell have successfully dismissed this assertion as unnecessarily one-dimensional.[206] Michaels, commenting on 4QpPs 37 2.19 and 4QFlor. 2.1, points out that in Qumran they seem "to have embraced both the

---

202. My translation.
203. My translation.
204. Sander, "ΠΥΡΩΣΙΣ and the First Epistle of Peter 4:12," 43–44, 49–50, 67, 85–86, 90–91, 93–94, 96, 103–4.
205. Sander, "ΠΥΡΩΣΙΣ and the First Epistle of Peter 4:12," 43–44, 49–50, 67, 85–86, 90–91, 93–94, 96, 103–4.
206. Campbell, "Honor, Shame," 203; Dubis, "Messianic Woes in First Peter," 126–28.

testing of the righteous and the final punishment of the wicked."²⁰⁷ Furthermore, the early church's understanding strengthens this reading even more. The Didache 16:5 reads:

> Τότε ἥξει ἡ κτίσις τῶν ἀνθρώπων εἰς τὴν πύρωσιν τῆς δοκιμασίας καὶ σκανδαλισθήσονται πολλοὶ καὶ ἀπολοῦνται, οἱ δὲ ὑπομείναντες ἐν τῇ πίστει αὐτῶν σωθήσονται ὑπ' αὐτοῦ τοῦ καταθέματος.

> Then shall the work of men come into the fire of trial, and many shall be offended, and shall perish; but they that endure in their faith shall be saved by the curse itself.²⁰⁸

The author of the Didache understands the "curse" as the eschatological sufferings through the false christs and shepherds to be the means through which believers will be purified and ultimately saved. Thus, this study affirms that one can see from the LXX, New Testament, and Qumran that "πύρωσις" and "πυρόω" frequently occur within metallurgical contexts.

This study contends, along with various scholars, that this metallurgical context is what lies behind Peter's use of the term.²⁰⁹ The Danker dictionary defines "πύρωσις" as the "process of burning . . . an intense degree of some painful occurrence or experience, *burning ordeal.*"²¹⁰ Clearly, then, one can deduce that Peter's use of the descriptor "πύρωσις" to define the believers' trials points to more than verbal abuse. Hiebert agrees that Peter uses "πύρωσις" "figuratively to denote the severity of the experience his readers are undergoing, an experience comparable to pain caused by exposure to fire."²¹¹ Thus, "πύρωσις" refers to an intense suffering that the believers are experiencing.²¹² Jobes and Achtemeier contend that there is not enough evidence to make a connection between "πύρωσις" and believers being set alight by Nero.²¹³ One can read these "fiery trials" metaphorically; however, Skaggs and Witherington III contend that there is no definite reason to

---

207. Michaels, *1 Peter*, 260–61.

208. Hitchcock and Brown, *Teaching of the Twelve Apostles*, 28.

209. For scholars who agree with this see, Achtemeier and Epp, *1 Peter*, 305; Davids, *First Epistle of Peter*, 164; Best, *1 Peter*, 162; Skaggs, *Pentecostal Commentary*, 62; Senior, *1 Peter*, 127; Hiebert, *1 Peter*, 284; Dubis, "Messianic Woes in First Peter," 120; Klausli, "Question of the Messianic Woes," 203–5; Kistemaker, *New Testament Commentary*, 174.

210. Danker, *Greek-English Lexicon*, 900 (emphasis original, bold removed).

211. Hiebert, *1 Peter*, 284.

212. Skaggs, *Pentecostal Commentary*, 62–63.

213. Jobes, *1 Peter*, 94; Achtemeier and Epp, *1 Peter*, 305–6.

do so.²¹⁴ The primary problem with this theory is that Nero's persecution was local to Rome, and Peter's audience was in Asia Minor.²¹⁵ However, it is plausible that among Peter's audience are those who fled the persecution in Rome, or who were ejected by the emperor.²¹⁶ These people would then be expecting the spread of that persecution to the provinces and seeking to understand why their friends/family members in Rome were being killed.²¹⁷ Skaggs concludes, therefore, that it is just as plausible "to see them as reflective of Nero's persecution in which the Christians were actually burned."²¹⁸ This also leaves room for the fact that, even in the ancient world, news travels fast.

Furthermore, as opposed to the "mere possibility" of trials in 1 Peter 3:17 using the optative tense; here the present participle "γινομένη" denotes that the sufferings are real, painful, and being experienced right now.²¹⁹ The purpose of these trials is again explained as "πρὸς πειρασμὸν." Achtemeier and Michaels show that "πρὸς πειρασμὸν" can be translated as "in order to test you."²²⁰ In 1 Peter 1:7, "δοκιμαζομένου" is used, and in 4:12, "πειρασμὸν" is used to convey the same idea.²²¹ Indeed, Kistemaker asserts that these trials purify the believers as a furnace purifies gold.²²² Finally, Peter's exhortation that the believers should "μὴ ξενίζεσθε" deserves some explanation.

How could Peter expect his readers to "not be surprised at the suffering that is coming upon them?"²²³ The Jews at this time had a developed theology of suffering and martyrdom.²²⁴ Also, they had grown accustomed

---

214. Skaggs, *Pentecostal Commentary*, 63; Witherington III, *Letters and Homilies*, 211.

215. Skaggs, *Pentecostal Commentary*, 63.

216. Skaggs, *Pentecostal Commentary*, 63. This point is also made in the audience section of chapter 2 where Jobes asserts that it was commonplace for emperors to expel noncitizens from Rome if the city became over-crowded.

217. Skaggs, *Pentecostal Commentary*, 63.

218. Skaggs, *Pentecostal Commentary*, 63n118.

219. Johnstone, *First Epistle of Peter*, 354–55; Skaggs, *Pentecostal Commentary*, 63.

220. Achtemeier and Epp, *1 Peter*, 305–6; Michaels, *1 Peter*, 261. More is said regarding the purpose function of this phrase in the next section.

221. Donelson, *I & II Peter and Jude*, 133.

222. Kistemaker, *New Testament Commentary*, 174.

223. My translation, 1 Pet 4:12.

224. Davids, *First Epistle of Peter*, 164; Best, *1 Peter*, 162; Donelson, *I & II Peter and Jude*, 133–35.

to being a cultural minority and operating on the fringes of society.[225] Furthermore, they had a distinct understanding of suffering as used by God to discipline and test them, as shown in the section above.[226] Therefore, this phrase would have been especially relevant for gentiles who had never been a cultural minority.[227] Moreover, as noted above, for the Greeks a true religion would have been expected to deliver one from "λύπη."[228] Even more, in the Greek mind, suffering usually signaled a break in one's relationship with the gods.[229] Therefore, for Peter to claim that suffering is "εἰ δέον ἐστίν" (since it is necessary) and "κατὰ τὸ θέλημα τοῦ θεοῦ" (according to the will of God) would have been a foreign idea to them. However, the reality is that by becoming part of the people of God, Peter's audience has already entered into the final judgment of God.[230] The reason they should not be surprised is that the Old Testament people of God suffered, Jesus himself suffered, and then he promised his followers that they too would suffer.[231] Furthermore, Peter himself suffered/was tested and found to be faithful.[232] Peter then places the ball in the audience's court and urges them to respond correctly.[233] Peter hopes that they too will be found faithful so that they might rejoice at Christ's coming.

This section shows that 1) "πύρωσις" points to more than "mere verbal abuse" as some scholars suggest. Furthermore, this understanding is bolstered by the Old Testament, intertestamental Judaism, the New Testament, and the early church fathers; 2) Peter again affirms the idea that this testing is for the purification of the saints; 3) "γινομένη" proves that there is not only a possibility of suffering but that it is their current experience;

---

225. Davids, *First Epistle of Peter*, 164; Best, *1 Peter*, 162; Donelson, *I & II Peter and Jude*, 133–35.

226. See section above.

227. Davids, *First Epistle of Peter*, 164; Donelson, *I & II Peter and Jude*, 134; Achtemeier and Epp, *1 Peter*, 305–6; Best, *1 Peter*, 162. However, this would have been a shock to Jews as well who expected the messianic age to bring about deliverance from their oppressors and the restoration of the kingdom to Israel.

228. Donelson, *I & II Peter and Jude*, 33.

229. Donelson, *I & II Peter and Jude*, 134.

230. Harink, *1 & 2 Peter*, 115–17; Achtemeier and Epp, *1 Peter*, 306; Skaggs, *Pentecostal Commentary*, 62–63.

231. Marshall, *1 Peter*, 150; Stibbs, *First Epistle General of Peter*, 158–59; Kistemaker, *New Testament Commentary*, 174; Best, *1 Peter*, 162; Senior, *1 Peter*, 127–28.

232. See chapter 2 under "Peter's Martyrdom."

233. Witherington III, *Letters and Homilies*, 211.

and 4) "μὴ ξενίζεσθε" reinforces the idea of the necessity of suffering for the Christian believer as did "εἰ δέον ἐστίν" in 1:6. This study continues in the next section with verses that function as the explanatory subclauses for the purpose clause introduced by "πρὸς πειρασμὸν."

First Peter 4:13–14

As noted above by Michaels and Achtemeier, it is possible to construe "πρὸς πειρασμὸν" as a purpose clause.[234] Therefore, they propose a translation "in order to test you."[235] Thus, it functions exactly like the "ἵνα" in 1:6. This study proposes 1 Peter 4:13–14 forms a subclause of 4:12. In other words, it explains the purpose of the "πυρώσει πρὸς πειρασμὸν" in greater detail. This study deals with these two verses in succession below.

First Peter 4:13 reads:

> ἀλλὰ καθὸ κοινωνεῖτε τοῖς τοῦ Χριστοῦ παθήμασιν, χαίρετε, ἵνα καὶ ἐν τῇ ἀποκαλύψει τῆς δόξης αὐτοῦ χαρῆτε ἀγαλλιώμενοι.
>
> But rejoice insofar as you share Christ's sufferings, that you may also rejoice and be glad when his glory is revealed.

Scholars are divided as it pertains to the meaning of "καθὸ κοινωνεῖτε τοῖς τοῦ Χριστοῦ παθήμασιν" (insofar as you share Christ's sufferings). Some assert that this "participation in Christ's sufferings"[236] refers to a participation in Christ's foundational suffering on the cross, i.e., his sacrifice which brings salvation.[237] Furthermore, these scholars propose that this participation then correlates with Peter's previous teaching on the *Imitatio Christi* (*Imitation of Christ*), i.e., to participate in Christ's suffering is to suffer in the way in which Christ suffered.[238] These scholars see a continuation of Peter's thoughts from 1 Peter 2:21:

---

234. Achtemeier and Epp, *1 Peter*, 305–6; Michaels, *1 Peter*, 261.

235. Achtemeier and Epp, *1 Peter*, 305–6; Michaels, *1 Peter*, 261.

236. My translation.

237. Schreiner, *1, 2 Peter, Jude*, 219; Donelson, *I & II Peter and Jude*, 135; Davids, *First Epistle of Peter*, 166–67; Grudem, *1 Peter*, 128; Michaels, *1 Peter*, 262; Forbes, *Exegetical Guide*, 155–56; Goppelt, *Commentary on 1 Peter*, 314–15. These scholars acknowledge that mystical participation in Christ through suffering is clear in Paul but prefer not to read that here in Peter.

238. Schreiner, *1, 2 Peter, Jude*, 219; Donelson, *I & II Peter and Jude*, 135; Davids, *First Epistle of Peter*, 166–67; Grudem, *1 Peter*, 128; Michaels, *1 Peter*, 262; Forbes, *Exegetical Guide*, 155–56; Goppelt, *Commentary on 1 Peter*, 314–15.

Exegetical Analysis

> ὅτι καὶ Χριστὸς ἔπαθεν ὑπὲρ ὑμῶν ὑμῖν ὑπολιμπάνων ὑπογραμμόν, ἵνα ἐπακολουθήσητε τοῖς ἴχνεσιν αὐτοῦ
>
> For to this you have been called, because Christ also suffered for you, leaving you an example, so that you might follow in his steps.

Here, Christ's suffering is explicitly mentioned to be "an example to be imitated."[239] They also point to 1 Peter 4:1:

> Χριστοῦ οὖν παθόντος σαρκὶ καὶ ὑμεῖς τὴν αὐτὴν ἔννοιαν ὁπλίσασθε
>
> Since therefore Christ suffered in the flesh, arm yourselves with the same way of thinking

which again urges the believers to think about suffering "like Jesus did." First Peter 3:17–18 reads:

> κρεῖττον γὰρ ἀγαθοποιοῦντας, εἰ θέλοι τὸ θέλημα τοῦ θεοῦ, πάσχειν ἢ κακοποιοῦντας. ὅτι καὶ Χριστὸς ἅπαξ περὶ ἁμαρτιῶν ἔπαθεν, δίκαιος ὑπὲρ ἀδίκων, ἵνα ὑμᾶς προσαγάγῃ τῷ θεῷ θανατωθεὶς μὲν σαρκί, ζῳοποιηθεὶς δὲ πνεύματι
>
> For it is better to suffer for doing good, if that should be God's will, than for doing evil. For Christ also suffered once for sins, the righteous for the unrighteous, that he might bring us to God, being put to death in the flesh but made alive in the spirit.

This verse further emphasizes this thought of suffering "like Jesus did," i.e., righteous for the unrighteous. Michaels says, "Christians share in Christ's sufferings neither sacramentally in baptism nor in mystical union with him, but simply by following the example of his behavior when facing similar circumstances."[240] This study affirms that the idea of *Imitatio Christi* is prevalent throughout the letter and is to be affirmed in this verse as well. However, is that the only meaning that one can glean from this verse? This study proceeds to answer this question with an excursus on the "κοινων" word group.

The Danker dictionary defines "κοινωνέω" as *"share, have a share."*[241] Furthermore, they define the noun "κοινωνία" as "close association involving mutual interests and sharing, *association, communion, fellowship, close*

---

239. My translation.
240. Michaels, *1 Peter*, 262.
241. Danker, *Greek-English Lexicon*, 552 (emphasis original, bold removed).

relationship . . . participation, sharing."²⁴² This word group occurs only once in 1 Peter; therefore, this study turns to other sources in order to ascertain its meaning. Interestingly, in Judaism, the "κοινων" word group is never used to denote fellowship with God.²⁴³ The Hebrew word that is translated "κοινωνία" in the LXX is "רבח." However, when the LXX translates it as "κοινωνία," it refers to man-to-man relationships.²⁴⁴ Hauck asserts that this is surprising because it is evident from the Old Testament that the Israelites regarded the sacrificial meal as a

> sacral fellowship between God and man . . . In Israel, too, the common meal implies a close relationship which binds the participants to one another. This applies not merely to the men who partake of it; it is equally true of the belief participation of God."²⁴⁵

Philo, a Hellenistic Jew and a contemporary to Peter and Paul, however, adopts the Hellenistic language of "κοινωνία" and applies it to the fellowship shared between God and man.²⁴⁶ In the New Testament, the "κοινων" word group occurs sporadically, but primarily, in the Pauline Letters. Hauck asserts that Paul uses the "κοινων" word group to refer to the "participation of the believer in Christ and Christian blessings, and for the mutual fellowship of believers."²⁴⁷ This is clear in 1 Corinthians 1:9:

> ἐκλήθητε εἰς κοινωνίαν τοῦ υἱοῦ αὐτοῦ Ἰησοῦ Χριστοῦ τοῦ κυρίου ἡμῶν
>
> God is faithful, by whom you were called into the fellowship of his Son, Jesus Christ our Lord.

Here Paul asserts that believers "have been called into fellowship/participation with the Son." These believers then enter into a spiritual communion with Christ. Paul, furthermore, uses this word to describe what happens at the Lord's Supper in close connection with the Jewish understanding of what happens at the sacrificial meal noted above. First Corinthians 10:16–21 reads:

---

242. Danker, *Greek-English Lexicon*, 553 (emphasis original, bold removed).
243. *TDNT*, 801.
244. Lev 6:2; Mal 2:14; Job 34:8; Prov 28:24.
245. *TDNT*, 801.
246. Borgen et al., *Works of Philo*, 1:158. "οὐχὶ καὶ μείζονος τῆς πρὸς τὸν πατέρα τῶν ὅλων καὶ ποιητὴν κοινωνίας ἀπέλαυσε προσρήσεως τῆς αὐτῆς ἀξιωθείς; "
247. *TDNT*, 804.

Τὸ ποτήριον τῆς εὐλογίας ὃ εὐλογοῦμεν, οὐχὶ κοινωνία ἐστὶν τοῦ αἵματος τοῦ Χριστοῦ; τὸν ἄρτον ὃν κλῶμεν, οὐχὶ κοινωνία τοῦ σώματος τοῦ Χριστοῦ ἐστιν; ὅτι εἷς ἄρτος, ἓν σῶμα οἱ πολλοί ἐσμεν, οἱ γὰρ πάντες ἐκ τοῦ ἑνὸς ἄρτου μετέχομεν. βλέπετε τὸν Ἰσραὴλ κατὰ σάρκα· οὐχ οἱ ἐσθίοντες τὰς θυσίας κοινωνοὶ τοῦ θυσιαστηρίου εἰσίν; Τί οὖν φημι; ὅτι εἰδωλόθυτόν τί ἐστιν ἢ ὅτι εἴδωλόν τί ἐστιν; ἀλλ' ὅτι ἃ θύουσιν, δαιμονίοις καὶ οὐ θεῷ [θύουσιν]· οὐ θέλω δὲ ὑμᾶς κοινωνοὺς τῶν δαιμονίων γίνεσθαι. οὐ δύνασθε ποτήριον κυρίου πίνειν καὶ ποτήριον δαιμονίων, οὐ δύνασθε τραπέζης κυρίου μετέχειν καὶ τραπέζης δαιμονίων.

The cup of blessing that we bless, is it not a participation in the blood of Christ? The bread that we break, is it not a participation in the body of Christ? Because there is one bread, we who are many are one body, for we all partake of the one bread. Consider the people of Israel: are not those who eat the sacrifices participants in the altar? What do I imply then? That food offered to idols is anything, or that an idol is anything? No, I imply that what pagans sacrifice they offer to demons and not to God. I do not want you to be participants with demons. You cannot drink the cup of the Lord and the cup of demons. You cannot partake of the table of the Lord and the table of demons.

Therefore, for Paul, those who partake of the Jewish sacrifice are "participating" in the altar of the temple. Also, those who partake of the feasts of pagan temples are "participating with demons." Consequently, when the believers participate in the Lord's Supper they do not merely eat bread and drink wine but they participate in Christ's body and blood. This includes the blessing of forgiveness, but in the words of Best "appears to imply much more than the imitation of Christ."[248] Indeed, Klauck affirms that

> This is not just a living again of Christ's sufferings. Nor is it a mere personal conformity. Nor is it a retrospective passion dogmatics. By spiritual participation in Christ the sufferings of the apostle are a real part of the total suffering which is laid on Christ (Col. 1:24)."[249]

Continuing this thought, "By participation in Christ's sufferings Paul has hope of analogous participation in his glory."[250] There is a definite spiritual participation in Christ himself that occurs when a Christian suffers for the

---

248. Best, *1 Peter*, 162; *TDNT*, 805.
249. *TDNT*, 806.
250. *TDNT*, 806.

Called to Suffer

name of Christ.²⁵¹ It is on this basis that scholars contend that these sufferings are a mystical participation in Christ himself.²⁵² Spicq asserts

> *le croyant, incorpre au Christ a par le bapteme, participle sa vie durant aux souffrances que le Christ a subies dans sa chair.*²⁵³

> The believer, incorporated into Christ by baptism, participates throughout his life (her life) in the sufferings that Christ endured in his flesh.²⁵⁴

In the same way, as a person is united to Christ spiritually in baptism and the Lord's Supper, the believer participates in Christ himself through suffering for his name. Indeed, according to Grudem, their participation in Christ

> involves not only union with him in his death and resurrection, but also union with him in the whole pattern of his life (Rom. 6:5), which includes his sufferings for righteousness (1 Pet. 2:20–21; 3:17–18; Rom. 8:17; Phil. 3:10; Col. 1:24; 2 Tim. 3:12; 1 Jn. 2:6).²⁵⁵

Hiebert, however, offers a good caution that the Christian does not rejoice in suffering simply as a good in itself.²⁵⁶ Rather, the Christian rejoices because of the fellowship that it brings with Christ.²⁵⁷ It is through rejoicing in the present sufferings that the believer is prepared for future glory.²⁵⁸ Therefore, for Peter, there is a clear connection between present resolve and future result.²⁵⁹ Furthermore, if one is to look at the second part of the verse "ἵνα καὶ ἐν τῇ ἀποκαλύψει τῆς δόξης αὐτοῦ χαρῆτε ἀγαλλιώμενοι" (that you may also rejoice and be glad when his glory is revealed), the participation in Christ's suffering leads to a participation in his glory. In the same way, baptism is a participation in Christ's death. One would surely

---

251. Plumptre, *General Epistles*, 147.

252. Best, *1 Peter*, 162; Dubis, "Messianic Woes in First Peter," 145; Campbell, "Honor, Shame," 204; Plumptre, *General Epistles*, 147; Lillie, *Lectures*, 288; Kistemaker, *New Testament Commentary*, 174; Cranfield, *I & II Peter and Jude*, 120.

253. Spicq, Les Epitres de Saint Pierre, 155.

254. I am indebted to Dr. Brad Embry from Regent University Divinity School for this translation.

255. Grudem, *1 Peter*, 179.

256. Hiebert, *1 Peter*, 285.

257. Hiebert, *1 Peter*, 285.

258. Masterman, *First Epistle of S. Peter*, 152.

259. Hiebert, *1 Peter*, 286.

EXEGETICAL ANALYSIS

not propose that this participation in Christ's glory is merely to be glorified "like" him or to be baptized "like" him, as if getting wet was the point of baptism.

Against this participatory view, Best asserts that these sufferings are a participation in that foundational suffering, but also the messianic woes.[260] However, it is not necessary to draw such a hard and fast distinction between the two.[261] Zerwick points out that "we must beware lest we sacrifice to clarity of meaning part of the fulness of meaning."[262] Bekker, insightfully as always, observes that it is imperative that Christians read the Scriptures in a Paleo-Orthodox manner.[263] By this Bekker means that the Protestant tradition needs to move away from one-dimensional interpretive strategies that are concerned with various linguistic, philosophical, or contextual studies.[264] Instead, there should be a *Ressourcement* of the Quadriga or fourfold interpretation of Scripture.[265] This study affirms Bekker, Campbell, and Zerwick's sentiments that it is more than possible for there to be multiple layers of meaning in a text. Consequently, that is true for the text of 1 Peter as well.

This reading is further strengthened by the adverbial conjunction "καθὸ" (in so far as). Robertson shows that "καθὸ" is an abbreviated form of "καθότι."[266] Elliott, Goppelt, and Forbes assert that instead of the more common rendering of "καθὸ" as "in so far as," one could translate it as "because/in view of the fact that."[267] There is precedent for this rendering in the LXX. For instance, 1 Esdras 1:48 (LXX) reads:

> καὶ ἀπέστειλεν ὁ θεὸς τῶν πατέρων αὐτῶν διὰ τοῦ ἀγγέλου αὐτοῦ μετακαλέσαι αὐτούς, καθὸ ἐφείδετο αὐτῶν καὶ τοῦ σκηνώματος αὐτοῦ

---

260. Best, *1 Peter*, 162.
261. Campbell, "Honor, Shame," 204n23; Dubis, "Messianic Woes in First Peter," 145.
262. Zerwick, *Biblical Greek*, 13.
263. Bekker, "Scriptural Formation," 99.
264. Bekker, "Scriptural Formation," 96.
265. Bekker, "Scriptural Formation," 98. It is not in the scope of this study to explicate the quadriga or how it is to be applied. See Bekker's text, as well as Leithart, "Quadriga or Something Like It," 110–11.
266. Robertson, *Grammar of the Greek New Testament*, 967.
267. Elliott, *1 Peter*, 774; Goppelt, *Commentary on 1 Peter*, 315; Forbes, *Exegetical Guide*, 155. This is also the way that it is used in 1 Esdras, 1:48.

The God of their ancestors sent his messenger to call them back, because he would have spared them and his dwelling place.[268]

This translation provides the rationale for their suffering.[269] It strengthens the view that there is a real participation that happens between the believer and Christ himself as one suffers in his name. Contrary to this view, Grudem, Selwyn, and others translate this word as expressing degree, i.e., "in the measure which"[270] or "in so far as."[271] While this study acknowledges that "καθὸ" is primarily translated as expressing degree, "καθότι" is primarily translated as expressing purpose.[272] This strengthens the *Imitatio Christi* view, i.e., insofar as you suffer like Christ, to this degree do you participate in his sufferings. Therefore, if Robertson's assertion that "καθὸ" is an abbreviated form of "καθότι" is correct, then both translations can stand grammatically.[273] Forbes furthermore asserts that one can garner contextual support for both interpretations.[274] This study proposes that in keeping with what is mentioned in the previous discussion on "κοινωνία" one must not "sacrifice to clarity of meaning part of the fulness of meaning."[275] There is ample reason to propose that there is a *double entendre* of sorts here.

Therefore, this study proposes that all three groups of scholars mentioned in this section are correct. For the believer to "κοινωνεῖτε τοῖς τοῦ Χριστοῦ παθήμασιν" means they: 1) participate in the foundational and atoning suffering of Christ; they participate in these sufferings by suffering "like Jesus did," i.e., the *Imitatio Christi*; 2) their participation in these sufferings brings about a deeper union between them and Christ, i.e., they participate in his being through their sufferings; and finally, 3) through their suffering they participate in the "messianic woes," which must be fulfilled before the end comes.

---

268. NRSV.

269. Forbes, *Exegetical Guide*, 155.

270. Selwyn, *First Epistle of St. Peter*, 221.

271. Grudem, *1 Peter*, 178. See also, Hiebert, *1 Peter*, 288; Schreiner, *1, 2 Peter, Jude*, 219; Donelson, *I & II Peter and Jude*, 135; Michaels, *1 Peter*, 262. NKJV, ESV, NRSV, NIV all propose similar translations.

272. See Danker, *Greek-English Lexicon*, 493; Liddell et al., *Greek-English Lexicon*, 855.

273. Robertson, *Grammar of the Greek New Testament*, 967.

274. Forbes, *Exegetical Guide*, 155.

275. Zerwick, *Biblical Greek Illustrated by Examples*, 13.

Before moving on it is necessary to say a few words regarding "παθήμασιν." This word can mean both physical and emotional suffering.[276] In 1 Peter 1:11, "εἰς Χριστὸν παθήματα" it refers to the sufferings of Christ. Moreover, 2 Corinthians 1:5 reads:

> ὅτι καθὼς περισσεύει τὰ παθήματα τοῦ Χριστοῦ εἰς ἡμᾶς, οὕτως διὰ τοῦ Χριστοῦ περισσεύει καὶ ἡ παράκλησις ἡμῶν
>
> For as we share abundantly in Christ's sufferings, so through Christ we share abundantly in comfort too

Here, Paul uses it to speak of Christ's sufferings. One finds the same usage in Colossians 1:24:

> Νῦν χαίρω ἐν τοῖς παθήμασιν ὑπὲρ ὑμῶν καὶ ἀνταναπληρῶ τὰ ὑστερήματα τῶν θλίψεων τοῦ Χριστοῦ ἐν τῇ σαρκί μου ὑπὲρ τοῦ σώματος αὐτοῦ
>
> Now I rejoice in my sufferings for your sake, and in my flesh I am filling up what is lacking in Christ's afflictions for the sake of his body, that is, the church

and in Hebrews 2:10:

> πολλοὺς υἱοὺς εἰς δόξαν ἀγαγόντα τὸν ἀρχηγὸν τῆς σωτηρίας αὐτῶν διὰ παθημάτων τελειῶσαι
>
> For it was fitting that he, for whom and by whom all things exist, in bringing many sons to glory, should make the founder of their salvation perfect through suffering.[277]

Certainly, in these texts where "πάθημα" (suffering) is used for the sufferings of Christ, it is not used to refer to emotional/verbal suffering/abuse. Therefore, this study concludes that the usage of "παθήμασιν" as it pertains to the suffering of believers points even further to the reality of physical suffering, i.e., physical abuse, torture, and martyrdom.

First Peter 4:14 reads:

> εἰ ὀνειδίζεσθε ἐν ὀνόματι Χριστοῦ, μακάριοι, ὅτι τὸ τῆς δόξης καὶ τὸ τοῦ θεοῦ πνεῦμα ἐφ' ὑμᾶς ἀναπαύεται
>
> If you are insulted for the name of Christ, you are blessed, because the Spirit of glory and of God rests upon you.

---

276. Danker, *Greek-English Lexicon*, 747; Liddell et al., *Greek-English Lexicon*, 1285.

277. This study returns to Hebrews' use of "τελειῶσαι" in the section on 1 Peter 5:9 below.

Elliott and Witherington III show that "εἰ" here is less conditional than it is temporal.[278] Thus, they reject the translation "if," which again emphasizes the "mere possibility," and propose "since" or "when" as a better rendering.[279] The reality that one must suffer in the name of Christ and not for doing evil is emphasized again. The phrase "ὅτι τὸ τῆς δόξης καὶ τὸ τοῦ θεοῦ πνεῦμα ἐφ' ὑμᾶς ἀναπαύεται" (because the Spirit of glory and of God rests upon you) is a difficult one. Selwyn proposes that this is a substantive reference to the Shekinah glory of God as in the Old Testament.[280] This leads to a translation of "the glory and the Spirit of God rest upon you."[281] Forbes and Davids, however, against this view assert that in other places in the New Testament where constructs such as this occur the sense of the neuter article is clear, whereas here that clarity is lacking.[282] Robertson proposes that the repetition of the article serves to emphasize the two genitives.[283] Elliot concurs and posits that this expression forms a hendiadys that expresses a single idea, thus providing the following translation *"because the divine Spirit of glory rests upon you."*[284] In keeping with this, Dubis and Turner propose that it is an epexegetical expression, which leads to a similar translation as Elliott's "the Spirit of glory, that is, the Spirit of God."[285] Davids further agrees and proposes this translation "'the Spirit

---

278. Elliott, *1 Peter*, 778; Witherington III, *Letters and Homilies*, 213.

279. Elliott, *1 Peter*, 778; Witherington III, *Letters and Homilies*, 213.

280. Selwyn, *First Epistle of St. Peter*, 222–24.

281. Davids, *First Epistle of Peter*, 168.

282. Forbes, *Exegetical Guide*, 156; Davids, *First Epistle of Peter*, 167.

283. Robertson, *Grammar of the Greek New Testament*, 785.

284. Elliott, *1 Peter*, 782 (emphasis original).

285. Dubis, "Messianic Woes in First Peter," 188; Turner, *Grammar of New Testament Greek*, 3:187. Davids's translation: "'the Spirit of glory and of God rests upon them,'" falls in line with this view. Davids provides the following reasons for why this translation is to be preferred: "The neuter article before 'of glory' (τὸ τῆς δόξης) appears to make the most sense if it anticipates 'Spirit' (also with a neuter article—καὶ τὸ τοῦ θεοῦ πνεῦμα), which follows after the 'and.' The reasons for this interpretation are that (1) 'the Spirit of God' was a stereotyped phrase that Peter would have tended not to break up, (2) naming glory first balances the 'insult' of the first part of the verse just as 'Spirit of God' balances the 'name of Christ,' and (3) the often-cited examples of the article's being used alone (Matt. 21:21; 1 Cor. 10:24; Jas. 4:14; 2 Pet. 2:22), which would argue for a translation something like 'the glory and the Spirit of God rest upon you,' all occur in stereotyped phrases, of which this is not one" (Davids, *First Epistle of Peter*, 167–68n10).

of glory and of God rests upon them."²⁸⁶ This study affirms these latter three translations but prefers Davids and Dubis's rendering.

Therefore, in this phrase, Peter explains why the believers should rejoice in their suffering, "because the Spirit of glory and of God is resting upon them."²⁸⁷ The idea that God's Spirit rests on his people is not a new one. In the Old Testament, God's spirit is said to rest upon his people and their leaders. Numbers 11:25–26 (LXX) reads:

> καὶ κατέβη κύριος ἐν νεφέλῃ καὶ ἐλάλησεν πρὸς αὐτόν, καὶ παρείλατο ἀπὸ τοῦ πνεύματος τοῦ ἐπ' αὐτῷ καὶ ἐπέθηκεν ἐπὶ τοὺς ἑβδομήκοντα ἄνδρας τοὺς πρεσβυτέρους, ὡς δὲ ἐπανεπαύσατο τὸ πνεῦμα ἐπ' αὐτούς, καὶ ἐπροφήτευσαν καὶ οὐκέτι προσέθεντο. ²⁶ καὶ κατελείφθησαν δύο ἄνδρες ἐν τῇ παρεμβολῇ, ὄνομα τῷ ἑνὶ Ελδαδ καὶ ὄνομα τῷ δευτέρῳ Μωδαδ, καὶ ἐπανεπαύσατο ἐπ' αὐτοὺς τὸ πνεῦμα—καὶ οὗτοι ἦσαν τῶν καταγεγραμμένων καὶ οὐκ ἦλθον πρὸς τὴν σκηνήν—καὶ ἐπροφήτευσαν ἐν τῇ παρεμβολῇ.

> So Moses went out and told the people the words of the Lord. And he gathered seventy men of the elders of the people and placed them around the tent. ²⁵ Then the Lord came down in the cloud and spoke to him, and took some of the Spirit that was on him and put it on the seventy elders. And as soon as the Spirit rested on them, they prophesied. But they did not continue doing it.

Furthermore, Dubis notes the various occurrences of God's Spirit coming upon judges (Judg 3:10; 11:29; 14:6, 19; 15:4), kings (1 Sam 10:6, 10; 11:6; 16:3; 19:23), and prophets (2 Kgs 2:9; 2 Chr 15:1; 20:14).²⁸⁸ In late Judaism, the outpouring of God's Spirit was perceived as an eschatological gift that God would give to his people in the messianic age.²⁸⁹ Most scholars propose that Isaiah 11:2 (LXX) is what lies behind this text in 1 Peter.²⁹⁰ It reads "καὶ ἀναπαύσεται ἐπ' αὐτὸν πνεῦμα τοῦ θεοῦ"²⁹¹ (And the Spirit of

---

286. Davids, *First Epistle of Peter*, 167.

287. My translation.

288. Dubis, "Messianic Woes in First Peter," 179–80.

289. Best, *1 Peter*, 164; Arichea and Nida, *Translator's Handbook*, 149; Dubis, "Messianic Woes in First Peter," 183–89.

290. Elliott, *1 Peter*, 783; Witherington III, *Letters and Homilies*, 213; Arichea and Nida, *Translator's Handbook*, 149; Achtemeier and Epp, *1 Peter*, 307–9; Dubis, "Messianic Woes in First Peter," 179–95; Kistemaker, *New Testament Commentary*, 176; Forbes, *Exegetical Guide*, 156; Goppelt, *Commentary on 1 Peter*, 323; Senior, *1 Peter*, 130; Skaggs, *Pentecostal Commentary*, 65.

291. Isa 11:2 (LXX).

the Lord shall rest upon him), and the parallel is self-evident. Peter, however, changes the original text by replacing the future verb "ἀναπαύσεται" (shall rest) with a present form "ἀναπαύεται" (rests). This, according to Elliott and Senior, denotes the present reality of God's presence with believers.[292] Achtemeier continues that this indicates that the prophecy from Isaiah regarding the future, at least in Peter's mind, had been fulfilled in the present.[293] Furthermore, Hunter, Holmrighausen, and Hiebert propose that there is an allusion to the Shekinah glory which filled the temple in the Old Testament, i.e., Exodus 40.[294] Other New Testament texts that affirm this idea of God's Spirit abiding with Christians during suffering abound. For example, John 16:7–15 speaks of the Spirit coming to help believers. Interestingly, however, this passage falls right after Jesus teaches the disciples about the hatred of the world towards them. Similarly, in Mark 13:11, Luke 12:11–12, and Matthew 10:19–20, the Spirit's helping of believers falls in the middle of a discourse regarding persecution. In Acts 7, Stephen experiences God's glory during his martyrdom. This leads Beare and Goppelt to argue that in Peter's pneumatology the Spirit does not abide with believers as in Paul.[295] Instead, Peter relies on the "gospel tradition" where the Spirit only comes sporadically when believers are suffering.[296] Achtemeier and Dubis sufficiently refutes this view.[297] Dubis convincingly shows that the Jewish expectation of return from exile and the outpouring of the Spirit in Joel 2 saw the Spirit as abiding permanently.[298] This is further attested by Peter's substitution of the future tense in Isaiah 11:2 for the present tense in 1 Peter 4:14, as noted above. This study proposes that Peter might be doing something else.

Instead of having an "earlier" understanding of the Spirit as coming and going depending on circumstances, Peter proposes a dual understanding of the Spirit in the life of the believer. In 1 Peter 1:3, Peter says the believer is called "in the sanctification of the Spirit," and in 3:18 and 3:21 he writes "made alive in the Spirit . . . through baptism," which would agree with Paul's understanding of having received the Spirit. Still further, this

---

292. Elliott, *1 Peter*, 783; Senior, *1 Peter*, 130.

293. Achtemeier and Epp, *1 Peter*, 308.

294. Hunter and Holmrighausen, *First Epistle of Peter*, 12:143; Hiebert, *1 Peter*, 287.

295. Beare, *First Epistle of Peter*, 192; Goppelt, *Commentary on 1 Peter*, 306.

296. Beare, *First Epistle of Peter*, 192; Goppelt, *Commentary on 1 Peter*, 306.

297. Achtemeier and Epp, *1 Peter*, 309; Dubis, "Messianic Woes in First Peter," 191.

298. Dubis, "Messianic Woes in First Peter," 191.

study proposes that there is a special "κοινωνία" (fellowship) that occurs when believers suffer. Indeed, Witherington III, Donelson, and Campbell assert that the Spirit of God is present when believers are suffering, in order to strengthen, comfort, and empower them.[299] This presence, however, is different from the Spirit's normal presence. This is further attested in the early Christian tradition;[300] the Martyrdom of Polycarp reads:

> Μακάρια μὲν οὖν καὶ γενναῖα τὰ μαρτύρια πάντα [τὰ] κατὰ τὸ θέλημα τοῦ Θεοῦ γεγονότα· δεῖ γὰρ εὐλαβεστέρους ἡμᾶς ὑπάρχοντας τῷ Θεῷ τὴν κατὰ πάντων ἐξουσίαν ἀνατιθέναι. τὸ γὰρ γενναῖον αὐτῶν καὶ ὑπομονητικὸν καὶ φιλοδέσποτον τίς οὐκ ἂν θαυμάσειεν; οἳ μάστιξι μὲν καταξανθέντες, ὥστε μέχρι τῶν ἔσω φλεβῶν καὶ ἀρτηριῶν τὴν τῆς σαρκὸς οἰκονομίαν θεωρεῖσθαι, ὑπέμειναν, ὡς καὶ τοὺς περιεστῶτας ἐλεεῖν καὶ ὀδύρεσθαι· τοὺς δὲ καὶ εἰς τοσοῦτον γενναιότητος ἐλθεῖν ὥστε μήτε γρύξαι μήτε στενάξαι τινὰ αὐτῶν ἐπιδεικνυμένους ἅπασιν ἡμῖν ὅτι ἐκείνῃ τῇ ὥρᾳ βασανιζόμενοι τῆς σαρκὸς ἀπεδήμουν οἱ μάρτυρες τοῦ Χριστοῦ, μᾶλλον δὲ ὅτι παρεστὼς ὁ Κύριος ὡμίλει αὐτοῖς.[301]

> Blessed therefore and noble are all the martyrdoms which have taken place according to the will of God (for it behooveth us to be very scrupulous and to assign to God the power over all things). For who could fail to admire their nobleness and patient endurance and loyalty to the Master? seeing that when they were so torn by lashes that the mechanism of their flesh was visible even as far as the inward veins and arteries, they endured patiently, so that the very bystanders had pity and wept; while they themselves reached such a pitch of bravery that none of them uttered a cry or a groan, thus showing to us all that at that hour the martyrs of Christ being tortured were absent from the flesh, or rather that the Lord was standing by and conversing with them.

While these martyrs are being beaten so that "their veins and arteries are visible,"[302] tortured, and finally killed, "the Lord was standing by them and talking to them."[303] Therefore, this study asserts that there is ample evidence to read the "κοινωνεῖτε τοῖς τοῦ Χριστοῦ παθήμασιν . . . τὸ τῆς

---

299. Witherington III, *Letters and Homilies*, 213; Donelson, *I & II Peter and Jude*, 136; Campbell, "Honor, Shame," 207.

300. See also the Passion of Perpetua and Felicita 1:3.

301. Lightfoot, *Apostolic Fathers*, Part II:365–66.

302. My translation.

303. My translation.

δόξης καὶ τὸ τοῦ θεοῦ πνεῦμα ἐφ' ὑμᾶς ἀναπαύεται" (participation in the sufferings of Christ . . . the spirit of God and of glory rests upon you) as a special/mystical fellowship that occurs between the believer and Christ through the Spirit specifically in the context of suffering. This conclusion, in turn, results that if the believer does not suffer there is a "fellowship" with Christ that they will never experience. There is a deep, intimate knowledge ("κοινωνία") that comes only through suffering for his name. Only when one embraces this suffering does one truly unite with Christ himself in a mystical way. Keener notes that this glory in verse 14 refers to God's palpable, manifest aura which shines around him.[304] That which God in the Old Testament proclaims he will give to no other (Isa 42:8) he gives to those who faithfully suffer in Christ's name.

First Peter 4:18

First Peter 4:18 reads:

> καὶ εἰ ὁ δίκαιος μόλις σῴζεται, ὁ ἀσεβὴς καὶ ἁμαρτωλὸς ποῦ φανεῖται;
>
> If the righteous is scarcely saved, what will become of the ungodly and the sinner?

Most scholars agree that 4:18 restates Peter's thought regarding God's judgment in 4:17.[305, 306] Schreiner notes that "μόλις" can either be translated "scarcely" or "with difficulty."[307] However, Peter's thought here is not to convey that they are scarcely snatched from the claws of destruction.[308] Instead, Peter continues his thought from 4:17 that it is through suffering that believers will be saved. Another parallel to this is found in Acts 14:22:

---

304. Keener, *1 Peter*, 88.

305. Kelly, *Epistles of Peter and Jude*, 193; Elliott, *1 Peter*, 802; Davids, *First Epistle of Peter*, 172; Senior, *1 Peter*, 132; Donelson, *I & II Peter and Jude*, 139; Goppelt, *Commentary on 1 Peter*, 333; Schreiner, *1, 2 Peter, Jude*, 228.

306. The arguments from 4:17 will not be repeated here, and this study assumes that the reader is keeping them in mind. These arguments can be found under the heading "Suffering as Judgment" in chapter 3 above.

307. Schreiner, *1, 2 Peter, Jude*, 228.

308. Schreiner, *1, 2 Peter, Jude*, 228.

ἐπιστηρίζοντες τὰς ψυχὰς τῶν μαθητῶν, παρακαλοῦντες ἐμμένειν τῇ πίστει καὶ ὅτι διὰ πολλῶν θλίψεων δεῖ ἡμᾶς εἰσελθεῖν εἰς τὴν βασιλείαν τοῦ θεοῦ

> strengthening the souls of the disciples, encouraging them to continue in the faith, and saying that through many tribulations we must enter the kingdom of God.

Here Paul urges the believers to remain faithful, asserting that "it is necessary for them through many trials and temptations to enter into the kingdom of God."[309] Nida and Arichea affirm that this idea of believers having to endure trials and persecutions in order to inherit eschatological salvation is precisely what "μόλις" refers to here.[310] Jesus promises the severity of believers' suffering in the Gospels. Mark 13:20 reads:

καὶ εἰ μὴ ἐκολόβωσεν κύριος τὰς ἡμέρας, οὐκ ἂν ἐσώθη πᾶσα σάρξ· ἀλλὰ διὰ τοὺς ἐκλεκτοὺς οὓς ἐξελέξατο ἐκολόβωσεν τὰς ἡμέρας.

> And if the Lord had not cut short the days, no human being would be saved. But for the sake of the elect, whom he chose, he shortened the days.

Here Jesus says that the suffering is so severe that the days have to be shortened for the elect to make it. Scholars note that it will be intensely difficult for the righteous to remain faithful to God and that it is only after faithfully enduring that they will be saved.[311] Donelson observes: "The advantage of the Christian does not lie in escaping judgment [i.e., suffering/temptation], but in the combination of redemption, inheritance, and a pattern of a righteousness and holiness."[312] Peter is emphasizing the universality and impartiality of God's judgment.[313] All people will have to give account to their creator without exception.[314] Peter uses this language of judgment and an imminent eschatological horizon to foster a greater impetus for holiness in his audience. Conversely, if one edits out this language of judgment, one loses this moral imperative as well.

---

309. My paraphrase.

310. Arichea and Nida, *Translator's Handbook*, 152.

311. Elliott, *1 Peter*, 801–2; Jobes, *1 Peter*, 294; Kistemaker, *New Testament Commentary*, 181; Senior, *1 Peter*, 132.

312. Donelson, *I & II Peter and Jude*, 139.

313. Elliott, *1 Peter*, 804.

314. Elliott, *1 Peter*, 804.

Furthermore, these scholars affirm that behind this verse lies Proverbs 11:31 (LXX), which reads:

εἰ ὁ μὲν δίκαιος μόλις σῴζεται, ὁ ἀσεβὴς καὶ ἁμαρτωλὸς ποῦ φανεῖται;³¹⁵

If the righteous is repaid on earth, how much more the wicked and the sinner!

Peter preserves the LXX text except for the addition of "καὶ" and the omission of "μὲν." The magnitude of lexical overlap makes Hiebert and Calvin's assertion that Peter is not quoting Proverbs, but rather a popular saying, highly unlikely.³¹⁶ Therefore, this study affirms that Proverbs 11:31 (LXX) is indeed what lies behind this text. However, this might not be the only thing Peter had in mind. It is clear if one reads the Codex Vaticanus, which is the oldest Greek extant manuscript of both Old and New Testaments, that there are no chapter or verse divisions as one finds in modern Bibles.³¹⁷ In the previous sections, it is noted that God uses suffering as a form of discipline for both corrective and purgative purposes.³¹⁸ This study proposes that Peter is saying that here as well. As noted, Proverbs 11:31 (LXX) is clearly behind this text; however, this study asserts that the very next line in the Codex Vaticanus is also in Peter's mind. Proverbs 12:1 (LXX) reads:

ὁ ἀγαπῶν παιδείαν ἀγαπᾷ αἴσθησιν, ὁ δὲ μισῶν ἐλέγχους ἄφρων.

Whoever loves discipline loves knowledge, but he who hates reproof is stupid.

The one who loves instruction develops the "capacity to understand."³¹⁹ Peter, therefore, develops the idea of suffering as God's judgment by affirming that this discipline is both purgative and educational.³²⁰ Marshall

315. Kelly, *Epistles of Peter and Jude,* 193; Elliott, *1 Peter,* 802; Davids, *First Epistle of Peter,* 172; Senior, *1 Peter,* 132; Donelson, *I & II Peter and Jude,* 139; Goppelt, *Commentary on 1 Peter,* 333; Schreiner, *1, 2 Peter, Jude,* 228; Marshall, *1 Peter,* 157; Witherington III, *Letters and Homilies,* 217; Jobes, *1 Peter,* 294.

316. Calvin, *Commentaries on the Catholic Epistles,* 312; Hiebert, *1 Peter,* 293.

317. "Codex Vaticanus."

318. See chapter 2 ("Jewish Understanding of Suffering," "Greek Understanding of Suffering") and chapter 3 ("Suffering as Judgment").

319. My translation. Quotation from Danker, *Greek-English Lexicon,* 29, his translation for "αἴσθησιν."

320. For more on this, see Talbert, *Learning through Suffering.*

proposes the reason that God wills this suffering for believers is that evil can only be destroyed through suffering.[321] This is to say that man's sinful nature can only be trained and conformed to the image of Christ through purgative and educational suffering. Furthermore, Hebrews 5:8–9 reads:

> καίπερ ὢν υἱός, ἔμαθεν ἀφ' ὧν ἔπαθεν τὴν ὑπακοήν, καὶ τελειωθεὶς ἐγένετο ...

> although he was a son, he learned obedience through what he suffered. And being made perfect ...

Christ learns obedience through his sufferings and is made perfect by them. If this is true of Christ, how much more is it true of his followers? It is through suffering that God judges, teaches, and perfects believers into the image of his beloved Son. Peter weaves two aspects of judgment into one statement: a judgment that cleanses them and instructs them to walk in his ways.

First Peter 5:9

The final section of this chapter looks at 1 Peter 5:9. It reads:

> ᾧ ἀντίστητε στερεοὶ τῇ πίστει εἰδότες τὰ αὐτὰ τῶν παθημάτων τῇ ἐν κόσμῳ ὑμῶν ἀδελφότητι ἐπιτελεῖσθαι.

> Resist him, firm in your faith, knowing that the same kinds of suffering are being experienced by your brotherhood throughout the world.

Scholars agree that "ᾧ ἀντίστητε στερεοὶ τῇ πίστει" refers to the believers resisting the devil.[322] Faith here refers to the orientation of one's entire life towards God, according to Goppelt, more so than the intellectual acknowledgment of facts.[323] Furthermore, faith here is living in obedience to God in the midst of testing; this is the true expression of faith.[324] Scholars provide two different translations for "εἰδότες." On the one hand, Marshall, Davids, Wand, Witherington III, and others assert that the

---

321. Marshall, *1 Peter*, 157.

322. Achtemeier and Epp, *1 Peter*, 342–43; Jobes, *1 Peter*, 314; Elliott, *1 Peter*, 861–63; Marshall, *1 Peter*, 170–171.

323. Goppelt, *Commentary on 1 Peter*, 362.

324. Goppelt, *Commentary on 1 Peter*, 362.

correct translation of this participle is "knowing that."³²⁵ Conversely, Beare, Best, and Bigg posit that it should be translated "knowing how."³²⁶ These scholars argue that "οἶδα" without "ὅτι" must mean "knowing how."³²⁷ Davids, however, asserts that in Luke 4:41 and in 1 Clement 62:3 "οἶδα" without "ὅτι" can mean "know that" when followed by an infinitive.³²⁸ This study affirms that the participle is best translated as "knowing that." One final contention arises regarding the word "ἐπιτελεῖσθαι." Most translations translate this word as "undergoing,"³²⁹ "experienced,"³³⁰ "going through,"³³¹ and "being experienced."³³² Jobes, Goppelt, Hiebert, and others agree with this translation.³³³ Others disagree.³³⁴ Dubis writes, "Such translations . . . fail to communicate the goal-orientation of ἐπιτελέω."³³⁵ Liddell and Scott define "τελέω" as "*fulfil, accomplish, execute, perform.*"³³⁶ The *TDNT*, furthermore, asserts that "ἐπιτελέω" is a strengthened form of τελέω with no special distinction in use."³³⁷ In the LXX, the meaning of "ἐπιτελέω is to accomplish, do something to someone, or carry through to the finish, i.e., to complete."³³⁸ First Esdras 4:55 (LXX) reads:

325. Marshall, *1 Peter,* 171; Davids, *First Epistle of Peter,* 193–94; Wand, "Lessons of First Peter," 387–99; Witherington III, *Letters and Homilies,* 239; Schreiner, *1, 2 Peter, Jude,* 244; Elliott, *1 Peter,* 861–63; Dubis, "Messianic Woes in First Peter," 106–9; Jobes, *1 Peter,* 314; Kistemaker, *New Testament Commentary,* 203; Senior, *1 Peter,* 148; Michaels, *1 Peter,* 300–301.

326. Beare, *First Epistle of Peter,* 205–6; Bigg, *Critical and Exegetical Commentary,* 125; Best, *1 Peter,* 175.

327. Beare, *First Epistle of Peter,* 205–6; Bigg, *Critical and Exegetical Commentary,* 125; Best, *1 Peter,* 175.

328. Davids, *First Epistle of Peter,* 193n23.

329. NRSV, NIV, NAB.

330. NKJV.

331. TEV, NEB.

332. ESV.

333. Jobes, *1 Peter,* 315; Goppelt, *Commentary on 1 Peter,* 363–64; Donelson, *I & II Peter and Jude,* 151; Campbell, "Honor, Shame," 226; Schreiner, *1, 2 Peter, Jude,* 224.

334. *TDNT,* 8:60; Kelly, *Epistles of Peter and Jude,* 211; Dubis, "Messianic Woes in First Peter," 106–9; Elliott, *1 Peter,* 862; Kistemaker, *New Testament Commentary,* 203; Senior, *1 Peter,* 148; Skaggs, *Pentecostal Commentary,* 72; Witherington III, *Letters and Homilies,* 239.

335. Dubis, "Messianic Woes in First Peter," 107.

336. Liddell et al., *Greek-English Lexicon,* 1771 (emphasis original).

337. *TDNT,* 8:60.

338. *TDNT,* 8:60.

EXEGETICAL ANALYSIS

καὶ τοῖς Λευίταις ἔγραψεν δοῦναι τὴν χορηγίαν ἕως ἧς ἡμέρας ἐπιτελεσθῇ ὁ οἶκος καὶ Ιερουσαλημ οἰκοδομηθῆναι

and likewise for the charges of the Levites, to be given them until the day that the house was completed, and Jerusalem built up

Speaking of the temple, the author uses "ἐπιτελεσθῇ" to speak of the "completion" of the temple. First Kings 3:9 (LXX) reads:

ἐν τῇ ἡμέρᾳ ἐκείνῃ ἐπεγερῶ ἐπὶ Ηλι πάντα, ὅσα ἐλάλησα εἰς τὸν οἶκον αὐτοῦ, ἄρξομαι καὶ ἐπιτελέσω.

On that day I will fulfill against Eli all that I have spoken concerning his house, from beginning to end.

God will "complete/ἐπιτελέσω" everything that he has spoken against Eli's house.[339] Zechariah 4:9 (LXX) affirms this usage:

Αἱ χεῖρες Ζοροβαβελ ἐθεμελίωσαν τὸν οἶκον τοῦτον, καὶ αἱ χεῖρες αὐτοῦ ἐπιτελέσουσιν αὐτόν.

The hands of Zerubbabel have laid the foundation of this house; his hands shall also complete it.

Here again, the author uses "ἐπιτελέσουσιν" to refer to the completion of something. This usage is carried over into the New Testament. Second Corinthians 7:1 reads:

Ταύτας οὖν ἔχοντες τὰς ἐπαγγελίας, ἀγαπητοί, καθαρίσωμεν ἑαυτοὺς ἀπὸ παντὸς μολυσμοῦ σαρκὸς καὶ πνεύματος, ἐπιτελοῦντες ἁγιωσύνην ἐν φόβῳ θεοῦ

Since we have these promises, beloved, let us cleanse ourselves from every defilement of body and spirit, bringing holiness to completion in the fear of God.

The believers' holiness is "completed/ἐπιτελοῦντες" by cleansing themselves from every defilement.[340] Acts 13:29 reads:

ὡς δὲ ἐτέλεσαν πάντα τὰ περὶ αὐτοῦ γεγραμμένα, καθελόντες ἀπὸ τοῦ ξύλου ἔθηκαν εἰς μνημεῖον

And when they had carried out all that was written of him, they took him down from the tree and laid him in a tomb

---

339. My translation.
340. See also *TDNT*, 8:60–61.

Here "all that had been written"[341] "was completed/ ἐτέλεσαν."[342] Second Corinthians 12:9 reads:

καὶ εἴρηκέν μοι· ἀρκεῖ σοι ἡ χάρις μου, ἡ γὰρ δύναμις ἐν ἀσθενείᾳ τελεῖται

But he said to me, "My grace is sufficient for you, for my power is made perfect in weakness

Here God's power is completed/brought to its fullness in Paul's weakness. Finally, Philippians 1:6 drives this point home:

πεποιθὼς αὐτὸ τοῦτο, ὅτι ὁ ἐναρξάμενος ἐν ὑμῖν ἔργον ἀγαθὸν ἐπιτελέσει ἄχρι ἡμέρας Χριστοῦ Ἰησοῦ.

And I am sure of this, that he who began a good work in you will bring it to completion at the day of Jesus Christ.

Paul contrasts "ἐναρξάμενος" with "ἐπιτελέσει"; "God started the work and will complete it."[343] The Shepherd of Hermas, furthermore, affirms this usage of "ἐπιτελέω":

οἷς παρέδωκεν ὁ κύριος πᾶσαν τὴν κτίσιν αὐτοῦ αὔξειν καὶ οἰκοδομεῖν καὶ δεσπόζειν τῆς κτίσεως πάσης· διὰ τούτων οὖν τελεσθήσεται ἡ οἰκοδομὴ τοῦ πύργου.

These are the holy angels of God, who were first created, and to whom the Lord handed over his whole creation, that they might increase and build up and rule over the whole creation. By these will the building of the tower be finished.[344]

Here the angels of the Lord are said to "complete/τελεσθήσεται" the building of the house. Clearly, in the LXX, New Testament, and the postapostolic fathers, "ἐπιτελέω" does not bear the meaning "experienced" but rather to complete. In agreement with Dubis, Elliott, and others, this study proposes that Peter uses "ἐπιτελέω" in the same way.[345] Indeed, this verb

341. My translation.
342. My translation.
343. My translation.
344. Shepherd of Hermas, "Shepherd of Hermas," Vision 3.4.1.
345. Dubis, "Messianic Woes in First Peter," 106–9; Elliott, *1 Peter*, 862; Kistemaker, *New Testament Commentary*, 203; Senior, *1 Peter*, 148; Skaggs, *Pentecostal Commentary*, 72; Witherington III, *Letters and Homilies*, 239; Kelly, *Epistles of Peter and Jude*, 211. Although most of these scholars prefer to translate "ἐπιτελέω" as "accomplished," it bears more or less the same meaning.

bears the meaning of "complete."³⁴⁶ The suffering believers are experiencing is not meaningless but come upon them to complete a purpose.³⁴⁷ Gartner concludes that *"Thus the Christian awaits not the end of suffering but its goal."*³⁴⁸ This study, therefore, proposes the following translation for 1 Peter 5:9: "Resisting the devil, firm in your faith, knowing that your sufferings are bringing the brotherhood to completion."³⁴⁹ The sufferings that the believers are experiencing are bringing them to completion. They are being cleansed, shaped, and conformed to the image of Christ. Indeed, this suffering is what facilitates their Christian formation.

This chapter shows seven things. Firstly, suffering is indeed necessary according to 1 Peter. Secondly, suffering comes from God and is in accordance with his will for the believer. Thirdly, however, suffering has to be "as a Christian" that is doing what is in keeping with God's commands. Suffering for doing evil has no value. Furthermore, their suffering is the beginning of God's final judgment. Fourthly, this suffering/judgment can be retributive (i.e., punishment for sin), educational (i.e., to correct the believer who has gone astray), or it can be purgative (i.e., to cleanse the believer from sin and shape them into the image of Christ). However, it can also be all three at once. Fifthly, and moreover, this chapter shows that "λυπηθέντας," "πειρασμοῖς," "δοκίμιον," "πυρὸς," "δοκιμαζομένου," "παθήματα," and "παθόντος" all affirm the conclusion from chapter 2 that the believers' suffering was not merely verbal or emotional, but physical—and painfully so. Sixth, in the discussion on "ἐπιτελέω," this study concludes that it does not refer to the believers' experience of suffering, but to the reality that this suffering completes them. This finding even further strengthens the necessity of suffering in Christian formation. Without suffering the believer cannot reach their goal, i.e., being formed into the image of Christ and thus attaining unto eschatological salvation. Finally, and most importantly, is the reality of a "special" "κοινωνία" that occurs between the believer and Christ as they suffer for his name. There is an entire dimension of Christ that will remain a mystery to the believer until they have embraced "ποικίλοις πειρασμοῖς" (various trials), which, according to Peter, facilitate "κοινωνεῖτε τοῖς τοῦ Χριστοῦ παθήμασιν" (the fellowship in the sufferings of Christ).

---

346. Elliott, *1 Peter*, 861.
347. Green, *1 Peter*, 175; Senior, *1 Peter*, 148; Skaggs, *Pentecostal Commentary*, 72.
348. Burkhard Gartner, "Suffering," 3:725 (emphasis added).
349. My translation.

Chapter 4

Conclusion

LET'S RECAP. EVERY CHRISTIAN will suffer at some point in their walk with Christ. This book endeavors to show that not only is it unavoidable, but it is also God ordained since this suffering forms an essential part of holistic formation. Based on Peter's first letter, chapter 2 provided contextual support and chapter 3 exegetical support for this statement. We now move on to extrapolate what the conclusions of these chapters mean for Christians today. How should we understand God's role in suffering, how does suffering bring about Christian formation, and what is its effect on our relationship with Christ?

PETER'S EXAMPLE

But first, allow me a short detour back to the questions of authorship and the nature of Peter's martyrdom. The question of authorship may seem mundane to the reader. In fact, in contemporary hermeneutical theory where the reader is the source of meaning, authorship is often deemed irrelevant.[1] The thought goes that whether Peter wrote it, or whether there was a Petrine circle, does not alter the meaning of the text. This is an unhelpful line of thinking. If we were to make sense of the letter's message, it matters a great deal who wrote it and how the author engaged with suffering. Moreover, if the Christian Scriptures are deemed to be the word of God, breathed out by God through the human authors for a specific purpose, then ambivalence to these details negates the reliability of the text. If one

---

1. See Vanhoozer, *Is There a* Meaning?, 43–97. His chapter on undoing the author provides an excellent overview of postmodern/contemporary hermeneutical theory.

CONCLUSION

is unable to trust the letter's self-attestation that Peter is indeed the author (1:1) then how could one be expected to trust the rest of the content? If one denies Petrine authorship, one might just as well deny that Jesus suffered and died for our sins (2:24), that Jesus is the model for us to follow (2:22–23), and that God is coming back to judge (1:17). This can lead to the inability to distinguish between Scripture and whatever devotional book one may be reading. To affirm Petrine authorship, then, is to affirm that the Scriptures are God-breathed and that they are true and trustworthy.

Regarding the matter of Peter's martyrdom, it might not be "scientifically" verifiable whether Peter was martyred in Rome or not. However, chapter 2 shows that all the evidence that we have from the early church is unanimous; Ignatius, Eusebius, Clement of Rome, Clement of Alexandria, Tertullian, Dionysus, Gaius, as well as the Acts of Peter all point to the fact that from AD 95 onwards the church has always believed that Peter was indeed martyred in Rome. This is further affirmed by Bauckham and Bockmuehl who show that the reception history in the first 200 years AD unanimously affirms Peter's martyrdom. It is striking that there are no competing traditions regarding the nature of his martyrdom. All existing evidence points to the fact that Peter was martyred in Rome under Emperor Nero.

Why does this matter? I would propose that it is Peter's martyrdom that provides legitimacy to his letter. Peter asserts that Jesus is the example who is to be followed (2:21–24). After writing this, contra some contemporary teachers who tell their followers to do things they themselves are unwilling to do, Peter paves the way by example. If Peter, an apostle, was willing to pay the ultimate price for his allegiance to Christ, how much more should we be willing to pay that price? The *Imitatio Christi* remains the core of all Christian formation. It is easy to emphasize this imitation when it comes to Jesus' miraculous endeavors or his caring for the disenfranchised. However, when it comes to suffering *like* Jesus did, there seems to be a serious disconnect. Benedictine monk Hubert van Zeller exclaims:

> If it was right for Christ to go by the way of suffering to the final possession of his glory, it is right also for us. We are members of his body. The limbs must go the way of the head; the parts may not choose one way of going to the father while the whole chooses another. What Christ endures, we endure; what Christ enjoys, we enjoy. There is only this difference: he does it in his degree, we in ours.[2]

2. Zeller, *Mystery of Suffering*, 1.

Peter not only exhorts us that God deems it commendable when we imitate Jesus through suffering, but he also follows his own advice through martyrdom.

GOD'S PROVIDENCE AND SUFFERING

It is plausible to accept that all of us go through undesirable experiences and that they can be transformative if we set our minds on responding in a constructive manner. Even nonbelievers can embrace this train of thought. Probably more unsettling is the fact that God brings certain forms of suffering into our lives. Peter describes this kind of suffering as "according to the will of God" (4:19). We understand from his letter that we can suffer in illegitimate ways when it is brought upon us by our own foolishness (2:20) or evil actions (3:14). Jesus also affirms this in John 5 when he says to the man that he had healed from paralysis at the pool of Bethesda: "See, you are well! Sin no more, that nothing worse may happen to you."[3] Blomberg and Thomas assert that for the believer to continue in sin will most definitely lead to more suffering.[4] However, it would be foolish to assume that when someone suffers the only logical deduction is that they are caught in sin. Ask Job's friends! Peter is saying that God deems it necessary for the believer to suffer certain things and that God brings these things into the believer's life. In this chapter's elaboration on suffering, the reader can assume that it is this kind of suffering that is under discussion.

The key, then, in suffering well lies in our trust in divine providence.[5] Providence, from the Latin word *providentia*, means to foresee, and provide.[6] Thus, providence refers to God's capacity to foresee what is in our best interest and provide exactly what we need in order to reach our ultimate good. Van Zeller describes it as follows: "that when we have to suffer, we can safely assume that God has allowed this particular trial for our sanctification."[7] The aim of life with God is not for us to experience the least amount of discomfort and the most pleasure possible;[8] rather, our aim should be to handle every situation, "whether pleasurable or painful,"

---

3. John 5:14 ESV.
4. Blomberg, *Can We Still Believe in God?*, 12; Thomas, "Stop Sinning," 3–20.
5. Zeller, *Mystery of Suffering*, 4.
6. Lewis and Short, *Harper's Latin Dictionary*, 1480.
7. Zeller, *Mystery of Suffering*, 4.
8. Zeller, *Mystery of Suffering*, 5.

Conclusion

in a way that displays our devotion to God.[9] Suffering, when embraced as something for our sanctification, becomes the ultimate expression of our trust in God.

It is essential that we remind ourselves that God possesses knowledge and wisdom that remains outside of our grasp. The prophet Isaiah proclaims, "For as the heavens are higher than the earth, so are my ways higher than your ways and my thoughts than your thoughts."[10] Compared to God's vision, humanity's vision is severely limited. We cannot even predict the weather with relative accuracy more than a week in advance. Yet, we feel comfortable to assume that we know what is necessary for us to be able to walk in God's purposes for our lives five years from now. Old Testament scholar Tom Keiser says that the essence of the original sin in Genesis 3 is the lack of trust that God knows what is in our best interest.[11] The fall happens because we usurp the role of determining what we need. We desire to be able to decide for ourselves what is going to be the best course of action. We deny God his right to call us wherever he deems fit. We assume that we know what we need in order to accomplish our purpose in this life. This is the very essence of sin. We forget that it is not our purpose that we are seeking to accomplish, but God's purpose for our lives and this world. Therefore, he is the only one who can determine what is necessary for us to achieve it. One must acquire the requisite amount of humility to accept the limitations that our fleshly and contingent existence places upon us. God is God, and we are not. It is in some ways blasphemous to even try to assume that our plans are better than his plans. In the same way, at least for this author, it is blasphemous to call God's goodness into question simply because things did not turn out the way that we wanted. Our capacity is so severely limited that to try and tell God what is good and what is not is the ultimate expression of arrogance and rebellion. God is the Good Shepherd, and he can see things that we cannot. First Peter 4:19 says, "Therefore let those who suffer according to God's will entrust their souls to a faithful Creator while doing good." Our disposition must be one of humility, submission, and trust in his goodness.

There are a couple of pitfalls which must first be addressed. The first is the position of the Stoic who simply knuckles down and does not allow the circumstances to get to them. The second is the one of the fatalist who does

---

9. Zeller, *Mystery of Suffering*, 5.
10. Isa 55:9 ESV.
11. Tom Keiser at a chapel event at Regent University in Fall of 2021.

nothing because what does it help to kick against what fate has decreed? The problem with these two approaches is that they invariably lead to simply enduring the suffering. If we can only make it through this, they will say, maybe greener pastures await us. Christians are not called to passively surrender to suffering but to embrace it. They can embrace the suffering not because they like to suffer more than anybody else, but because they have glimpsed its origin, i.e., from a God who cares for them and wants their good. Furthermore, they have discerned its purpose, i.e., to form Christ within them. This must in no way be perceived as a one-off process.

The Christian response includes all the variations of human emotions and just a cursory reading of the book of Psalms illustrates how the Christian can grapple with hardship through grief and lament. Perhaps this is best illustrated by Jesus' prayer in the garden of Gethsemane. The text in Luke's Gospel portrays Jesus in this manner: "being in agony he prayed more earnestly; and his sweat became like great drops of blood falling down to the ground."[12] There is clear engagement with God about the reality that Jesus does not want to go down this road. He prays: "Father, if you are willing, remove this cup from me."[13] However, this engagement brings about surrender: "Nevertheless, not my will, but yours, be done."[14] He does not embrace God's will for his life because it happened to be what he wanted to do anyway. He also doesn't exhibit indifference (stoicism) or passive resignation (fatalism). He petitions God to release him from the suffering, but he is willing to surrender himself to the will of the Father.

We would be mistaken to assume that this process of embracing divine providence is a one-off process. Louise Kretzschmar's framework for conversion is helpful to illustrate how believers go through various steps in this process of surrender.[15] Kretzschmar proposes five conversions that take place in believers as we grapple with the Scriptures, namely: intellectual, affective, volitional, relational, and moral. Whilst Kretzschmar's work is primarily in hermeneutical practice and theory, it can also be instructive for Christian formation as one orients oneself to God in the process of suffering as well.[16]

---

12. Luke 22:44 ESV.
13. Luke 22:42 ESV.
14. Luke 22:42 ESV.
15. Kretzschmar, "Authentic Christian Leadership," 41–60.
16. Bekker, "Scriptural Formation," 99–100. The table below is owed to Bekker's masterful analysis and exposition of Kretzschmar's work. Please refer to it in future

CONCLUSION

1. **Intellectual Conversion**—A reformation of the believer's thoughts and perceptions occurs as one evaluates one's own moral framework, as well as the moral framework of society at large, against that of the Scriptures. The purpose is to reach "prudence" or "correct judgment" through the assimilation of a biblical thought world.[17]

2. **Affective Conversion**—As one engages with the Scriptures, the believer's values are converted to reflect that of the scriptural witness. It should lead to the embracing of what Bekker calls "*orthokardia*" or a "right heartedness towards God." One evaluates one's ultimate affections and adopts various biblical, historical, and ascetic disciplines "in service to the world" so that one's affections might be transformed.[18]

3. **Volitional Conversion**—This involves seeking "a redeemed human will that moves from willfulness (identified as arrogant self-sufficiency) to willingness (described as flexible receptivity) in a quest to be formed and to serve."[19]

4. **Relational Conversion**—As the Scriptures are read one seeks to have one's moral conscience formed as a community. As a result, with a renewed understanding of relationships one engages these personal and communal relationships with an emphasis on how one can best serve one's neighbor.

5. **Moral Action**—Finally, once the previous four conversions have been achieved, it motivates moral action that can transform the communities within which we live.

The reader can see why this framework is so helpful. Intellectual conversion results in a reformation of what the believer deems to be good and evil. If one's framework has taken a scriptural shape rather than a cultural one, then suffering can be embraced because it is no longer viewed from a societal morality which despises suffering and views the goal of life as happiness and pleasure. Furthermore, in affective conversion, the believer is forced to consider that which one values the most: God's will or one's own definition of the good life and the consequent pursuit of flourishing.

---

citation.
17. Bekker, "Scriptural Formation," 99.
18. Bekker, "Scriptural Formation," 100.
19. Bekker, "Scriptural Formation," 100.

As right-heartedness is formed in the believer, it causes one to become able to gladly embrace God's will.

Affective conversion encapsulates a three-step framework for embracing suffering suggested by van Zeller, namely 1) resignation, 2) acceptance, and 3) choice.[20] It starts with resignation "to the will of God" in whatever circumstance one finds oneself, and acceptance of whatever God deems necessary to send into one's life.[21] As a created being, the believer resigns himself to God as the Creator, and recognizes that submission to God's plan brings him glory and results in one's own sanctification.[22] There are some who would view this "resignation" to something that is contrary to one's own desires as inauthentic, but that is a terribly postmodern way of perceiving reality. Van Zeller comments: "Resignation in the true sense does not make people impervious, indifferent; it makes them hopeful. It means that they have refused to be defeated by their sufferings, and as a result they come through with a deeper realization of what suffering is designed to do."[23] It frees the believer from the temptation to complain about one's troubles and from the obsession to constantly look for a way out.[24] Consequently, one moves up the ladder towards "acceptance."[25] This assumes a more cooperative stance where the believer is willing to cooperate with God's will. It looks at both the past and future and remains undisturbed, because the believer has become content to trust in God's providence, i.e., God's capacity and willingness to love, care, and provide, regardless of circumstance.

To return to Bekker and Kretzschmar's table above, point three is where the rubber hits the road. During volitional conversion, one's will, or volition, is transformed from "willfulness" to "willingness."[26] The believer willingly embraces whatever God sends into one's life because one can accept that it is good. One moves from "resignation" to what van Zeller calls "welcome."[27] The believer does not only accept God's will but embraces it as a good and perfect gift. This then leads to relational conversion and moral

20. Zeller, *Mystery of Suffering*, 75–91.
21. Zeller, *Mystery of Suffering*, 75.
22. Zeller, *Mystery of Suffering*, 75–76.
23. Zeller, *Mystery of Suffering*, 78–79.
24. Zeller, *Mystery of Suffering*, 79.
25. Zeller, *Mystery of Suffering*, 81.
26. Bekker, "Scriptural Formation," 100.
27. Zeller, *Mystery of Suffering*, 88.

action where the believer can look past his or her own desires and start acting in a manner beneficial to the community, even at the expense of himself. Reinhold Niebuhr's prayer is a fitting conclusion:

> God, grant me the serenity to accept the things I cannot change, courage to change the things I can, and wisdom to know the difference. Living one day at a time, enjoying one moment at a time, accepting hardship as the pathway to peace. Taking, as Jesus did, this sinful world as it is, not as I would have it. Trusting that he will make all things right if I surrender to his will. That I may be reasonably happy in this life, and supremely happy with him forever in the next.[28]

SUFFERING EMPOWERS THE BELIEVER

Dovetailing on the need for relational conversion and moral action in the process of conversion, allow me to propose that suffering has the unique ability to grow a person's capacity for sacrifice. Sacrifice, or forsaking our own interests, is a key component of our walk with Christ and probably one of the most striking indicators of Christian maturity. When we offer our lives to him and to one another in an effort to love as he has loved us (John 15:12) it more often than not includes making choices that we would rather avoid. What if suffering helps us to mature into believers who are able to choose sacrifice when we have the option to choose otherwise? In other words, what if unavoidable hardship creates resilience in us that empowers us to willingly embark on difficult paths for the sake of Christ? Van Zeller describes it as follows:

> The Christian who runs away from the first suggestion of discomfort will back away from the challenge of sacrifice. And the challenge to sacrifice himself on one or other altar of life—whether in marriage, in a religious vocation, supplying the needs of others, and the demands of a job, political principle, or simply as a witness to truth—is inevitably bound to present itself.[29]

If one shirks from discomfort, then one will remain unwilling to lay down one's life for God and neighbor. None of us are particularly disposed to embracing sacrifice or discomfort. When situations present themselves

---

28. Niebuhr, "Serenity Prayer," lines from full version. Replaced "he" with "Jesus" to reflect the original.
29. Zeller, *Mystery of Suffering*, 7.

where we need to choose the good of the other at our own expense, it takes maturity to resist our own needs and desires, a maturity that develops as we endure hardship. Insert times of unexpected suffering and suddenly we find ourselves in an environment where our capacity for hardship is expanded. Paul writes about this process to the Romans: "Not only that, but we rejoice in our sufferings, knowing that suffering produces endurance, and endurance produces character, and character produces hope, and hope does not put us to shame, because God's love has been poured into our hearts through the Holy Spirit who has been given to us."[30] When we are forced by suffering to endure discomfort, we can more easily choose voluntary discomfort for the sake of others when the situation presents itself. The book of Hebrews says that "Christ learned obedience through the things he suffered."[31] The resistance that Jesus experienced presented him with the opportunity to act in holiness and obedience to God. It is somewhat of a mystery that the Son of God "learned obedience," but it is safe to assume that if Jesus needed to learn obedience, you and I surely need to learn it too. If we embrace it, suffering can be a wonderful teacher that comes alongside us to mature us and build our resilience for godly living.

Suffering does not only enlarge one's capacity for self-sacrifice, but it also comes with a promise of increased power. This might sound paradoxical, but it is the same paradox that is present in Paul's words to the Corinthians: "For when I am weak, then I am strong."[32] This statement is preceded by Paul describing his thorn in the flesh. In 2 Corinthians 12:7–8, Paul laments to God to remove a "thorn in his side" which is "harassing" him.[33] The Greek term behind "harass" here is "κολαφίζῃ," which means "to strike sharply *with the fist*" or to "*beat*" in order "to cause physical impairment, *torment*."[34] Paul is taking a serious beating from this "messenger of Satan." Three times Paul asks God to intervene in this serious and painful situation. Yet, God responds: "My grace is sufficient for you, for my power is made perfect in weakness."[35] Not only does God give sufficient grace to us in trials, but his power is perfected in our weakened state. Thus, Paul

---

30. Rom 5:3–5 ESV.

31. Heb 5:8, my translation.

32. 2 Cor 12:10 ESV.

33. ESV.

34. Danker, *Greek-English Lexicon*, 555 (emphasis original; bold removed from original).

35. 2 Cor 12:7–8 ESV.

says: "Therefore I will boast all the more gladly of my weaknesses, so that the power of Christ may rest upon me."[36] There is an important lesson to learn here: the power of God comes to rest on the believer in a situation of weakness precipitated by suffering. It might not sound pleasant, but that is the scriptural witness. If we do not embrace the situation, we might never experience the power of God to the degree that he wants us to. In 2 Corinthians 4:7–11, Paul, in a similar vein, says:

> But we have this treasure in jars of clay, to show that the surpassing power belongs to God and not to us. We are afflicted in every way, but not crushed; perplexed, but not driven to despair; persecuted, but not forsaken; struck down, but not destroyed; always carrying in the body the death of Jesus, so that the life of Jesus may also be manifested in our bodies. For we who live are always being given over to death for Jesus' sake, so that the life of Jesus also may be manifested in our mortal flesh."[37]

Suffering reminds us that any virtue, gift, or blessing is from God and not from within ourselves. Thus, all glory is ascribed to his name and not us. Also, Paul defines his affliction, despair, crushing, and persecution as carrying in his body "the death of Jesus"; this points to a participation in the mystery of Christ's death. This participation leads to the manifestation of life, both in Paul's life and in the lives of his followers. There will be no life without death, and certainly no resurrection without a cross. As disciples of Jesus and ministers of the gospel we can only experience eternal change if God's life and power are present amongst us. We might think that this happens when we are strong and successful, but the nature of Jesus' death and the ministry of his followers shows us otherwise. It is amidst the presence of weakness and death where true life and power arises.

SUFFERING FACILITATES UNION WITH CHRIST

To restate something from chapter 3, suffering presents believers with an interesting paradox.[38] These trials have the potential both for glory and tragedy.[39] They can either develop and deepen the spiritual life of the believer,

---

36. 2 Cor 12:7–8 ESV.
37. ESV.
38. Green, *1 Peter*, 30.
39. Green, *1 Peter*, 30.

or they can stunt and corrupt it.⁴⁰ It's much like hot water which hardens the egg but softens the potato. Indeed, to quote Green: "'testing' comprises a crisis of decision, of faithfulness, of outcome, since it is at one and the same time the opportunity for the refiner's fire to carry out its work of purifying faith and the opportunity for diabolic forces to wrestle God's people away from their faith through temptation."⁴¹ The key to which purpose prevails lies in the response of the believer to this "suffering." If the believer assumes that suffering cannot be from God, or that it points to their lack of faith that can be fixed by embracing the right mindset, their response will be one of confusion and resistance. The enemy might then be able to tempt the believer to turn away from God because of a discontentment with how things are panning out. However, if the believer understands that God prunes and purifies us through suffering, it can be embraced and subsumed under a higher purpose. In fact, it can then lead to one of the ultimate outcomes of suffering: union with God.

Union with God can be described as a deep "κοινωνία/fellowship" with the Godhead. For Peter, suffering is nothing less than a participation in the sufferings of Christ himself, and as Christians embrace suffering it becomes the vehicle through which they can enter into "the mystery of Christ's passion."⁴² This is the apex of suffering: without it, there is an entire dimension of God that will remain unknowable to the believer. Recall the phrase, the "Spirit of glory and of God rests upon you." It refers to God's palpable glory that shines around him. That which God will share with no other (Isa 42:8) he causes to rest on those who suffer faithfully in his name. In other words, there is a special abiding of the Spirit on the believer as they endure suffering as a Christian. An example from church history helps parse this out.

In "The Martyrdom of Perpetua and Felicitas," the following story is recounted.⁴³ Perpetua, a young, twenty-two-year-old woman, well-educated and from a family of means, becomes a Christian.⁴⁴ Due to her conversion, she is thrown into a dungeon along with other Christians.⁴⁵ At the

40. Green, *1 Peter*, 30.
41. Green, *1 Peter*, 227.
42. Zeller, *Mystery of Suffering*, 8.
43. For the entire story, see Roberts et al., "Martyrdom."
44. Roberts et al., "Martyrdom," 699–700.
45. Roberts et al., "Martyrdom," 699–700.

CONCLUSION

time, she is also nursing her young child.[46] Her father seeks to persuade her to recant and thus be set free, even using her son as leverage.[47] She then asks her father a question:

> 'Father,' said I, 'do you see, let us say, this vessel lying here to be a little pitcher, or something else?' And he said, 'I see it to be so.' And I replied to him, 'Can it be called by any other name than what it is?' And he said, 'No.'[48] She then with great resolve answers to him "Neither can I call myself anything else than what I am, a Christian."[49]

Her father then abandons her, and she is left to face whatever the Romans have in store for her.[50] Her brother, who is in prison with her, comes to her and says, "My dear sister, you are already in a position of great dignity, and are such that you may ask for a vision, and that it may be made known to you whether this is to result in a passion or an escape."[51] Then something extraordinary happens. Perpetua replies: "And I, who knew that I was privileged to converse with the Lord . . . asked, and this was what was shown me."[52] She then goes on to recount the vision that she received from the Lord about her impending martyrdom.[53] Theologically, there is the assumption in this martyrdom account that if one is faithful to suffer for the name of Christ then one receives the privilege to receive visions and insight from the Lord. This is no different from the "κοινωνία" that results from "Spirit of glory and of God resting upon you." There is a special communion that happens between the believer and God when one embraces suffering for his name. The same pattern can be seen with Stephen, the first martyr in the book of Acts. Consider this passage:

> Now when they heard these things they were enraged, and they ground their teeth at him. But he, full of the Holy Spirit, gazed into heaven and saw the glory of God, and Jesus standing at the right hand of God. And he said, "Behold, I see the heavens opened, and the Son of Man standing at the right hand of God." But they

---

46. Roberts et al., "Martyrdom," 699–700.
47. Roberts et al., "Martyrdom," 699–700.
48. Roberts et al., "Martyrdom," 699–700.
49. Roberts et al., "Martyrdom," 699–700.
50. Roberts et al., "Martyrdom," 699–700.
51. Roberts et al., "Martyrdom," 700.
52. Roberts et al., "Martyrdom," 700.
53. Roberts et al., "Martyrdom," 700.

cried out with a loud voice and stopped their ears and rushed together at him. Then they cast him out of the city and stoned him. And the witnesses laid down their garments at the feet of a young man named Saul. And as they were stoning Stephen, he called out, "Lord Jesus, receive my spirit." And falling to his knees he cried out with a loud voice, "Lord, do not hold this sin against them." And when he had said this, he fell asleep.[54]

Consider the state of a natural person whose body is being killed slowly by rocks that dig into your flesh. The natural or expected response is not one of awe and mercy. Stephen displays both as he receives a vision of Christ and echoes his Lord's dying words: "do not hold this sin against them." Something is at work here that is far greater than any good intentions that we might be able to muster up when we consider how we'll react when martyred for Christ. God's Spirit has taken hold of Stephen, and there is a union between Stephen and the Lord that enables him to imitate Jesus as he experiences the same kind of suffering that his Lord did.

In this union the believer sees God in a special way, and this "seeing" leads to transformation. The church fathers termed this the "beatific vision."[55] This vision of God does not only inform the believer but transforms and perfects him. John describes it in this way: "Beloved, we are God's children now, and what we will be has not yet appeared; but we know that when he appears we shall be like him, because we shall see him as he is."[56] It is a misnomer to assume that we can see God without transforming. John states that his appearance will transform us; when we see him in his full glory the only logical result will be that we become like him. Although this is a future event, we are already able to "know [him] in part,"[57] and this knowing takes place in a special way as we participate in the sufferings of Jesus.

CONCLUSION

The way of the cross is not one of the ways to God, but *the way* to God. Hebrews 12:14 says that without holiness no one will see the Lord. For Peter, suffering is the primary agent that God uses to produce this holiness in believers. Suffering's purpose can therefore be described as "ἐπιτελεῖσθαι" (to be completed). The believer is brought to completion because suffering

54. Acts 7:54–60 ESV.
55. Boersma, *Seeing God*, .
56. 1 John 3:2.
57. 1 Cor 13:12 ESV.

CONCLUSION

purges the believer from sin, shapes and forms the believer into the image of Christ, and facilitates union with God. This is what the early Christian mystics would refer to as "deification."[58] Ignatius of Antioch understood his impending martyrdom as the means through which he would attain unto God.[59] Like Ignatius, Christians today would do well to view suffering not as a possibility, but a necessity, in order to attain unto God.

Contrary to the modern notion that suffering only serves to weaken us, Athanasius of Alexandria asserts: "Because the saints saw that the divine fire would cleanse them and benefit them, they did not shrink back from or get discouraged by the trials which they faced. Rather than being hurt by what they went through, they grew and were made better, shining like gold that has been refined in a fire."[60] God is with the believer in the fire through his ever-present Spirit, and the Spirit is the perfecting cause who leads people to their divinely appointed ends. Cole describes this process as "the story of a movement from imperfection to perfection, with perfection understood as a complete realization of the divine purpose."[61] This includes both the completion of the person's formation into the image of Christ and the restoration of this world.

If believers shrink away from suffering, they will not become holy as they should; and quite frankly, according to Peter, nor will they inherit the eternal crown of glory. Many people limit suffering as a phase of preparation for a special blessing or breakthrough in this life. Thus, the purpose of suffering is to prepare them for the blessing God has for them in the near future. However, Peter looks beyond this life and connects suffering with the eschaton, or the coming of God's kingdom. The kingdom is not only a future reality; rather, when Jesus was resurrected this new kingdom already started to break into this world. It is as Christians lay down their lives as Christ did that the kingdom continues to break into this world to restore the brokenness of the world around us. N. T. Wright contends that the kingdom comes when Christians "live as Resurrection people between Easter and the final day, with our Christian life, corporate and individual, in both worship and mission, as a sign of the [Resurrection] and a foretaste of the [the new kingdom]."[62] Suffering may be linked to temporal or earthly benefits, but it is ultimately linked to God's coming kingdom. Paul

---

58. McGinn and McGinn, *Early Christian Mystics*, 9–17.
59. Ignatius of Antioch, *Corpus Ignatianum*, 47.
60. Athanasius's 10th Festal Letter, quoted in Bray, *James, 1–2 Peter*, 71.
61. Cole, *He Who Gives Life*, 116.
62. Wright, *Surprised by Hope*, 29–30.

says in Acts 14:22 that we enter God's kingdom "through many tribulations (sufferings)."[63] Without suffering the believer will not inherit the new kingdom. This means two things: first, they will not experience God's reign and power in this life, and second, that they will not participate in the new heavens and the new earth when Jesus returns to judge the living and the dead. This is a stark reminder. Those who shirk from suffering or deny its place in God's purposes are risking way more than they think. This is affirmed by the Didache 12:5–6: "the work of men shall come under testing and many shall turn away, but the ones who remain in the faith until the end shall be saved by the curse itself."[64] For Peter and the early church, suffering is what saves us. Suffering is not one way; it is the only way.

> Be on the alert for your life, do not let your lamps be extinguished and do not be unprepared, but be ready, for you do not know the hour in which our Lord comes. And be assembled together frequently, seeking what is fitting for your souls. For the full time of your faith will be of no benefit to you unless you are found perfect at the final moment. For in the final days false prophets and corrupters shall be multiplied, and the sheep will be turned into wolves and love will be turned into hate. For as lawlessness increases, they will hate and they will persecute and they will betray one another. And then the deceiver of the world shall appear as a son of God and he will perform signs and wonders, and the earth will be handed over into his hands and he will do incessantly vile things which have never happened before since time began. Then the creation of mankind shall come to the burning ordeal of testing. And many will be led astray and will be destroyed, but the ones enduring in their faith will be saved by the *curse itself*. And then the signs of the truth shall appear: first, a sign of an opening in heaven; then a sign of the sound of a trumpet; and the third *sign*, the resurrection of the dead. Now, not all *of the dead* but as was said, the Lord shall come and all the holy ones with him. Then the world will see the Lord coming upon the clouds of heaven.[65]

---

63. Note added for clarity.

64. My paraphrase and translation.

65. The Didache in *The Apostolic Fathers in English,* 16.1–8 (emphasis original). Brannan translates verse 5 as referring to "the accursed one," as in Christ. I disagree with this translation and rather see the antecedent as suffering; therefore, I have adapted his translation to reflect that with the addition of *"curse itself."* The Greek of verse 5 reads "οἱ δὲ ὑπομείναντες ἐν τῇ πίστει αὐτῶν σωθήσονται ὑπ' αὐτοῦ τοῦ καταθέματος." I translate it as "the one who endures in the faith shall be saved by the curse itself."

Bibliography

Achtemeier, Paul J. "Newborn Babes and Living Stones: Literal and Figurative Language in 1 Peter." In *To Touch the Text: Biblical and Related Studies in Honor of Joseph A. Fitzmeyer.* ed., M. P. Horgan and P. J. Koleski, 207–36. New York: Crossroad, 1989.

Achtemeier, Paul J., and Eldon Jay Epp. *1 Peter: A Commentary on First Peter.* Minneapolis: Fortress, 1996.

Aeschylus. *Agamemnon.* Translated by George Theodoridis. https://www.poetryintranslation.com/theodoridisgagamemnon.php.

———. *Persians.* Translated by George Theodoridis. *BacchicStage,* 2009. https://bacchicstage.wordpress.com/aeschylus-2/persians/.

Aland, K., et al. *Novum Testamentum Graece,* 28th Edition. Stuttgart: Deutsche Bibelgesellschaft, 2012.

Ali, Shirin. "Harvard Ditching Standardized Testing Requirements for Admissions for Next Four Years." *The Hill,* December 17, 2021. https://thehill.com/changing-america/enrichment/education/586321-harvard-ditching-standardized-testing-requirements-for.

Allen, George C., trans. *The Didache or The Teaching of the Twelve Apostles Translated with Notes.* London: Astolat, 1903.

Allison, Dale C. *The End of the Ages Has Come: An Early Interpretation of the Passion and Resurrection of Jesus.* Philadelphia: Fortress, 1985.

American Psychiatric Association. "History of the DSM." https://www.psychiatry.org/psychiatrists/practice/dsm/history-of-the-dsm.

Anderson Scott, C. "'The Sufferings of Christ': A Note on 1 Peter 1:11." *Expositor* 12, 6th series (1905) 234–40.

The Apocrypha: King James Version. Bellingham, WA: Logos Research Systems, 1995.

The Apostolic Fathers in English. Translated by Rick Brannan. Bellingham, WA: Lexham, 2012.

Arichea, Daniel C., and Eugene A. Nida. *A Translator's Handbook on the First Letter from Peter.* New York: United Bible Societies, 1980.

Balch, David L. *Let Wives Be Submissive: The Domestic Code in 1 Peter.* Atlanta: SBL, 1980.

Baucham, Voddie. *Fault Lines: The Social Justice Movement and Evangelicalism's Looming Catastrophe.* Washington, DC: Salem, 2021.

Bauckham, Richard. "The Martyrdom of Peter in Early Christianity." *ANRW* 26.1 (1992) 539–95.

Beare, Francis W. *The First Epistle of Peter.* Oxford: Blackwell, 1970.

BIBLIOGRAPHY

Bechtler, Steven R. *Following in His Steps: Suffering, Community, and Christology in 1 Peter.* Socity of Biblical Literature Dissertation Series 162. Atlanta: Scholars, 1998.

Bekker, Cornelius J. "Scriptural Formation: The Power of the Biblical Story." In *The Holy Spirit and Christian Formation: Multidisciplinary Perspectives*, edited by Diane J. Chandler, 91–106. Cham, Switzerland: Palgrave Macmillan, 2016.

Benko, Stephen. *Pagan Rome and the Early Christians.* Bloomington: Indiana University Press, 1984.

Best, Ernest. *1 Peter.* The New Century Bible Commentary. Sheffield: Sheffield Academic Press, 1971.

Bigg, Charles. *A Critical and Exegetical Commentary on the Epistles of Peter and Jude.* The International Critical Commentary. Edinburgh: T. & T. Clark, 1902.

Blomberg, Craig L. *Can We Still Believe in God?: Answering Ten Contemporary Challenges to Christianity.* Grand Rapids: Brazos, 2020.

Bockmuehl, Markus. *The Remembered Peter.* Tübingen: Mohr Siebeck, 2010.

Boersma, Hans. *Seeing God: The Beatific Vision in Christian Tradition.* Grand Rapids: Eerdmans, 2018.

Borchert, Gerald L. "The Conduct of Christians in the Face of the 'Fiery Ordeal' (4:12—5:11)." *Review & Expositor* 79 (Summer 1982) 451–62.

Borgen, Peder, et al. *The Works of Philo: Greek Text with Morphology.* 10 vols. Bellingham, WA: Logos Bible Software, 2005.

Boring, Eugene M. *1 Peter.* Abingdon New Testament Commentary Nashville: Abingdon, 1999.

Bowler, Kate. *Blessed: A History of the American Prosperity Gospel.* New York: Oxford University Press, 2013.

Brannan, Rick, et al., eds. *The Lexham English Septuagint.* Bellingham, WA: Lexham, 2012.

Bray, Gerald, ed. *James, 1–2 Peter, 1–3 John, Jude.* Ancient Christian Commentary on Scripture. Downers Grove, IL: InterVarsity, 2000.

Brown, Raymond E., and John P. Meier. *Antioch and Rome.* New York: Paulist, 1983.

Burkert, Walter. *Greek Religion.* Cambridge: Harvard University Press, 1985.

Calvin, John. *Commentaries on the Catholic Epistles.* Translated by John Owen. Bellingham, WA: Logos Bible Software, 2010.

Campbell, Barth Lynn. "Honor, Shame, and the Rhetoric of 1 Peter." PhD diss., Fuller Theological Seminary, School of Theology, 1995.

Chandler, Diane J. *Christian Spiritual Formation: An Integrated Approach for Personal and Relational Wellness.* Downers Grove, IL: InterVarsity, 2014.

Charles, R. H. *Apocalypse of Baruch.* Macon, GA: Scholars, 1976.

Christensen, Sean M. "Solidarity in Suffering and Glory: The Unifying Role of Psalm 34 in 1 Peter 3:10–12." *Journal of the Evangelical Theological Society* 58/2 (2015) 351.

Clowney, Edmund P. *The Message of 1 Peter: The Way of the Cross.* Leicester: InterVarsity, 1988.

"Codex Vaticanus." https://digi.vatlib.it/view/MSS_Vat.gr.1209.

Cole, Graham A. *He Who Gives Life: The Doctrine of the Holy Spirit.* Chicago: Crossway, 2007.

Copeland, Kenneth. "Should I Expect to Die for Jesus?" *Kenneth Copeland Ministries.* https://www.kcm.org/read/question-of-the-day/should-i-expect-die-jesus.

———. "Why Do Bad Things Happen?" *Kenneth Copeland Ministries.* https://www.kcm.org/real-help/spiritual-growth/learn/why-do-bad-things-happen?language_content_entity=en-US.

Bibliography

Cost, Ben. "Critics Lambast Coddling Schools for Eliminating 'D' and 'F' grades." *New York Post*, December 9, 2021. https://nypost.com/2021/12/09/coddling-schools-under-fire-after-dropping-d-and-f-grades/.

Cranfield, C. E. B. *I & II Peter and Jude: Introduction and Commentary*. Torch Bible Commentaries. London: SCM, 1960.

Croy, N. Clayton. *Endurance in Suffering: Hebrews 12:1–13 in Its Rhetorical, Religious, and Philosophical Context*. Society for New Testament Studies Monograph Series 98. New York: Cambridge University Press, 1998.

Danker, Frederick William, ed. *A Greek-English Lexicon of the New Testament and Other Early Christian Literature*. 3rd ed. Chicago: University of Chicago Press, 2000.

———. *Invitation to the New Testament: Epistles, Vol. 4: A Commentary on Hebrews, 1 and 2 Peter, 1, 2 and 3 John and Jude, with Complete Text from the Jerusalem Bible*. 20 vols. Garden City, NY: Doubleday, 1980.

Davids, Peter H. *The First Epistle of Peter*. NICNT. Grand Rapids: Eerdmans, 1990.

De Villiers, Jan Lodewyk. "Joy in Suffering in 1 Peter." *NeoTestamentica* 9.1 (1975) 64–86.

Donelson, Lewis R. *I & II Peter and Jude: A Commentary*. The New Testament Library. Louisville: Westminster John Knox, 2010.

Dryden, J. de Waal. *Theology and Ethics in 1 Peter: Paraenetic Strategies for Christian Character Formation*. WUNT. Tübingen: Mohr Siebeck, 2006.

Dubis, Kevin Mark. "Messianic Woes in First Peter: Suffering and Eschatology in 1 Peter 4:12–19." PhD diss., Union Theological Seminary, Virginia, 1998.

Earley, Dave, and Rod Dempsey. *Spiritual Formation Is: How to Grow in Jesus with Passion and Confidence*. Nashville: B&H Academic, 2018.

Elliott, John Hall. *1 Peter: A New Translation with Introduction and Commentary*. 1st ed. Vol. 37B. New York: Doubleday, 2000.

———. "1 Peter, Its Situation and Strategy: A Discussion with David Balch." In *Perspectives on First Peter*. edited by Charles H. Talbert, 61–78. Macon, GA: Mercer University Press, 1986.

———. *A Home for the Homeless: A Sociological Exegesis of 1 Peter, Its Situation and Strategy*. Philadelphia: Fortress, 1981.

Epictetus. *Discourses of Epictetus*. Translated by George Long. New York: Appleton and Co., 1904.

Eusebius. *Ecclesiastical History*. Translated by A. C. McGiffert. N.p.: Pantianos Classics, 2007.

Filson, Floyd V. "Partakers with Christ: Suffering in First Peter." *Interpretation* 9 (1955) 400–12.

Foakes-Jackson, F. J. *Peter: Prince of Apostles: A Study in the History and Tradition of Christianity*. New York: Doran, 1927.

Forbes, Greg W. *Exegetical Guide to the New Testament: 1 Peter*. Nashville: B&H, 2014.

Frank, Tenney. *Aspects of Social Behavior in Ancient Rome*. Oberlin, OH: Oberlin College Press, 1932.

Frend, William H. C. *Martyrdom and Persecution in the Early Church: A Study of the Conflict from the Maccabees to Donatus*. New York: 1967.

Gadamer, Hans-Georg. *Plato's Dialectical Ethics: Phenomenological Interpretations Relating to the Philebus*. Translated by Robert M. Wallace. New Haven: Yale University Press, 1991.

Gartner, Burkhard. "Suffering." In *The New International Dictionary of New Testament Theology*, edited by Colin Brown, 3:719–26. 3 vols. Grand Rapids: Zondervan, 1976.

BIBLIOGRAPHY

Geertz, Clifford. *The Interpretation of Cultures*. New York: Basic, 1973.

Goppelt, Leonard. *A Commentary on 1 Peter*. Translated by James E. Alsup. Grand Rapids: Eerdmans, 1993.

Goulder, Michael D. "Did Peter Ever Go to Rome?" *Scottish Journal of Theology* 57 (2004) 377–97.

Green, Bernard. *Christianity in Ancient Rome: The First Three Centuries*. London: T. & T. Clark, 2010.

Green, Joel B. *1 Peter*. The New Horizons New Testament Commentary. Grand Rapids: Eerdmans, 2007.

Grudem, Wayne. *1 Peter*. Tyndale New Testament Commentary Series. Downers Grove, IL: IVP Academic, 1988.

Grundmann, Walter. "Δεῖ, Δέον Ἐστί." In *TDNT*, 2:22..

Guthrie, Donald. *New Testament Introduction*. Downers Grove, IL: InterVarsity, 1970.

Guthrie, William K. C. *The Greeks and Their Gods*. London: Methuen, 1950.

Haidt, Jonathan, and Greg Lukianoff. *The Coddling of the American Mind: How Good Intentions and Bad Ideas Are Setting Up a Generation for Failure*. New York: Penguin, 2018.

Hall, M. Elisabeth Lewis. "Suffering as Formation: The Hard Road to Glory." In *The Holy Spirit and Christian Formation: Multidisciplinary Perspectives*, edited by Diane J. Chandler, 69–88. Cham, Switzerland: Palgrave Macmillan, 2016.

Hall, Randy. "For to This You Have Been Called: The Cross and Suffering in 1 Peter." *Restoration Quarterly* 19.3 (1976) 137–47.

Harink, Douglas Karel. *1 & 2 Peter*. Grand Rapids: Brazos, 2009.

Haslam, Nick. "Concept Creep: Psychology's Expanding Concepts of Harm and Pathology." *Psychological Inquiry* 27.1 (2006) 1–17.

Hesiod. "Works and Days." Translated by Hugh G. Evelyn-White. http://www.sacred-texts.com/cla/hesiod/works.htm.

Hiebert, D. Edmond. *1 Peter*. Chicago: Moody, 1984.

Hillyer, Norman. "First Peter and the Feast of Tabernacles." *Tyndale Bulletin* 21 (1970) 39–70.

Hitchcock, Roswell D., and Francis Brown, eds. *The Teaching of the Twelve Apostles: Greek*. London: Nimmo, 1885.

Homer. *The Odyssey: A Translation into English Prose by A. S. Kline*. London: Poetry in Translation, 2004.

Horrell, David G. *1 Peter*. New Testament Guides. London: Bloomsbury, 2008.

———. *Epworth Commentaries: The Epistles of Peter and Jude*. Peterborough, UK: Epworth, 1998.

Hort, Fenton J. A. *The First Epistle of St. Peter: The Greek Text with Introductory Lecture, Commentary and Additional Notes*. London: Macmillan, 1898.

Hunter, Archibald M., and Elmer G. Holmrighausen. *The First Epistle of Peter*, vol. 12 of the Interpreter's Bible. 12 vols. New York: Abingdon, 1957.

Ignatius of Antioch. *Corpus Ignatianum: Greek Text, Middle Recension*. Berlin: Asher and Co., 1849.

Jobes, Karen H. *1 Peter*. BECNT. Grand Rapids: Baker Academic, 2005.

———. "'O Taste and See': Septuagint Psalm 33 in 1 Peter." *Stone-Campbell Journal* 18 (2015) 241.

Joel Osteen Ministrie. "Our Ministry." https://www.joelosteen.com/our-ministry.

Bibliography

Johnson, Dennis E. "Fire in God's House: Imagery from Malachi 3 in Peter's Theology of Suffering (1 Pet 4:12-19)." *Journal of the Evangelical Theological Society* 29.3 (September 1986) 285–94.

Johnson, Lauren M. "Colorado Judge Finds Christian Baker Broke State Discrimination Law by Refusing to Bake a Birthday Cake for a Trans Woman." *CNN*, June 18, 2021. https://www.cnn.com/2021/06/18/us/jack-phillips-colorado-baker-discrimination-trnd/index.html.

Johnstone, Robert. *The First Epistle of Peter: Revised Text with Introduction and Commentary*. Edinburgh: T. & T. Clark, 1888.

Jones, David W., and Russell S. Woodbridge. *Health, Wealth, and Happiness: How the Prosperity Gospel Overshadows the Gospel of Christ*. Grand Rapids: Kregel, 2011.

Jonge, Marinus de, ed. *The Testament of the Twelve Patriarchs: A Critical Edition of the Greek Text*. Leiden: Brill, 1978.

Josephus, Flavius. *The Works of Flavius Josephus*. Translated by William Whiston. Peabody, MA: Hendrickson, 1980.

Jung, Jaewoong. "Between Texts and Sermon: 1 Peter 2:18–25." *Interpretation* 76.1 (2022) 57–59.

Keener, Craig S. *1 Peter: A Commentary*. Grand Rapids: Baker Academic, 2021.

Kelly, J. N. D. *The Epistles of Peter and of Jude*. BNTC. Grand Rapids: Baker Academic, 1993.

Kirby, Peter, trans. "The Ascension of Isaiah." *Early Christian Writings*. http://www.earlychristianwritings.com/text/ascension.html.

Kistemaker, Simon J. *New Testament Commentary: Exposition of the Epistles of Peter and the Epistle of Jude*. Grand Rapids: Baker, 1987.

Klausli, Markus Theron. "The Question of the Messianic Woes in 1 Peter." PhD diss., Dallas Theological Seminary, Dallas, 2007.

Knox, John. "Pliny and 1 Peter: A Note on 1 Pet 4:14–16 and 3:15." *Journal of Biblical Literature* 72.3 (September 1953) 187–89.

Kraemer, David. *Responses to Suffering in Classical Rabbinic Literature*. New York: Oxford University Press, 1995.

Kretzschmar, Louise. "Authentic Christian Leadership and Spiritual Formation in Africa." *Journal of Theology for Southern Africa* 128 (2002) 41–60.

Krodel, Gerhard. "1 Peter." In *The General Letters: Hebrews, James, 1–2 Peter, Jude, 1-2-3 John*, edited by Gerhard Krodel, 42–83. Revised and enlarged edition. Proclamation Commentaries. Minneapolis: Fortress, 1995.

Leaney, A. R. C. *The Letters of Peter and Jude*. CBC. Edited by Peter R. Ackroyd et al. Cambridge: Cambridge University Press, 1967.

Leithart, Peter J. "The Quadriga or Something Like It: A Biblical and Pastoral Defense." In *Ancient Faith for the Church's Future*, edited by Mark Husbands and Jeffrey P. Greenman, 110–26. Downers Grove, IL: IVP Academic, 2008.

Lenski, Richard C. H. *The Interpretation of the Epistles of St. Peter, St. John and St. Jude*. Columbus, OH: Lutheran Book Concern, 1938.

Lentz, Carl. *Own the Moment*. New York: Simon & Schuster, 2017.

Le Roux, Elritia. *Ethics in 1 Peter: The Imitatio Christi and the Ethics of Suffering in 1 Peter and the Gospel of Mark—A Comparative Study*. Eugene, OR: Pickwick, 2018.

Levin, Yuval. *A Time to Build: From Family and Community to Congress and the Campus: How Recommitting to Our Institutions Can Revive the American Dream*. New York: Basic, 2020.

BIBLIOGRAPHY

Lewis, Charlton T., and Charles Short. *Harper's Latin Dictionary*. Oxford: Clarendon, 1891.

Liddell, Henry George, et al, eds. *A Greek-English Lexicon*. Oxford: Clarendon, 1996.

Lightfoot, Joseph B. *The Apostolic Fathers, Part I: S. Clement of Rome: Revised Text*. New York: Macmillan, 1890.

———. *The Apostolic Fathers, Part II: S. Ignatius, S. Polycarp: Revised Texts*, Second Edition, Vol. 3. New York: Macmillan, 1889.

Lillie, John. *Lectures on the First and Second Epistles of Peter*. Minneapolis: Klock & Klock, 1978.

Lindstrom, Fredrik. *Suffering and Sin: Interpretations of Illness in the Individual Complaint Psalms*. Stockholm: Almqvist and Wiksell, 1994.

Lohse, Eduard. "Parenesis and Kerygma in 1 Peter." In *Perspectives on First Peter*, edited by Charles H. Talbert, 37–60. Macon, GA: Mercer University Press, 1986.

Lutz, Cora E. "Musonius Rufus, The Roman Socrates." *Yale Classical Studies* 10 (1947) 3–147.

MacIntyre, Alisdaire. *After Virtue: A Study in Moral Theory*. 2nd ed. London: Duckworth, 1985.

Magie, David. *Roman Rule in Asia Minor to the End of the Third Century after Christ*. 2 vols. Princeton: Princeton University Press, 1950.

Magno, Hector. *Sufffering Is Not God's Will*. Bloomington, IN: Author House, 2016.

Marshall, I. Howard. *1 Peter*. Downers Grove, IL: InterVarsity, 1991.

Martin, Troy W. *Metaphor and Composition in 1 Peter*. Edited by Pheme Perkins. SBL Dissertation Series 131. Atlanta: Scholars, 1992.

Masterman, J. Howard B. *The First Epistle of S. Peter: Greek Text*. London: Macmillan, 1990.

McGinn, Bernard, and Patricia Ferris McGinn. *Early Christian Mystics: The Divine Vision of the Spiritual Masters*. New York: Crossroad, 2003.

McKnight, Scot. *1 Peter: The NIV Application Commentary from Biblical Text to Contemporary Life*. Grand Rapids: Zondervan, 1996.

McNally, Richard. "If You Need a Trigger Warning, You Need PTSD Treatment." *The New York Times*, September 13, 2016. https://www.nytimes.com/roomfordebate/2016/09/13/do-trigger-warnings-work/if-you-need-a-trigger-warning-you-need-ptsd-treatment.

Michaels, J. Ramsey. *1 Peter*. WBC 49. Waco, TX: Word, 1988.

———. "Eschatology in 1 Peter 3:17." *New Testament Studies* 13.4 (July 1967) 394–401.

Miller, Chuck. *The Spiritual Formation of Leaders: Integrating Spiritual Formation and Leadership Development*. Maitland, FL: Xulon, 2007.

Miller, Donald G. *On This Rock: A Commentary on First Peter*. Edited by Dikran Hadidian. PTMS 34. Allison Park, PA: Pickwick, 1993.

Moffatt, James. *The General Epistles: James, Peter and Judas*. Edited by James Moffatt. MNTC. London: Hodder & Stoughton, 1928.

Morris, Andrea. "Judge Rules in Favor of Christian Professor after His Wrongful Termination for Challenging Students' Beliefs on Sexuality." *CBN News*, July 27, 2019. https://www1.cbn.com/cbnnews/us/2018/november/california-professor-fired-for-challenging-students-beliefs-about-sexuality-is-reinstated.

MyNorthwest Staff. "Seattle Pride Speaks Out against Upcoming Dave Chapelle Performance." *MyNorthwest*, December 15, 2021. https://mynorthwest.com/3283458/seattle-pride-speaks-out-dave-chappelle-climate-pledge-arena/.

BIBLIOGRAPHY

Niebuhr, Reinhold. "Serenity Prayer." *Belief Net*. https://www.beliefnet.com/prayers/protestant/addiction/serenity-prayer.aspx.

Osteen, Joel. *Every Day a Friday: How to Be Happier 7 Days a Week*. New York: Faith Words, 2012.

———. *Next Level Thinking: 10 Powerful Thoughts for a Successful and Abundant Life*. New York: Faith Words, 2018.

Parker, David C. "The Eschatology of 1 Peter." *Biblical Theological Review* 24 (Spring 1994) 27–32.

Pelikan, Jaroslav, and Helmut T. Lehmann. *Luther's Works, American Edition*. 55 vols. Philadelphia: Muehlenberg and Fortress; St. Louis: Concordia, 1955–86.

Penner, Ken, and Michael S. Heiser. *Old Testament Greek Pseudepigrapha with Morphology*. Bellingham, WA: Lexham, 2008.

Pettit, Paul, ed. *Foundations of Spiritual Formation: A Community Approach to Being Like Christ*. Grand Rapids: Kregel Academic, 2008.

Piper, John. "Hope as the Motivation for Love: 1 Peter 3:9–12." *New Testament Studies* 26 (1980) 212–31.

Platt, Richard H., Jr., ed. *The Forgotten Books of Eden*. New York: Alpha House, 1927.

Pliny the Younger. "Letters of Pliny the Younger and the Emperor Trajan." *PBS Frontline*. Translated by William Whiston. https://www.pbs.org/wgbh/pages/frontline/shows/religion/maps/primary/pliny.html.

Plumptre, E. H. *The General Epistles of St. Peter & St, Jude, with Notes and Introduction*. Cambridge Bibles for Schools and Colleges 48. Cambridge: Cambridge University Press, 1879.

Pobee, John S. *Persecution and Martyrdom in the Theology of Paul*. JSNTSup 6. Sheffield: JSOT, 1986.

Porter, Stanley E. "Tribulation, Messianic Woes." In *Dictionary of the Later New Testament and Its Development*. edited by Ralph P. Martin and Peter H. Davids, 1672–76. Downers Grove, IL: InterVarsity, 1997.

Price, Simon R. F. *Rituals and Power: The Roman Imperial Cult in Asia Minor*. Cambridge, MA: Cambridge University Press, 1984.

Richard, Earl. "Functional Christology in First Peter." In *Perspectives on First Peter*, edited by Charles H. Talbert, 121–40. Macon, GA: Mercer University Press, 1986.

Rieff, Philip. "Reflections of Psychological Man in America." In *The Feeling Intellect: Selected Writings*, edited by Jonathan B. Imber, 3–10. Chicago: University of Chicago Press, 1990.

———. *Triumph of the Therapeutic: Uses of Faith after Freud*. 40th anniversary edition. 1963;. Reprint, Wilmington, DE: ISI, 2006.

Roberts, Alexander, et al., eds. "The Martyrdom of Perpetua and Felicitas." In *Latin Christianity: Its Founder, Tertullian*, 699–706. Translated by R. E. Wallis. ANF 3. 10 vols. Buffalo, NY: Christian Literature, 1885.

Robertson, A. T. *A Grammar of the Greek New Testament in the Light of Historical Research*. 4th ed. Nashville: Broadman, 1934.

Robinson, H. Wheeler. *Suffering Human and Divine*. New York: Macmillan, 1939.

Roser, Max. "Mortality in the Past—Around Half Died as Children." *Our World in Data*, June 11, 2019. https://ourworldindata.org/child-mortality-in-the-past.

Rouse, Ted. *Why Suffering Cannot Be God's Will*. Chicago: Insight, 2003.

Russell, David S. *The Method and Message of Jewish Apocalyptic: 200 BC—100 AD*. London: SCM, 1964.

BIBLIOGRAPHY

Russell Sage Foundation. "Real Mean and Median Income, Families and Individuals, 1947–2012, and Households, 1967–2012." https://www.russellsage.org/sites/all/files/chartbook/Income%20and%20Earnings.pdf.

Sachdeva, Maanya. "Harry Potter Fans Criticise JK Rowling after New 'Transphobic' Tweet: 'Please Stop Causing Pain.'" *The Independent*, December 13, 2021. https://www.independent.co.uk/arts-entertainment/books/news/harry-potter-jk-rowling-transphobic-terf-b1974984.html.

Sander, Emilie T. "ΠΥΡΩΣΙΣ and the First Epistle of Peter 4:12." PhD diss., Harvard University, Massachusetts, 1966.

Savelle, Jerry. *If Satan Can't Steal Your Joy . . . He Can't Keep Your Goods*. Tulsa, OK: Harrison House, 2002.

Schoedel, William R. *Hermeneia: Ignatius of Antioch: A Commentary on the Letters of Ignatius of* Antioch. Philadelphia: Fortress, 1985.

Schreiner, Tom. *1, 2 Peter, Jude*. NAC 37. Nashville: Broadman & Holman, 2003.

Schutter, William L. *Hermeneutic and Composition in 1 Peter*. Tübingen: Mohr Siebeck, 1989.

Scott, C. Anderson. "'The Sufferings of Christ': A Note on 1 Peter 1:11." *Expositor* 12.6 (1905) 234–40.

Selwyn, Edward G. *The First Epistle of St. Peter*. London: Macmillan, 1958.

Seneca. *Epistles, Volume I: Epistles 1–65*. 2 vols. Translated by Richard M. Gummere. Cambridge, MA: Harvard University Press, 1917.

———. *Moral Essays, Volume I: De Providentia. De Constantia. De Ira. De Clementia*. 2 vols. Translated by John W. Basore. Cambridge, MA: Harvard University Press, 1928.

———. *On Consolation: To Helvia, Marcia, and Polybius*. Translated by Frank Justus Miller. London: Heinemann, 1917.

———. *On Providence, Moderation, and Constancy of Mind*. Translated by Robert L'Estrange. Edited by Keith Seddon. Morrisville, NC: LULU, 2010.

Senior, Donald P. *1 Peter*. Sacra Pagina Series. Collegeville, MN: Liturgical, 2003.

Septuaginta: A Reader's Edition. Peabody, MA: Hendrickson, 2018.

Shepherd of Hermas. "Shepherd_b." https://www.ccel.org/l/lake/fathers/shepherd_b.htm.

Skaggs, Rebecca. *The Pentecostal Commentary on 1 Peter, 2 Peter, Jude*. London: T. & T. Clark International, 2004.

———. "The Spirit in 1 Peter, 2 Peter, and Jude: Transformation and Transcendence." *Pneuma* 43 (2021) 538.

Skehan, Patrick W. *The Wisdom of Ben Sira*. New York: Doubleday, 1987.

Slevin, Colleen, "Christian Baker Sued Again for Refusing to Bake a Cake." *Christianity Today*, March 24, 2021. https://www.christianitytoday.com/news/2021/march/colorado-christian-baker-jack-phillips-sued-lgbt-cake-court.html.

Sordi, Marta. *The Christians and the Roman Empire*. Translated by Annabel Bedini. Norman: University of Oklahoma Press, 1986.

Spicq, Ceslas. *Les Epitres de Saint Pierre*. Sources Bibliques. Paris: Gabalda & Cie, 1966.

———. *Theological Lexicon of the New Testament*. 3 vols. Edited by J. D. Ernest. Peabody, MA: Hendrickson, 1994.

Starke, Rodney. *The Cities of God: The Real Story of How Christianity Became an Urban Movement and Conquered Rome*. New York: Harper One, 2006.

Ste Croix, G. E. M. "Why Were the Early Christians Persecuted?" *Past and Present* 26 (November 1963) 24–31.

Bibliography

———. "Why Were the Early Christians Persecuted?—A Rejoinder." *Past and Present* 27 (April 1964) 28–33.
Stibbs, Alan M. *The First Epistle General of Peter*. Tyndale New Testament Commentaries Grand Rapids: Eerdmans, 1959.
Suetonius. "The Life of Augustus." University of Chicago. Suetonius' *Twelve Caesars*. http://penelope.uchicago.edu/Thayer/E/Roman/Texts/Suetonius/12Caesars/Augustus*.html.
———. "The Life of Claudius." University of Chicago. Suetonius' *Twelve Caesars*. https://penelope.uchicago.edu/Thayer/E/Roman/Texts/Suetonius/12Caesars/Claudius*.html.
Tacitus. "The Annals." http://classics.mit.edu/Tacitus/annals.4.iv.html.
Talbert, Charles H. *Learning through Suffering: The Educational Value of Suffering in the New Testament and in Its Milieu*. Collegeville, MN: Liturgical, 1991.
Taleb, Nassim N. *Antifragile: Things that Gain from Disorder*. New York: Random House, 2012.
Taylor, Charles. *A Secular Age*. Cambridge: Harvard University Press, 2007.
———. *Modern Social Imaginaries*. Durham, NC: Duke University Press, 2003.
———. *Sources of the Self: The Making of the Modern Identity*. Cambridge: Harvard University Press, 1989.
Thiede, Carsten Peter. *From Galilee to Rome*. Grand Rapids: Zondervan Academic, 1988.
Thiessen, Matthew. *Jesus and the Forces of Death: The Gospels' Portrayal of Ritual Impurity within First-Century Judaism*. Grand Rapids: Baker Academic, 2020.
Thomas, John Christopher. "Stop Sinning Lest Something Worse Come upon You." *JSNT* 59 (1995) 3–20.
Thuren, Lauri. *Argument and Theology in 1 Peter: The Origins of Christian Paraenesis*. Sheffield: Sheffield Academic, 1995.
———. *The Rhetorical Strategy of 1 Peter with Special Regard to Ambiguous Expressions*. Turku, Finland: Åbo Akademis Förlag, 1990.
Tiedke, Erich and Hans George Link. "Necessity." In *The New International Dictionary of New Testament Theology*, edited by Colin Brown, 2:64–66. 3 vols. Grand Rapids: Zondervan, 1976.
Trueman, Carl R. *The Rise and Triumph of the Modern Self: Cultural Amnesia, Expressive Individualism, and the Road to Sexual Revolution*. Wheaton, IL: Crossway, 2020.
Turner, Nigel. *A Grammar of New Testament Greek*. Edited by James H. Moulton. 3 vols. Edinburgh: T. & T. Clark, 1976.
Tweng, Jean M. *iGen: Why Today's Super-Connected Kids Are Growing Up Less Rebellious, More Tolerant, Less Happy—and Completely Unprepared for Adulthood—and What That Means for the Rest of Us*. New York: Atria, 2017.
UCA News. "Scottish Christian Leaders Say Hate Crime Bill Limits Freedom to Disagree." https://www.ucanews.com/news/scottish-christian-leaders-say-hate-crime-bill-limits-freedom-to-disagree/91453.
Vanhoozer, Kevin J. *Is There a Meaning in This Text?: The Bible, the Reader, and the Morality of Literary Knowledge*. Grand Rapids: Zondervan, 2009.
Van Rensburg, Fika J. "A Code of Conduct for the Children of God Who Suffer Unjustly: Identity, Ethics and Ethos in 1 Peter." In *Identity, Ethics, and Ethos in the New Testament*, edited by Francois S. Malan and Jan G. Van der Watt, 473–510. Berlin: de Gruyter, 2006.

Vermes, Geza. *The Dead Sea Scrolls in English*. 4th Edition. Sheffield: Sheffield Academic Press, 1995.

Wallace, Daniel B. *Greek Grammar Beyond the Basics: An Exegetical Syntax of the New Testament with Scripture, Subject, and Greek Word Indexes*. Grand Rapids: Zondervan Academic, 1997.

Wallace, Harold D., Jr., "Power from the People: Rural Electrification Brought More than Light." *National Museum of American History*, February 12, 2016. https://americanhistory.si.edu/blog/rural-electrification.

Wand, John W. C. "The Lessons of First Peter." *Int* 9 (1955) 387–99.

Watson, Dale L. "The Implications of Christology and Eschatology for a Christian Attitude for the State of 1 Peter." PhD diss., Harvard University, Massachusetts, 1970.

Webb, Robert L. "The Apocalyptic Perspective of First Peter." ThM Thesis, Regent College, Canada, 1986.

Wendland, Ernst R. "'Stand Fast in the True Grace of God!' A Study of 1 Peter." *JOTT* 13 (2000) 25–102.

"Why Is Scotland's Hate Crime Bill So Controversial?" *BBC News*, December 15, 2020. https://www.bbc.com/news/uk-scotland-scotland-politics-53580326.

Wilken, Robert Louis. *Christians as the Romans Saw Them*. New Haven: Yale University Press, 1984.

Wilson, Walter T. *The Hope of Glory: Education and Exhortation in the Epistle to the Colossians*. Leiden: Brill, 1997.

Witherington, Ben, III. *Letters and Homilies for Hellenized Christians*. Downers Grove, IL: IVP Academic, 2006.

Woo, Kenneth J. "Suffering as a Mark of the Church in Martin Luther's Exegesis of 1 Peter." *CTQ* 77 (2013) 307.

Wright, N. T. *Surprised by Hope: Rethinking Heaven, the Resurrection, and the Mission of the Church*. New York: Harper One, 2008.

Young, Douglas. *Theognis*. Leipzig: Teubner, 1961.

Zeller, Hubert van. *The Mystery of Suffering*. Notre Dame: Christian Classics, 1964.

Zerwick, Maximilian. *Biblical Greek Illustrated by Examples*. Translated and adapted from the 4th Latin edition by Joseph Smith, Scripta Pontificii Instituti Biblici, 114. Rome: Biblical Institute, 1963.

www.ingramcontent.com/pod-product-compliance
Lightning Source LLC
Chambersburg PA
CBHW051106160426
43193CB00010B/1338